THE ORGANIZATIONAL COMMUNICATOR

THE ORGANIZATIONAL COMMUNICATOR

CAL W. DOWNS
University of Kansas

DAVID M. BERG
Purdue University

WIL A. LINKUGEL
University of Kansas

HARPER & ROW, Publishers
New York   Hagerstown   San Francisco   London

Sponsoring Editor: *Larry Sifford*
Project Editor: *Renée E. Beach*
Designer: *Frances Torbert Tilley*
Production Supervisor: *Kewal K. Sharma*
Photo Researcher: *Myra Schachne*
Compositor: *American Book–Stratford Press, Inc.*
Printer and Binder: *Halliday Lithograph Corporation*
Art Studio: *Danmark & Michaels Inc.*

THE ORGANIZATIONAL COMMUNICATOR

Library of Congress Cataloging in Publication Data

Downs, Cal W   1936–
   The organizational communicator.

   Includes index.
   1. Communication in organizations. 2. Inter-
viewing. 3. Discussion. 4. Public speaking.
I. Berg, David M., joint author. II. Linkugel,
Wil A., joint author. III. Title.
HD38.D66   658.4'5   76–22768
ISBN 0–06–041734–X

CONTENTS

PREFACE

Communication is an exciting field of study, and communicating effectively is quite a challenge. This book examines the part of communication study that pertains to the organizational context. Human communication is similar regardless of context; at the same time, there are contextual factors that assist or constrain the organizational communicator. Our attempt, thus, is to wed our knowledge of communication theory with our knowledge of organizational theory. The book is heavily grounded in theory but always has a practical bent, striving to make concrete the principles and guidelines that should help the manager or executive be an effective communicator. The target readership is the college student taking a basic course in organizational communication and the adult professional searching for assistance with his or her communication endeavors.

The book is divided into five parts: (I) Organizational Communication, (II) Interviewing, (III) Group Conferences, (IV) Personal Presentations, and (V) The Book in Perspective. Each of these sections is introduced with a general overview and a statement of behavioral objectives, with the chapters being geared toward those objectives. Each chapter is introduced with a preview and concludes with a brief recapitulation that places the main points in perspective. We think educational objectives can best be met through this approach.

The first part of the book introduces the reader to the nature of human organizations, explains the organization-communication interface, and explores fundamental communication concepts with an eye toward the problem areas that commonly present themselves.

The next three parts of the book spring from a survey that identifies the vital communication activities of the organizational executive. *The Report of the Manpower Resources Study Committee* of the International Communication Association (April 23, 1975) shows that executives in business and industry rely heavily on communication abilities related to interviewing, conference discussion, and personal presentations. We have therefore focused on vital principles pertaining to these forms of interpersonal communication.

Since interviewing involves a one-to-one relationship, we take it up first. We begin with a discussion of interviewing theory, tactics, and problems, and conclude with three important forms of interviewing: the selection interview, the appraisal interview, and the persuasive interview. After each type of interviewing has been discussed, we present either an example of such an interview or a case study for thought and discussion. We think that in this manner the reader will be able to develop a concrete perspective concerning each type of interviewing activity.

Part III analyzes group conferences. This section discusses strengths and weaknesses of group discussion, analyzes the dynamics of groups at work, and concludes with a series of practical suggestions for effective participation and leadership in groups.

Part IV focuses on personal presentations. The *Manpower Resources* report reveals that personal presentations are of great importance to organizational communicators. Personal address is often the communication activity that generally concerns executives the most because it involves that special moment when they are standing entirely on their own, revealing their talents, knowledge, and preparation—or lack of it. This part of the book begins by examining the fundamental anatomy of all discourse; it discusses the problems of preparation and presentation, and takes a specific look at various types of personal presentations. Explaining, reporting, briefing, good-will speaking, selling ideas, and many other types of personal address are discussed.

Part V recapitulates the book and places its ideas into a final perspective. It ends by stressing the problem of selecting communication channels in relation to messages and purposes. A fundamental position of this book is that selecting the most appropriate communication channel is a vital consideration for the organizational communicator. The book ends with two cases concerning channel selection.

We think the organizational breakdown of the book, the specificity with which communication activities are examined, and the theoretical grounding of vital concepts should make this book a helpful agent for introducing and orienting the average college student to organizational communication activities.

This book can also be used in a basic speech course, especially if the course is designed to take the student through various levels of interpersonal communication, from dyadic, through small group, to public. Since a great percentage of college graduates will at one time or another be part of an organization of some type, the organizational aspects of the book may well be an asset rather than a hindrance to the beginning speech student.

In addition, this book should prove useful in an adult course in organizational communication. It touches on things a professional adult can relate to, and the examples used are drawn directly from organizational activities.

Finally, the individual adult reader, looking for assistance in fulfilling his or her communication requirements, should find this book useful. It is the type of book that can be read entirely for general information, but it is also constructed so that the reader can easily go back to particular sections as he or she confronts communication situations. Sections of the book giving the reader special help in dealing with problems are readily located.

Each of the authors has had some experience with all the communication activities discussed in the book. At the same time, each has also had a special focus that has allowed him to bring particular expertise to the writing of certain sections of the book. We hope this combination of authorship has produced a relevant, authoritative, helpful, and interesting book for the reader.

Cal W. Downs
David M. Berg
Wil A. Linkugel

Miller, Monkmeyer

PART I
ORGANIZATIONAL COMMUNICATION

This section is a basic introduction to the area of organizational communication. Chapter 1 describes the general nature of organizations and identifies some of the structural elements that influence the way people communicate in their respective organizations. Chapter 2 examines several functions of communication in organizations and identifies several different subsystems in which people communicate. Chapter 3 sets out the authors' frame of reference for examining the process of communication and pinpoints some of the most important dimensions that should be considered as one seeks to improve one's communicative skills. These three chapters lay the theoretical foundation on which the rest of the book is based.

When the reader has finished this section, he or she should be able to

1) Enumerate and define the most important structural qualities of organizations.
2) Describe three different perspectives for analyzing organizations.
3) Describe the communication process, and define its most important dimensions.
4) Analyze the chief functions of communication in organizations.
5) Take any communication situation in an organization and analyze the communication and organizational factors that influence it.
6) Identify some common communication problems in organizations and design strategies to overcome them.

CHAPTER 1

THE ORGANIZATION: A CONTEXT

Preview

The organizational communicator must understand how his communication is affected by the basic structural characteristics of the organization.

- Hierarchy
- Span of control
- Division of labor
- Line and staff functions
- Chain of command
- Role relationships

Organizational theory has been influenced by three major theoretical perspectives.

- Scientific management
- Human relations
- The contingency approach

The kinds of prescriptions that people will make about effective communication will be determined by their choice among these three perspectives.

Organizations dominate our lives. Almost everything we do and every decision we make is shaped by some kind of organized effort. One way to demonstrate this is to make a list of the organizations with which we interact each week. Last week, for example, one of the authors

was the father in a *family*
taught in a university communication *department*
consulted with an international packaging *company*
attended a *church*
shopped in a *supermarket*
voted in a *city* election
played on a basketball *team* in a city *league*
attended a *PTA* meeting
solicited funds for a philanthropic *organization*
rode in a *car pool*

At some time, then, he was a member of each of these organizations. The interesting thing is that no two of them were alike. His participation in each one was different, of course, but they also differed in size, purpose, the products they produced, and perhaps most important of all, the way they were structured. Some were formal, others informal; some were tightly structured, others organized quite loosely.

In this chapter we want to explore formal organizations, primarily the work organization. It is the one that pays our salaries and helps us pursue a career. In fact, this is the organization that dominates us most of all. We even identify ourselves in terms of what work we do. When asked who we are, we are likely to respond, "I am director of personnel for Acme Corporation" or "I teach at the state university." Such statements do not really tell "who" we are, but we use them to give a primary identification.

Another reason why we shall concentrate on the work organization is that this is the one that has been studied most frequently by organizational theorists; thus we have a lot of data that will help us understand it. While we shall examine what most organizations have in common, the reader should always keep in mind that organizing is not an exact science. It still involves a lot of trial and error. The advantage of looking at some of the theories, however, is that it makes us aware of some of the options we have. We also become aware that different approaches to organization are often based on rational decisions that somehow fit into a strategy for accomplishing our goals. As H. R. Bobitt writes:

If we were to go out today to observe different modern organizations in action— a church, school, hospital, manufacturing concern, military unit—we should perhaps be more impressed with their similarities than with their differences. This would be particularly true of their structural characteristics: e.g., their structure of authority, system of control, definite lines of communication, and division of labor. It should be evident that these similarities are not simply the result of chance. Common threads of thought run through all formal organizations. They are threads woven into not only the practice of organization but its theory as well. The threads . . . are found in virtually every organization in existence, from the very simple to the most complex.

STRUCTURAL CHARACTERISTICS OF FORMAL ORGANIZATIONS

Some degree of organization emerges whenever people interact with one another. A formal organization can be differentiated, however, from a social organization in terms of both the explicitness with which its purpose is stated and the degree to which its structure is defined. Whenever we speak of organizations we are in fact speaking of formal organizations. And we define *organization* as people making some input and using some technologies (in some structured relationship) in order to produce some output.

This definition allows us to account for the social worker operating in a government agency, the sergeant in the military, and the minister in a church as well as the person on the factory assembly line.

A good analysis of the nature of organization must account for *all* its principal components: people, structure, technologies, and tasks or goals. In this chapter our main focus will be on structure, but the discussion will obviously be based on assumptions about people, tasks, and technologies. It is virtually impossible to discuss one without talking about its relation to the others.

There are many ways of classifying organizations, but one of the most useful for our purposes is to classify them according to the people who benefit from them. Blau and Scott describe four basic classifications of people identified with any organization:

1) Members or rank-and-file workers
2) Owners or managers of the organization
3) Clients or public in contact (shoppers in a supermarket, students in a university, patients in a hospital, recipients of welfare, etc.)
4) Public at large, i.e., the external society in which the organization exists[2]

In a sense each one of these groups represents a different constituency for the organization, and the decision-makers in that organization have to take into account all four constituencies. Any one organization, however, may need to consider one of these groups as its primary beneficiary, and therefore this is a useful way of examining some of the most pressing problems of the organization.[3]

Organization	Prime beneficiary	Basic problem
Mutual benefit association	Rank-and-file	Internal democratic control
Business	Owners or managers	Efficient operation
Service organization	Client group	Professional service
Commonwealth organization	Public at large	External democratic control

The structure of an organization may be influenced to a great extent by the primary beneficiary group and the resulting problems. This is why we find so many different types of structure in organizations and also why what is acceptable in some types of organizations may not be as acceptable in others. Government structure, for example, is often dictated by public sentiment, and may operate in ways quite different from what would be accepted in a business enterprise, where structure may be dictated by economic considerations.

There are many ways of structuring work organizations. In fact, if you were to look closely at any one large organization you would probably find wide differences in the way the various divisions or departments within that company are organized. Nevertheless, there are some concepts that are common to all organizations, and these have a great impact on the communication flow in the organization.

HIERARCHY There are always elements of hierarchy present in every organization. Perhaps they are most evident in large industries and the military, but they are present in every social organization, too. Of course there are degrees of hierarchy. For example, two of the basic ways of organizing are the highly centralized (tall) organization and the decentralized (flat) organization.

The *tall* organization consists of a hierarchy with many levels, and it produces close supervision and control. Decisions are centralized, and control is sometimes regarded as tending toward the autocratic style. The more steps in the hierarchy, the more information moving up the organization is filtered, censored, and distorted. Workers at low levels are not expected to participate, and the success of the system depends to a great extent on the initiative, skill, and judgments of those at the top. The tall organization has been characteristic of most American work organizations, and the organization chart in Figure 1.1 is representative of those in many large organizations.

If one examines this relatively centralized organizational chart closely, one may notice variances within the total organization. "Essentially, the American Airlines organization might be described as having centralized planning and control but with decentralized management at the local level. The city areas are free to operate, however, only within certain defined staff plans."[4]

The *flat* organization, by contrast, has few levels of hierarchy, and more people report to each supervisor. Consequently supervision tends to be rather loose, and the individual in the job is given greater responsibility for his own success. Whereas military and manufacturing organizations work well with a tall, centralized system, government, service, research, and sales organizations can often be very productive with a flat structure. The organization chart in Figure 1.2 illustrates a relatively flat organization at the managerial level.

Even this chart shows that there are still significant levels of hierarchy, but it also shows an attempt to decentralize the managerial structure.

The flat organization is inherently neither better nor worse than the tall organization; they are simply two different options. The decision as to which to choose may be based on many factors. Some people need control; others do not. Some tasks require more centralized supervision than others. Size or geographic spread may dictate the decision. In the long run the decision will rest primarily on which type of organization is likely to give the best economic standing.

Figure 1.1 American airlines corporate organization.

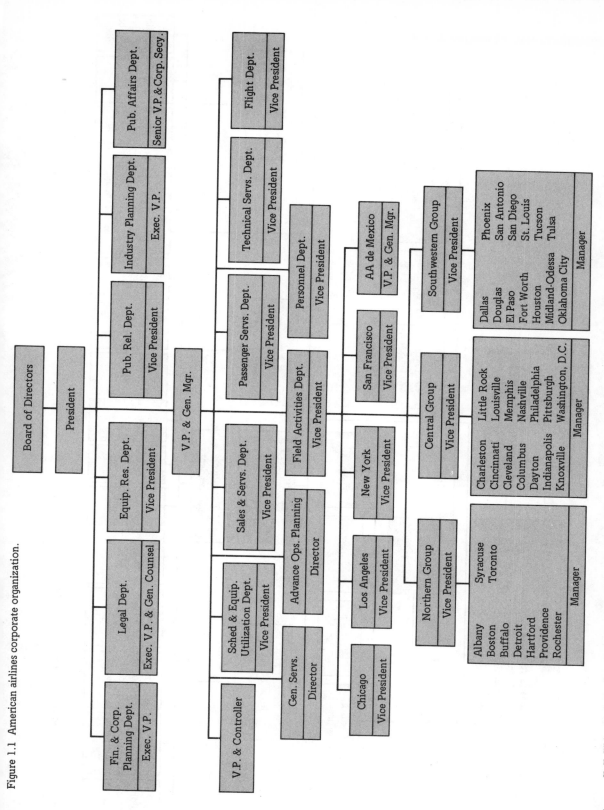

Source: K. K. White, *Understanding the Organization Chart* (New York: American Management Association, 1963), p. 80. Used by permission.

Figure 1.2. Continental Can Company Top Management.

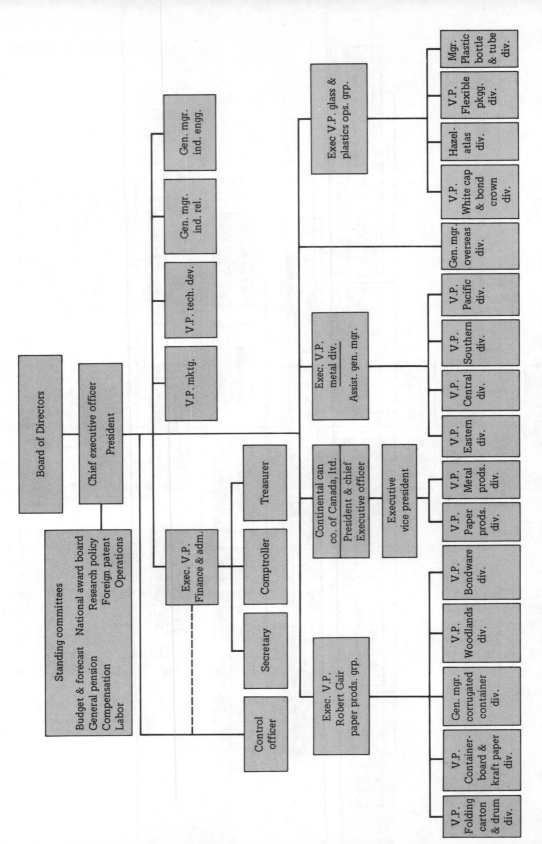

Source: K. K. White, *Understanding the Organization Chart* (New York: American Management Association, 1963), p. 105. Used by permission.

SPAN OF CONTROL

V. A. Graicunas apparently originated the concept of span of control in the 1930s as a means of indicating the number of subordinates a manager can effectively control at one time. People have argued over the correct number, but the basic concept is a viable one. Proponents of a tall structure tend to like a relatively narrow span of 6–12 people. Proponents of the flat structure realize that their system calls for less supervision and may want to enlarge the number.

One important consideration in determining an appropriate span of control is the managerial level of the position in the organization. Foremen, for example, often have 20 or 30 people working directly under them, whereas chief executives have only 3–8 people reporting directly to them. One reason for this is that the nature of the task at the various levels differs. Foremen are generally concerned with production of one product. At upper levels, however, managers try to coordinate several highly differentiated operations, each of which requires a great deal of effort even to comprehend. In such cases it would be unwise to expect the manager to maintain a fairly close knowledge of what is happening in too many distinct areas.

The span of control has many implications for communication flow within the organization. In classical organization theory, for example, the optimum span of control ranged from 5 to 15. The rationale was that supervising more than 15 people—with all the communication that would involve—would seriously dilute the manager's ability to supervise any one subordinate very effectively. Decisions about span of control are designed, on the one hand, to prevent communication overload; on the other hand, they are a way of putting distance between the manager and other workers, managers, and specialists in the organization.

DIVISION OF LABOR

The industrial revolution produced the assembly line, and ever since then workers and managers have been restricted to only part of the work on a given product. *Division of labor* has become a key concept in organization theory. Basically, it refers to how the work is divided. The general idea is that efficiency and productivity increase with task specialization and with departmentalization on the basis of function.

Dividing up the work has been productive. Nevertheless, we want to be more aware of the communication implications of division of labor. First, the more divided an organization is, the more it separates people. Engineers are housed in one area to work together, but are separated from others; assembly lines are organized so that workers produce only part of a product, and they may not see anyone else who works on it; the personnel department has separate areas for recruiting, training, and handling grievances; and advertising people work in their area trying to attract attention to the company and its products. Each is relatively isolated from the others—unless there are formal communication channels designed to give them some interaction. As a result the individual's loyalties are centered on his or her own work group, not the organization as a whole. And these loyalties influence the way people communicate.

Second, in such a structure the individual's perceptions of the total organization revolve around his own task. This often causes conflicts because each person perceives his own job as the important part of the company and often lacks a view of the total context. This is why superiors and subordinates or marketing and production departments often have different viewpoints. Theoretically, the perspective ought to become more general as one moves up the organization. The foreman, for example, is interested in his own group's productivity and is aware of its problems. The plant manager is interested in these, too, but he also has to view this group in terms of the information that he has about all divisions in the plant. The corporate vice president, in turn, must weigh what is happening in the plant in terms of what is happening in other plants as well as trends throughout the industry. These differences in perception often are the apparent result of division of labor, and they often account for much of the conflict communicated throughout the organization.

Third, division of labor makes the overwhelming communicative task of management the coordination of all the various divisions and functions in the organization.

LINE AND STAFF A corollary to the division of labor is the separation of work units into *line* and *staff*. While these terms are used in different ways and therefore do not have concrete definitions, *line* generally refers to the people who are actively involved in the work that produces the product or primary service of the organization. In a packaging industry, these are the people who are actively involved in making the packages. In a small-loan company, these are the people who make the loans.

Staff, on the other hand, refers to all the support services the line may use. It includes personnel departments, advertising, legal departments, and sometimes research divisions. These are the people whose contribution to overall production is really difficult to measure. The staff's relation to the line is usually advisory. In some defined circumstances, however, they may have some authority over the line. For example, a member of the industrial relations department may prohibit some action in the line because it is a violation of a contract, or the lawyer in the legal department may throw out a suggestion made in a conference because it is illegal. In most cases, however, the line has the prerogative of either accepting or rejecting the input from the staff.

CHAIN OF COMMAND The organizational chart identifies who interacts with whom. When these interactions are viewed in a hierarchical sense, as in identifying which subordinates interact with which superiors, we refer to them as the *chain* *of command.* In terms of communication, the chain of command is important for two reasons. First, each subordinate is expected to report to only one supervisor. Second, as information flows either up or down the organization, no level in the chain is to be bypassed. In other words, it has long been an axiom in organizational communication that each person is to funnel information only through the person next to him in the hierarchy. This idea does not always work in practice because one link in the hierarchy can become a communicative bottleneck, but it is still in general use.

ROLE The concepts of hierarchy, division of labor, and chain of command influence the differentiation of people's roles in the organization. Basically, a role includes the behaviors associated with a given position in the organization. It may include behaviors that are prohibited as well as those that must be done. Sometimes these are rather clearly spelled out in a job description, but most of the time there are still a lot of unstated expectations. For example, the role of a university student includes enrolling in a course, paying fees, attending classes, and taking whatever examinations are given. But this may be just the beginning. Throughout the term his role is expanded into doing research projects, making reports, reading assignments, and communicating in certain ways with the instructor and his classmates. In fact, the earlier role *prescription* may be quite different from the role *description* he might make about what he actually did in class. In similar ways we can identify the role behavior of any position. Part of the role of a military officer is to avoid fraternizing with enlisted men. A supervisor expects his subordinates to anticipate his needs for information. A patient in a hospital expects the nurses to be kind and considerate. All of these behaviors are expected because of the position a person has.

Even looking at the hierarchy without knowing the task or the people involved, we can tell some things about the roles of the people involved. (See Figure 1.3.) A's role permits him to give orders to B and C with the expectation that they will accept them. It is also generally expected that A will channel most of the information he wants D to have through B. D is expected to take orders from B and possibly A, but not from C. Strict adherence to the formal chain of command would dictate that C will have to go through B if he wants to communicate with D or E. G is also expected to go through C if he wants to communicate with A. This example demonstrates how structure determines many aspects of role relationships.

Examining roles has great implications for analyzing communication within the organization. First, the clarity of a role relationship influences the communication flow. Communication is easiest and most comfortable when we know what to expect of the other person. When the situation is ambiguous and we don't know what the other people's roles are, we are often unsure as to how we ought to approach them. Recently one of the

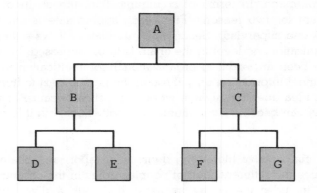

Figure 1.3.

authors encountered such a situation. He was attending a meeting in which a consultant was describing to some executives his way of conducting attitude surveys. The author was also a consultant with the company and was conducting a survey. The moment the author was introduced to him, the situation became strained because he had not been told what the author's role was going to be in relation to him. After a few minutes of discomfort, he asked directly how the author was going to be involved. When it was explained that the author was working on a different project, his role was clearer to him and the interaction was a productive one.

Second, most jobs place a person in several different roles. He will have to learn to be flexible in order to operate in each different situation. To some people, a manager is their "boss." To people higher in the organization, he is their subordinate. And for others he is just a member of the peer group. These three different relationships require different ways of communicating. We've asked hundreds of managers what they themselves do in relation to their bosses that makes them good subordinates. Generally, the two descriptions are quite different, and so are the problems of the individual manager in the two relationships.

Third, roles are ranked so that each position has a certain amount of *status* associated with it. To some people this is a dirty word because it shows that we are not all equal. It is a fact of life, however, that any organization gives greater or less value to the various positions in the organization. Consequently we need to know how status affects communication.

A woman in charge of a department in a government agency reported the following incident. She had regular meetings with her staff, and she usually told her boss when they were planned. He began to attend them, and being quite gregarious, he participated fully. She began to notice that people would not say much after he had expressed his opinions. Few questions were asked, no one would disagree with him, and sometimes the facts were embellished so that they came out a little better than they actually were. She concluded that these things might be caused by her staff's response to the boss' higher status. She summoned her courage and explained to her boss that he was quite unintentionally ruining her meetings. After that he did not come to every meeting; when he came, he held his own comments until after others had participated in the discussion. His actions resulted in greater participation by the staff, and the meetings proceeded quite successfully.

In the preceding example status got in the way of communication. But status can sometimes enhance communication. We recognize this when we say that important messages for general consumption should come from as close to the top as possible. This idea is illustrated by the following incident. A plant manager had repeatedly and very unsuccessfully told his employees to keep the area around the water fountain clean. Yet crushed cups, gum wrappers, and waste paper continued to litter the floor. One day the president of the company was touring the plant, saw the mess, and promptly put up a sign with the message: "Keep this area clean. Signed, J. Harvey Smith, President." It worked.

DIFFERENT PERSPECTIVES ON ORGANIZATION

A few years ago one of the authors had an opportunity to consult with a public utilities firm. He quickly learned that he was the latest in a long line of consultants. Several years earlier, a consulting firm had completely restructured the entire company. Old departments were abolished and new ones created, and in order to make them more efficient the functions of some departments were modified drastically. Years later the members of management were not pleased with the results, but because they felt that it would be too traumatic to try to return to the prior arrangement they had learned to live with the new structure. However, they were still searching for the right key to organizational success, so they employed some new consultants. This time the thrust was toward a change in people, and a number of new training programs were initiated. Their motives were good, but unfortunately the training function was placed under two people who did not know much about training. So this did not turn out to be the key management was looking for. The search continued, and more consultants were hired. Some studied the company's work technologies to help develop better ways of doing things, while the author worked on the internal communication flow.

We can learn much from this example. People have different perspectives on what is important in organizations. Some of the consultants concentrated on *structure*, others concentrated on *technology*, and still others focused their attention on the *people* in the organization. Because their perspectives were different, their suggestions were different. But none of them produced the magic formula for success that management would have liked. Nevertheless, all of these attempts at changing the organization, whether successful or not, taught the managers some important lessons about organizing. And one of the most important lessons to be learned is that there is not necessarily a right or wrong way of organizing, but the way we organize is a kind of strategy that we develop to accomplish our goals. And most of our decisions about organizing strategy are based on some kind of philosophy or perspective. Consequently we want to look at three of the major perspectives that have influenced organizations in the United States: (1) the scientific management movement, (2) the human relations school, and (3) the contingency approach.

SCIENTIFIC MANAGEMENT

Scientific management was the earliest movement, beginning before World War I. Sometimes called the classical theory of organization, it was concerned primarily with finding the best structure for formal organizations; the ideas of work specialization, authority, chain of command, division of work, and span of control were developed rather extensively. The classical notion of bureaucracy, as developed by Max Weber, stems from this movement, and it is characterized by the following principles:

1) Official business is conducted on a continuous basis.
2) It is conducted in accordance with stipulated rules in an administrative agency.
3) Every official's responsibility and authority are part of a hierarchy of authority.
4) Officials and other administrative employees do not own the resources necessary for the performance of their assigned functions but are accountable for their use of these resources.
5) Offices cannot be appropriated by their incumbents in the sense of private property that can be sold and inherited.
6) Official business is conducted on the basis of written documents.[5]

The advantages claimed for this system are that a person is paid in accordance with the amount of work he does, official tasks are depersonalized, centralized administration increases efficiency, promotions have a leveling effect on social and economic differences, and the bureaucratic authority relationship is very stable, that is, practically indestructible.

Another main thrust was standardization, not only of equipment and products but also of people and the work they do. Efficiency studies analyzed jobs in detail to determine exactly how they could be done in the least amount of time and with the greatest productivity.

Finally, the decisions of the scientific manager about structure, economics, and productivity were based on some fundamental assumptions about people. McGregor calls them Theory X assumptions and characterizes them as follows:

1) The average human being has an inherent dislike of work and will avoid it if he can.
2) Because of this human characteristic of dislike of work, most people must be coerced, controlled, and directed, threatened with punishment to get them to put forth adequate effort toward the achievement of organizational objectives.
3) The average human being prefers to be directed, wishes to avoid responsibility, has relatively little ambition, and wants security above all.[6]

As it developed, scientific management came to be identified with efficiency techniques such as bonus systems, time and motion studies, and a piecemeal reward system. Nevertheless, the pioneers of scientific management, including Taylor, Gantt, Emerson, Cooke, and Gilbreth, feel that theirs was a revolution in management and organizational values. To them it was a new way of thinking that was rational, efficient, and empirically supportable. And despite the modifying impact of later movements, scientific management is very much in evidence today.

HUMAN RELATIONS In 1929 a group of researchers from Harvard Business School began to explore the relationship between work environment and productivity. Whereas the scientific management movement viewed the organization as a formal work system, these researchers exposed it as a social system. They uncovered informal communication networks, a desire by some workers to participate in the organization, and an increase in productivity when workers were given attention.

From this beginning, the human relations movement mushroomed throughout the 1940s and 1950s. In part it was a reaction against scientific management, and people were emphasized over structure and technology as the key to organizational effectiveness. It produced a completely different set of assumptions about workers, popularized by McGregor as Theory Y:

1) The expenditure of physical and mental effort in work is as natural as play or rest. The average human being does not inherently dislike work. Depending on controllable conditions, work may be a source of satisfaction (and will be voluntarily performed) or a source of punishment (and will be avoided if possible).
2) External control and the threat of punishment are not the only means for bringing about effort toward organizational objectives. Man will exercise self-direction and self-control in the service of objectives to which he is committed.
3) Commitment to objectives is a function of the rewards associated with their achievement. The most significant of such rewards, e.g., the satisfaction of ego and self-actualization needs, can be direct products of effort directed toward organizational objectives.
4) The average human being learns, under proper conditions, not only to accept but to seek responsibility. Avoidance of responsibility, lack of ambition, and emphasis on security are generally consequences of experience, not inherent human characteristics.
5) The capacity to exercise a relatively high degree of imagination, ingenuity, and creativity in the solution of organizational problems is widely, not narrowly, distributed in the population.
6) Under the conditions of modern industrial life, the intellectual potentialities of the average human being are only partially utilized.[7]

Although its primary concern was people instead of structure, the human relations movement produced some new conceptualizations of organizational structure, too. It concentrated, for example, on the informal organization, the grapevine, and the networks that are not on the organizational chart. Emphasizing a need to reduce power and authority as a regulating influence, it called for changes in the organization such as decentralization, democratic leadership, and participative management. Better communications and organizational climate became overriding concerns, and job satisfaction was thought to be the way to attain better productivity.

The claims of the human relations movement were very popular, particularly among academic behavioral scientists, who published a great amount of research to support this new approach. Many managers also found it quite useful, and new innovations among workers received much publicity.

As the movement grew, however, it developed its critics, who raised three objections. First, "human relations" lost its identification as an approach to organizing and became identified with techniques of training such as case studies, T-groups, sensitivity training, awareness training, transactional analysis, and managerial grid. Since such techniques did not always lead to greater productivity or job satisfaction, they became quite controversial.

Second, some critics claimed that the human relations approach was very manipulative, that it taught managers how to use people. Scott describes this attitude as follows:

The human relations strategy is for the managers to work with the small group, with the informal leader to his side, and tune in on the grapevine to find out how things are going. Therefore, the skillful manager can put the small group to work for the cause of formal organization objectives by operating within the framework of natural human social tendencies rather than against it.[8]

Finally, behavioral scientists could not always support the claims of the movement. For example, decentralization was not always shown to work the kind of miracle claimed for it. And for every study that supported the claim that satisfaction and productivity were related one could find another study that showed some workers to be happy but unproductive. Furthermore, there was some indication that high productivity leads to higher satisfaction rather than satisfaction causing productivity.

Perhaps the human relations movement was not *the* answer, but its pioneers—Mayo, Roethlisberger, Dickson, McGregor—can be credited with some very important innovations in our thinking about organizations. Their emphases on people, communication, climate, job satisfaction, and job enrichment have had a marked impact on organizational life, and particularly on the expectations of the new generation of workers.

CONTINGENCY APPROACH   The contingency concept is based on the idea that each work situation is a unique configuration of tasks, organizational structure, types of subordinates, and manager preferences. Consequently it is assumed that no one managerial or organizational style will be equally successful across all situations. Fred Fiedler has been one of the chief pioneers of this approach, and his research seems to indicate that any style can succeed if the contingencies are right. Therefore one thrust of the contingency approach is to make each organization aware of its own unique features.

One aspect of the contingency approach that distinguishes it from some of the others is its emphasis on differences among tasks. Morse and Lorsch's research, for example, concluded that "the appropriate pattern of organization is *contingent* on the nature of the work to be done and on the particular needs of the people involved."[9] Their field research showed that industrial organizations might need to be organized and managed quite differently from research organizations. They also found significant differences even within the same type of industry.

The scientific management and human relations approaches to organization tended to be heavily oriented toward the "one best way." The contingency approach avoids this trap, and nowhere is this more clearly demonstrated than in the kinds of assumptions its proponents make about people:

1) Human beings bring varying patterns of needs and motives into the work organization, but one central need is to achieve a sense of competence.
2) The sense of competence motive . . . may be fulfilled in different ways by different people depending on how this need interacts with the strengths of the individual's other needs.
3) Competence motivation is most likely to be fulfilled when there is a fit between task and organization.
4) Sense of competence continues to motivate even when a competence goal is achieved; once one goal is achieved, a new, higher one is set.[10]

The contingency approach has made two major contributions to our thinking about organizations. First, it leads to a systematic approach in which an organization has to be examined in terms of its totality and all the important components have to be considered. Second, it treats organization as a kind of purposive strategy. It emphasizes that the organizer has some legitimate alternatives available to him in achieving his goals.

THE CHAPTER IN PERSPECTIVE

A kind of evolution has been taking place in organizational theories, with each stage making its contributions. Scientific management was useful in terms of understanding formal organization, but it was deficient in dealing with people. The human relations approach made a major contribution to our thinking about people. The contingency approach is now asking important questions about the proper balance among the components of organizations. It is obvious that management has been able to use ideas from each movement effectively, or they would not have been adopted so widely. Nevertheless, it is important to keep the evolutionary perspective, to realize that no movement or theory has yet provided the ultimate answer in terms of organizational effectiveness. And it is interesting to note that organizational theorists and behavioral scientists are already asking, "Where do we go from here?"

Although the chapter has focused primarily on the principles of organization, the aim is not to teach one how to organize. Rather, the real aim is to give the reader enough background in organizational theory so that he or she can identify the most important elements of organizational structure and begin to see how these elements influence the way people communicate. With this background, the reader is now ready to examine the role of communication in various organizational subsystems as described in Chapter 2.

REFERENCES

1. H. R. Bobitt, Jr., et al., *Organizational Behavior* (Englewood Cliffs, N.J.: Prentice-Hall, 1974), p. 17.

2. Peter Blau and W. R. Scott, *Formal Organizations: A Comparative Approach* (San Francisco: intext, 1962), pp. 42–45.

3. Ibid., p. 43.

4. K. K. White, *Understanding the Company Organization Chart* (New York: American Management Association, 1963), p. 79.

5. Reinhard Bendix, "Max Weber on Bureaucracy," in W. B. Wolf, ed., *Management* (Belmont, Calif.: Wadsworth, 1964), pp. 33–37.

6. Douglas McGregor, *The Human Side of Enterprise* (New York: McGraw-Hill, 1960), pp. 33–34.

7. Ibid., pp. 47–48.

8. William G. Scott, Organization Theory (Homewood, Ill.: Irwin, 1967), p. 413.

9. J. J. Morse and J. W. Lorsch, "Beyond Theory Y," *Harvard Business Review* (May 1970), 62.

10. Ibid., p. 67.

CHAPTER 2
THE ORGANIZATION–COMMUNICATION INTERFACE

> ## Preview
>
> The organization can be analyzed as a complete communication system made up of several subsystems.
>
> Some subsystems are classified by communicative functions:
>
> - Informative
> - Persuasive
> - Command/regulative
> - Integrative
>
> Some subsystems are classified by kind of network:
>
> - Formal
> - Informal
>
> Some subsystems are classified by organizational direction:
>
> - Downward
> - Upward
>
> Each subsystem performs a vital role in the general functioning of the organization.

As pointed out in the preceding chapter, most organization theories tend to concentrate on some part of the organization to the exclusion of the other parts, but there is merit in attempting to examine the organization as a whole. The complete system is characterized by Churchman as "a set of components that work together for the overall objective of the whole."[1] According to this definition, the system is greater than the sum of its individual parts and their internal relationships.

In this chapter we focus on the organization as a complete communication system. In order to examine the system, however, it is necessary to be aware of the subsystems that operate within it and the suprasystem or total environment in which the system operates.

SUPRASYSTEMS

Each system is also part of a *suprasystem*, or total environment in which a number of systems are operating. IBM, for example, is an entity by itself in that it has some boundaries, but it exists in the suprasystem of American business. And what happens in the suprasystem directly affects the internal workings of the system. When business is down in the auto industry, for example, the auto manufacturers do not need as many computers. So IBM is affected internally. As technologies are upgraded, universities need the latest computer equipment to teach their students. Again IBM may be affected internally. These examples demonstrate that a thorough understanding of a system may necessitate some investigation of how that system operates within its own environment, that is, its suprasystem. Furthermore, each system or organization usually builds communication networks designed to monitor the system's relationship with its suprasystem. Advertising, sales, and legal departments are different networks that tap the suprasystem at different points and bring important feedback to the organization that affects it internally.

SUBSYSTEMS

When we look at the subsystems of any organization, we find that there are many different types. On the one hand, we find that the organization can be subdivided structurally, because almost all organizations are divided into different departments. For example, most large manufacturing companies have a legal department, an industrial relations department, a manufacturing division, and a sales department. To understand the company as a whole, we have to understand the internal workings of each of these departments. But at the same time we must constantly be aware of the interdependent relationships among these departments. These interdependent relationships may not always be apparent—even to members of the organization—but they are always there, and they must be identified if one is to understand the total system.

Subsystems can also be classified as formal or informal. All of the processes identified earlier are formal in that they are consciously built into and controlled within the system. On the other hand, the human relations movement made us aware of a number of informal systems that operate in the organization. These include the grapevine, the rumor mill, the social preferences workers have for one another, and some nonverbal interaction processes. These ordinarily grow out of the social needs of the members of the organization. And while they have a great impact on the formal organization, they are not controlled by the formal system.

There are other subsystems that can be identified. In some cases it may be wise to consider the individual as a subsystem, or the physical setting in which jobs are done may turn out to be an important subsystem. The contingency approach would indicate that different organizational systems will have different kinds of subsystems that are important. The important points we wish to emphasize are that we need to define the subsystems and that we should be able to identify the ways in which they are interdependent. And the thrust of our analysis will focus on communication within the organization.

COMMUNI- CATION SUBSYSTEMS

In considering the organization as a communication system, we want to examine the role of communication in the organization, as well as some of its important subsystems.

In *The Human Organization*[2] Rensis Likert tried to show how some of the subsystems or variables in an organization fit together. In doing so, he described communication as an intervening variable that might have several different results: (1) productivity, (2) satisfaction, (3) good union-management relations, and (4) profit. In a sense this may be a good way to conceptualize the role of communications in organizations. There are only two major drawbacks to Likert's model. First, it appears to be linear. In reality, one's job satisfaction may affect the way one communicates as much as communication affects one's satisfaction. Furthermore, not only is communication affected by leadership behavior, but it also has the capacity to affect leadership behavior. So the relationship among these variables is not a linear one.

Second, Likert, like so many of us, seems to treat communication in a unidimensional sense, as an "it." But there are a great many dimensions of communication, as we shall see in Chapter 3. In addition to sources, receivers, and channels, there are different functions, different types of content, and different reactions to it. For example, it would be easy to suggest that some aspects of communication might lead an employee to be satisfied with his job, but some altogether different aspects of communication might lead him to greater productivity. In other words, we are suggesting that communication may have several different functions in any organization.

FUNCTIONS AS SUBSYSTEMS

Traditionally communication has been said to have four primary functions within the organizational context: (1) an informative function, (2) a command and regulative function, (3) a persuasive function, and (4) an integrative function.[3] An investigation of each of these should help us understand the important role of communication in the organization. Nevertheless, we must keep in mind that these functions are not mutually exclusive. Any given message or channel may fulfill several functions.

The informative function Information is the basic ingredient on which an organization thrives. And from a communication point of view it is possible to examine any organization as an information-processing system. Our primary concern is that all the members of the organization have the information that enables them to do their work. Management, for example, makes choices among the products that can be produced because it gets information from the suprasystem. This can be illustrated by the automobile industry. In the mid-1970s the public began to buy fewer large cars; management increased production of smaller, more economical cars. Workers, too, need information to do their jobs. In a system of management by objectives, for example, each worker sets new goals and develops new ways of working because he gets specific information about his own job performance.

Although we can see that informative communication is necessary to the performance of tasks, much of the information desired by members of an organization has little to do with their actual tasks. We have found, for example, that employees generally like to know the company's financial standing, how other divisions in the organization are doing, how government regulations affect their organization, and some of the personal achievements of employees. Such information does not assist the actual work flow in any direct sense, but employees express a need to know it, and the organization should therefore ensure that they get it.

One supervisory practice that highlights the informative function is the Monday morning meeting that is traditional in many organizations. The supervisor has regularly scheduled meetings with representatives from the different sections reporting to him. They may actually pass along information that is necessary for each to accomplish his task. But they also often simply report their plans for the week, relate how problems have been overcome and what additional problems might be anticipated, and explain the current status of their work. Knowing these things about Smith's operation may not necessarily help Jones do a better job, but it does serve a general informative function.

The command and regulative function A whole communication network of manuals, policies, orders, instructions, and directives comprises the guidelines by which the entire organization is run, and by its nature it not only tells people what to do but at the same time rules out all their other alternatives. In other words, the command and regulative function is the means by which management exercises control of the system, and management's ability to coordinate all the activities of the organization depends on how well it executes this control.

There are two primary characteristics of the communications that comprise the command and regulative function. First, they are peculiarly a management prerogative. Orders and instructions always flow from a superior downward to a subordinate; there can be no commands among peers. An order presumes that the communicator is in a position of authority to issue the command and to expect the receiver to comply. Compliance, however, is not always automatic. Chester Barnard suggests that an employee's acceptance of an order depends on (1) his understanding it, (2) the order's perceived consistency with the organization's purpose and the communicator's position, (3) its compatibility with his own personal interests, and (4) his physical and mental ability to comply.[4]

Second, the content of the command and regulative messages is essentially work oriented. They center primarily on the tasks necessary to do one's job. This means, of course, that there must be a rather elaborate communication system because employees at every level of the organization need to know what is expected of them and what restrictions are placed on their freedom to use their own judgment.

The persuasive function

There are many instances when people in an organization want to influence one another but attempts to control through the use of power and authority are either impossible or inappropriate. The following examples typify some attempts at persuasion. A subordinate will try to convince his boss to give him or her a raise; a manager may ask a secretary to perform some task that goes beyond his or her regular duties; a group of managers may meet to iron out the best solution to a problem; the editor of the employee newspaper may write an editorial designed to influence employee attitudes; the industrial relations manager may make a speech to upper management in which he tries to convince them that a system of flexible work hours should be adopted.

As these examples suggest, the persuasive function operates throughout the organization wherever people find it necessary to build a case for their ideas and their behaviors. Both managers and nonmanagers use it. It is important to see how the persuasive function supplements the command and regulative function, because much of what happens in any organization happens because of persuasion rather than orders. Even in superior-subordinate situations many managers prefer to try to persuade their employees to do things a certain way and will resort to commands only as a last resort. Their strategy is based on the idea that voluntary compliance breeds less resentment than the use of commands and authority.

The integrative function

There is a whole range of communication activities designed by management to cause the employee to identify with the organization and, it is hoped, to feel that he or she is a vital part of it. We want to concentrate on four of these activities:

1) Management has designed some formal channels of communication to keep the employee informed about the company as a whole. These include company newspapers and newsletters, films and filmstrips to explain the company financial picture or changes within the company, visits by top management, and yearly progress reports. These cost a lot of money, but most managements feel that building up the employee's identification with the total company is worth the expenditure.

2) Integration comes from the type of information a person gets about his particular job. In our surveys we have found that the people who are best integrated into the organization are those who are told what the goals and objectives of their departments are, how their jobs fit into the total picture, and what kind of progress they are making in their jobs.

3) In recent years many organizations have concentrated on upward channels of communication not only to get good ideas from their workers but also to give the worker a greater sense of participation in the organization. Suggestion systems and attitude surveys are popular instruments for accomplishing this, and many work conferences are designed in terms of the integrative function.

4) It has been demonstrated that many employees get a sense of integration through informal communications in the organization. Because social relations among employees perform an integrative function, some managements provide places for visiting during coffee breaks, company picnics, Christmas parties, athletic teams, and informal reports of personal achievements.

NETWORKS AS SUBSYSTEMS

Another way of examining the role of communication in an organization is to look at some of the principal communication networks that are present in most large organizations. Guetzkow identifies three formal networks that operate as subsystems of the organization, and we add a fourth, informal system.[5]

Authority

The principal channel of communication is the chain of command. The lines of authority are defined in terms of position power, and this network is a way of identifying who has the power to make decisions and who is accountable for every identifiable function in the organization. Generally, the flow of communication in the authority network is vertical, primarily downward, and it is through this network that the command and regulative function is fulfilled.

Information exchange

This network supplements the authority network in terms of both content and direction. Its messages concentrate on the internal state of the organization and the way the organization is affected by the environment, and much of the information flows upward rather than downward. A good example of this network would include all the work reports that a management requires of its employees.

Task expertise

Most companies rely on expert consultants either inside or outside the organization, and the task expertise network "handles the communication involved in bringing technical knowhow to task performance."[6] It does not follow the chain of command but is part of the adaptive mechanism of the organization that responds to whatever problems arise. In doing so, it may create new communication channels. In fact, the overall network may be quite segmented. A consultant, for example, is part of this network, and he may tap the organization at any level. The personnel department may also become a part of this network when called upon to help solve personnel problems. One characteristic that differentiates this network from the previous two is that its communication is likely to flow up and down, whereas communication in the others is predominantly upward or downward.

Informal networks

The informal communication subsystem does not appear in any organization chart, and it is often difficult to pinpoint because it includes everything outside the formal channels, that is, chance meetings in the lounge, the grapevine, and messages shared at social gatherings. It is usually oral and very fast. In fact, several studies have shown that information moves faster through the informal circuit than through the formal channels. The informal networks disseminate information in all directions—upward, downward, and horizontally—but it is not necessarily a random movement. Employees seem to build their own informal structures so that there are definite patterns with certain people occupying key roles.

It is a mistake to think of only one informal network in an organization. A number of informal subsystems that include different people and different types of messages operate in most organizations. Moreover, they arise for a number of different reasons. First, people are social beings and want to talk about what is happening to them at work as well as away from it. In this sense all organizational activities have social value, and it is through the informal channel that much of the integrative communication function takes place. Second, the informal subsystem supplements the formal ones. Sometimes it creates better and quicker channels of communication that overcome some of the formal barriers.

On the other hand, many people fear the informal networks because they cannot control them and any attempt to do so is resisted. Furthermore, informal networks sometimes cause difficulty because messages get distorted and it is difficult to correct them.

In conclusion, we may say that the informal networks are a fascinating aspect of organizational life. They have some benefits for management and some potential liabilities. A wise management will take both into consideration. And while it cannot be controlled or manipulated by management, the informal network can at least be tapped so that management can receive feedback about what kind of information is being processed through it.

COMMUNI-CATION DIRECTION AS A SUBSYSTEM

The fact that organizations function in hierarchies makes the direction of communication flow a significant variable in organizations, and it has become traditional to examine communication in terms of upward, downward, and horizontal subsystems. In this chapter we limit our discussion to upward and downward communication. While direction is the major difference between the two, we also find that each of these subsystems has some unique channels, processes different kinds of information, and performs different communicative functions.

Downward communication

Downward communication includes all interaction that flows from superior to subordinate. While this subsystem may perform any of the four communication functions described earlier, its most obvious function is the command and regulative function.

The downward subsystem also processes certain information that cannot come through any other subsystem. Research by Downs and Hazen identified three general types of information that employees want to have coming downward:[7] (1) Work requirements tell them exactly what they are to do and what is expected of them. This also involves knowing how problems are being handled, how their jobs relate to others, departmental goals and policies, and information about pay and benefits. (2) At every level employees want personal feedback as to how they are doing in their jobs, how they are being judged, and how their jobs compare with others. Such feedback not only helps them set new goals but also performs an integrative function by giving the individual some recognition for his efforts. Our research has demonstrated that this is the kind of information most employees feel they are not being given adequately. (3) Most employees feel a need for information that gives them the corporate perspective. They want to know the company's financial standing, its policies and goals, and its mistakes as well as its accomplishments.

Management has any number of channels available for sending such information to its employees. Not every message, however, would be equally appropriate for any given channel. For example, personal feedback should not be given through any channel that has general distribution; it is best given through a personal channel. Therefore one of the strategic choices of management is to find out which channel would be best for the message. Some of the most common channels available for downward communication are the following:

A. Personal Channels
 1. Formal interviews
 2. Conferences
 3. Telephone
 4. Letter
 5. Memo
 6. Planned floor contacts
 7. Nonverbal interaction

B. Impersonal Channels
 1. Handbooks and manuals
 2. Bulletin boards
 3. Employee publications
 4. Radio and television
 5. Training programs
 6. Conferences
 7. Reports
 8. Payroll inserts
 9. Annual financial reports
 10. Films and filmstrips
 11. Speeches

All of these channels would be available to most large organizations. Unfortunately, however, they are not always used well. There has been a tendency to copy communication practices from other organizations, and it may turn out that a given management has no means of evaluating its own communicative practices. Consequently the following guidelines might be useful in helping any organization mold its downward communication subsystem.

1) The channels and the types of information they carry should be definitely known by management and employees alike. This may occasionally require some publication about channels, since people tend to forget what is available to them.

2) Management should know exactly what it wants its communication to achieve. This is so obvious that it is sometimes forgotten. A consultant once pointed this out dramatically to a railway company by asking what it hoped to achieve through its house organ. Apparently no one had ever asked that question, and no one could give an answer. Even the editor showed great discomfort because he did not have identifiable goals in mind.

3) Lines of communication should be as direct and as short as possible. Generally, personal channels are preferred by employees because of their speed, the kind of information that goes through them, and the opportunity to get clarification of the message.

4) Human communication is never exact, and management may need to spend extra effort in an attempt to be clear and consistent. Clarity and consistency are judged by the receiver, so management needs to be oriented toward employee reactions.

5) Timeliness is important. There may be an optimum time to disseminate information. It is possible to communicate too early as well as too late. During labor negotiations, for example, it may be extremely unwise to announce the company's position before the negotiations are completed. Or a company may censor information about a new product in order to maintain its competitive edge. But these are special situations. A more common complaint is that it takes too long to process information or information does not get to the worker until it's too late. It's like getting an invitation after the event has already taken place.

6) Distribute the information when and where it is most likely to be comprehended. Some plants have grappled, for example, with the decision as to whether to distribute company newspapers at the plant or mail them to the home. Some people feel that mailing them to the home is likely to encourage other family members to read them; others feel that workers would not read them because they don't like to be bothered at home. Similarly, some conferences are held away from the work area in order to maximize comprehension. A company may have to study the unique behavior of its workers in order to make such a decision. And just because a policy works in another organization does not ensure that it will work in your company.

7) Use finances as a means of evaluating the communication program. Usually management will have some choices as to how information should be delivered. One may wonder, for example, whether it is more economical to pull employees off their jobs to listen to a speech on new staff benefits or to prepare an elaborate written explanation and mail it to their homes.

8) Generally, sending messages through two channels rather than one is more effective.

9) Even though it may be necessary to pay special attention to periods of stress and change, communication must be continuous. Employees will not tolerate a communicative vacuum.

Upward communication

In recent years great stress has been placed on the necessity of communicating upward. The formal organization, of course, has always required a full complement of task-related work reports be sent upward, but now there is a feeling that additional kinds of information need to be sent upward. The result is that upward communication is not always easily defined; Redding complains that it now encompasses "a confusing variety of concepts such as empathic listening, question and answer, participative decision-making, and suggestion systems."[8] What we learn from this is that different organizations have different philosophies and practices about upward communication. The important point is that some provision be made for employees to communicate upward.

A good rationale can be developed for paying considerable attention to employees' upward communication. First, it improves downward communication. It is only through the upward feedback that management can readily assess how effective its downward communication has been. Consequently upward communication becomes an important vehicle for identifying and solving problems. Second, upward communication keeps management attuned to what is going on throughout the organization. It is a good barometer of what employees are thinking and feeling. Third, upward communication performs an important integrative function by giving the employee a sense of participation and involvement in the organization. Finally, it pays off economically through creative suggestions and information that helps prevent mistakes.

Even with such a good general rationale, however, there is still the question of what messages should be sent upward. We've asked many executives if a good boss should always listen to his subordinates, and most have reservations. One manager was willing to listen to any questions about an assignment, but he could not care less about hearing that the employee did not want to do the assignment or whether he thought it was important. In another case a company recognized the value of upward communication and spent a lot of effort organizing an elaborate suggestion system. It wanted all the good suggestions employees could give, but management was a little disgruntled when one of the first suggestions was to have a "Miss Company" contest. Another study indicated that employers were perfectly willing to have employees talk *about* their feelings, but they were unwilling to have them communicate their feelings. In other words, it was acceptable for someone to say "I'm angry," but it was unacceptable for the same person to visibly portray that anger by his language or behavior. All of these examples suggest that upward communication in the abstract receives widespread endorsement but that there are some limitations placed on it, too. These limitations need to be clarified if an effective upward communication subsystem is to develop.

What, then, should be communicated upward? Pragmatically, we can answer: anything management requests or is willing to tolerate. Most managements will be receptive to reports about work or problems, creative suggestions for doing things better or increasing profitability, and certain types of employee reactions and feelings.

The most frequent channels for upward communication are the following:

A. Personal
  1. Informal social contacts
  2. Formal interviews
  3. Conferences
  4. Letters
  5. Telephone
  6. Reports
  7. Nonverbal interaction
  8. Planned floor contacts

B. Impersonal
  1. Training programs
  2. Suggestion systems
  3. Employee publications
  4. Consultants
  5. Attitude surveys
  6. Union publications
  7. Reports

The greatest difference between the channels used for upward communication and those used for downward communication occur on the impersonal side. There are special channels such as suggestion systems, attitude surveys, and outside consultants that have a unique upward function. On the other hand, it is interesting to note that most of the channels used for downward communication can also be used for upward communication. The training program, for example, is designed primarily to tell employees how to do their jobs, but it can also be used as a way of picking up employee reaction to the company and how things are being done. The interview, too, can be a means of putting upward and downward communication together. Even the company newspaper can be an instrument for upward communication. The president of a national finance agency has a column in the company paper in which he does nothing but answer employee questions.

Upward communication, like the downward subsystem, needs some guidelines for use. The following will be useful in most organizations:

1) Management should know what kinds of information it wants to have communicated upward and provide appropriate channels to get it.
2) Upward communication must be solicited. Many employees feel that communication is not wanted unless it is specifically requested.
3) Upward communication cannot be forced; it can only be invited. Open upward communication requires a basic trust of management. Even though information is solicited, some employees will be reluctant to give it if it involves any information that is potentially damaging to them. People generally communicate in ways that protect them and their jobs. This is why many employees are very suspicious of attitude surveys. The following experience, reported by

a director of employee communications for an international packaging firm, illustrates why people become suspicious. After a conference he was sent a reaction form that guaranteed his anonymity and asked him to evaluate the conference. He decided that he would not fill it out, and two weeks later he received an identical form in the mail with instructions to fill it out, since he had not filled out the first one. The experience in which promises of anonymity are not respected has been replicated thousands of times.

4) In general, personal channels are preferable to impersonal ones, except in cases where the employee feels a need to remain anonymous. Consequently both types should be available to the employee.

5) Listening must be active. There should be a concerted attempt to understand the messages employees send.

6) Upward communication requires a downward response. Employees who ask questions expect that they will be answered; employees who make suggestions expect that they will receive some feedback as to how they are evaluated. Employees who set goals for themselves and reach them expect their supervisors to give them recognition for doing so.

THE CHAPTER IN PERSPECTIVE

Each organization is a unique communication system made up of several different subsystems, each processing different kinds of messages and perhaps performing different kinds of communicative functions. Ultimately, however, organizations must be interpreted in terms of people—people interacting in various kinds of groupings. And as we try to place this chapter in perspective we wish to emphasize three points about people.

First, remembering the four classifications of communicative functions in an organization will be vital to understanding the rest of this book. Information, command and regulation, persuasion, and integration are not just what communication does in the impersonal *system;* they are the purposes *people* have as they communicate in interviews, conferences, and speeches: They are the end products that the organizational communicator tries to achieve.

Second, the upward, downward, and horizontal subsystems are not really discrete. They offer a useful framework for analyzing organizations; but in this book we are examining communication in terms of personal interactions, and these can always involve communication going in all directions at once.

Third, communicating in organizations is a complex process, but to a great extent people control their own communicative behavior. Consequently they can learn to communicate more effectively and more efficiently if they have a thorough understanding of what is involved in communicating with others. Chapter 3 analyzes in detail some of the important dimensions of the communication process and gives the conceptual framework for the remainder of the book.

REFERENCES

1. Brent Ruben, "General Systems Theory," in R. W. Budd and Brent Ruben, eds., *Approaches to Human Communication* (Rochelle Park, N.J.: Hayden, 1972), p. 124.

2. Rensis Likert, *The Human Organization* (New York: McGraw-Hill, 1967).

3. Lee Thayer, *Communication and Communication Systems* (Homewood, Ill.: Irwin, 1967), pp. 187–252.

4. Chester Barnard, *The Functions of the Executive* (Cambridge, Mass.: Harvard University Press, 1938), pp. 165–166.

5. Harold Guetzkow, "Communications in Organizations," in James March, ed., *Handbook of Organizations* (Chicago: Rand McNally, 1965), pp. 543–547.

6. Ibid., p. 545.

7. Cal W. Downs and Michael D. Hazen, "Dimensions of Communication Satisfaction," unpublished manuscript, 1975.

8. Charles Redding, *Communication Within the Organization* (New York: Industrial Communication Commission, 1972), p. 341.

CHAPTER 3
COMMUNICATION: A FRAME OF REFERENCE

Preview

There are eight vital dimensions of communication:

1. It is a joint process.
2. Each person performs several communication functions.
3. It is purposive.
4. Feedback is essential.
5. Each person is a unique communication filter.
6. Communicators often differ in their meanings for the same message.
7. The channel influences the interpretation of the message.
8. Each communicator will have many stimuli competing for his attention.

Effectiveness of communication is judged in terms of the communicator's expectations and purpose.

The greatest obstacle to effective communication is the illusion that it has occurred when in fact it has not. Consider the following real incidents reported by managers in a training program.

It was the morning before a regular monthly inventory in our plant, and the metallurgist in charge of the blast furnace wanted to smelt a large pile of fine dust before the inventory party could put it on the books as a by-product material. He left orders with the foreman to get rid of the pile before morning.

Fine dust, in small amounts, will not harm the operation of a blast furnace, but the amount on hand was too much for a 24-hour period. The foreman was an experienced operator and knew this; but he also did not like the metallurgist, so he followed orders to the letter.

On inventory morning the pile of dust was in the blast furnace but the furnace was not operating; it was dead.

. . . .

In the engineering development phase of a designated system, the program manager called into his office the head of the radar organization. Between them they chose a course of action for the radar design. The program manager failed to communicate the decision to the head of the system engineering department or to the head of the computer design department. He went on vacation. By the middle of the following week there were two system designs being implemented, one by the radar organization and the other by the system engineering organization. It was the contention of the system engineering head that the fix being implemented by the radar organization would minimize the radar problem at the expense of the overall system and would degrade the system's performance considerably.

System engineering undertook a complete analysis of the problem and demonstrated that its opinion was backed by the facts. Two weeks went by before the program manager returned. Then a long, frustrating, acrimonious meeting was held, and a reversal of the decision was made. In the meantime a significant amount of manpower had been wasted, precious schedule time lost, and some personal relationships weakened—all because of ineffective communication.

Cases like these are numerous, and we have all become aware of the tremendous damages that can result from such communication breakdowns. In other words, our frequent problems have made us realize that communication is important. All our interpersonal relationships and all our organizational coordination depend to some extent on our competence as communicators.

The foundation for developing communication skills and competence is an adequate understanding of the communication process. This chapter is designed to explore the vital dimensions of communication and offer a frame of reference that will wipe away some false illusions about communication. It is our premise that every person has some control over his communication activities—more so than one might realize—so that some of his difficulties can be prevented, changed, remedied, or at least perceived differently.

COMMUNICATION AS A PROCESS

The most basic principle of communication is that it is a process. This process notion is important because it emphasizes the fact that communication is dynamic interaction, forever changing. People are never completely predictable, and there is something potentially unique about each new communication encounter. Moreover, there are many variables that interact over a period of time, and therefore one can never produce the formula that is going to guarantee success in communicating. At best one can identify some of the contingencies that seem to be responsible for different kinds of communication effects. This means that the competent communicator is a good strategist who takes into account as many relevant factors as possible, and he is also a tactician who can adapt readily when he encounters problems.

As a dynamic process, communication can legitimately be studied from many points of view. George Gerbner has a verbal model that not only defines communication but also indicates the various areas of study that one might pursue in examining communication phenomena.

The Gerbner communication model[1]

1. Someone	6. to make available materials
2. perceives an event	7. in some form
3. and reacts	8. and context
4. in a situation	9. conveying content
5. through some means	10. of some consequence.

Thayer, on the other hand, approaches communication from a systems point of view and analyzes it in terms of the ways information is treated. He identifies four communication functions: (1) generating data, (2) disseminating information, (3) acquiring information, and (4) processing data.[2]

In this book we focus on communication processes involving oral face-to-face interactions that take place in an organizational setting. From this vantage point we feel that *communication can best be viewed as people in relationships sharing messages by exchanging them with one another through some communication channel with some consequence.* A simple model of communication at this level might look something like Figure 3.1. We shall use it as a point of departure to refine our concept of communication by looking at some vital dimensions of communication.

Figure 3.1. Communication model.

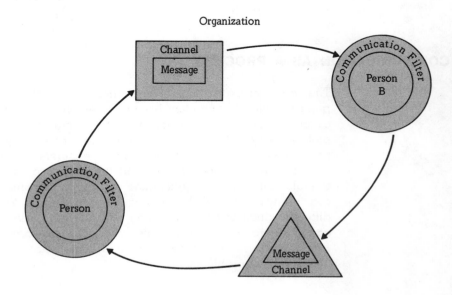

VITAL DIMENSIONS OF COMMUNICATION

1. *Communication is a joint process.* Both A and B contribute to the interaction, and the success of their communication encounter depends on both of them. Frequently we catch ourselves thinking the communicator controls the situation. But when we examine our model we find that both individuals are communicators and that neither has exclusive control over the other. One can be successful only if the other cooperates. In fact, in a poll conducted in 1974 Christopher Spicer discovered that the number one competence required by organizational communicators is the understanding that "we never have complete control over how our messages may be interpreted."[3]

2. *Each communicator performs several different communicative functions.* Sometimes, for example, A acts as the initiator or sender of a message; at other times A acts primarily as a listener. Actually he may do both simultaneously, but it facilitates our analysis if we separate the two. Therefore we will refine our model as shown in Figure 3.2.

As we have already intimated, it is almost always inappropriate to refer to one person as the source and the other as the receiver. In any sustained interaction they each use the processes of sending and receiving. And it is important that we realize that receiving skills are just as important as sending skills.

While it does represent the ideal in most interpersonal communication

Figure 3.2.

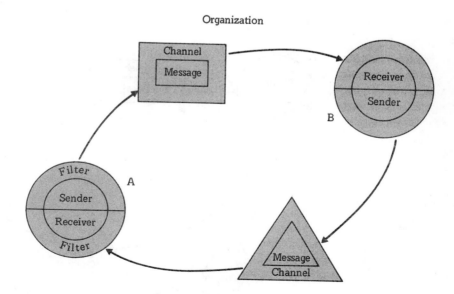

situations, even this model may not accurately represent what is occurring. The following are some realistic variations.

In some situations one functions entirely as a sender or as a receiver. In the classic speech situation, for example, there is a time when one person, the speaker, is the sender and the members of the audience are the receivers. In such cases the model might look like Figure 3.3.

During a forum or question-and-answer period, however, the source and receiver functions become more balanced again.

In meetings, too, the larger the size of the group, the more likely one is to find some people functioning as primary sources and the others as receivers. (See Figure 3.4.)

Finally, the relationships that sometimes exist within an organization dictate that one person function primarily as the source and the other as the receiver. For example, a manager once described his relationship with his boss in this way:

My superior calls me in to get my ideas or opinions on a particular issue. He first states his position and then asks, "What do you think?" Before I really respond, he concludes with "Fine," or "That will do." Sometimes he will even listen to my comments but then tell me why they won't work. Basically, rather than getting my input or advice, he is looking for someone to whom he can tell his plans.

Figure 3.3.

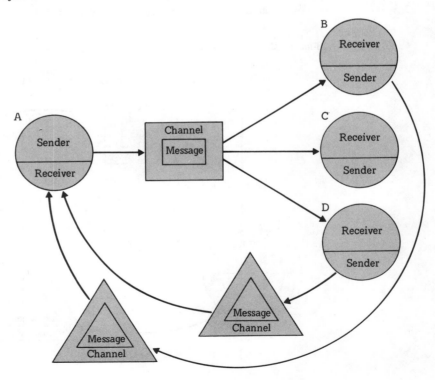

Figure 3.4.

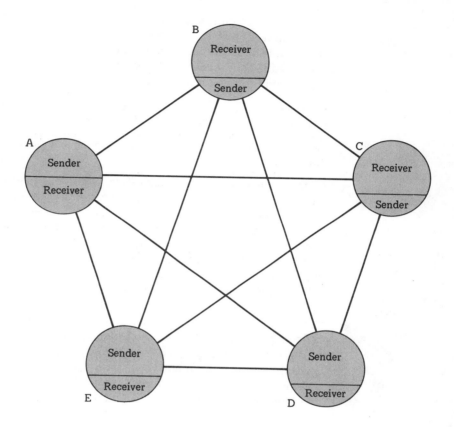

Such interaction is not inherent in the superior-subordinate relationship, but it does occur frequently.

3. *Communication is purposive.* The role a person plays in a given communication encounter depends partly on his purposes. And it is a common mistake to identify purpose only with the initiator. Both the sender and the receiver have their reasons and purposes for interacting with one another. The sender will initiate messages in order to persuade, inform, encourage, entertain, reprimand, and so forth. The receiver, on the other hand, will listen if he wants what the sender is offering or if he sees that the message or the relationship is somehow advantageous to him. It is important to reemphasize here that effective interaction is sometimes determined by the compatibility of the people's goals. If one is truly determined not to buy a given product but the salesman is equally determined to sell the product, one of the two is not going to be successful in achieving his goals. A lot of communication may take place, but part of it is doomed from the start.

If we say that communication is purposive, we must also recognize that the lack of it is also frequently purposive. People avoid others when the relationship is unpleasant, and they also sometimes withhold information from others out of spite, jealousy, or competition. In all these instances there is a definite purpose behind the reluctance to communicate.

4. *Feedback is essential to communication effectiveness*, and the context should provide for it. Feedback refers to

the process of correction through incorporation of information about effects received. When a person perceives the results produced by his own actions, the information so derived will influence subsequent actions. Feedback thus becomes a steering device upon which learning and the correction of errors are based.[4]

In its broadest sense, feedback refers to any response we get from someone who has received our message. Basically, it is necessary because we cannot be certain that the person has received the message and interpreted it as we hoped until we get some response. If feedback shows that the receiver does not understand, the communicator can repeat, elaborate, and explain the message. If the response indicates that the receiver rejects the message, the communicator may use this response in making his own response, that is, in shaping his future messages. To communicate without feedback is to put too much trust in the communication process and in people's abilities; eventually some breakdowns are bound to occur.

Because feedback has so much value, three additional points should be made. First, feedback must often be sought because people do not always give it voluntarily. When one employee was asked by a consultant whether he understood the instructions his boss had just given him, the employee replied, "No . . . but you don't think I was going to tell him, do you?" This employee would rather risk doing the task incorrectly than ask a question. Second, feedback consists of nonverbal messages as well as verbal ones. Sometimes people speak loudest with their feet; that is, they avoid contact. Third, bogus feedback is rather common. Like the person who is bored during a church service but tells the minister on the way out what a fine sermon it was, most of us are fairly adept at feeding back messages that do not really represent our true reactions. We call it tact, human relations, or sometimes self-preservation.

The following example demonstrates how feedback can be helpful. Although we do not necessarily recommend what happened, it is significant that both the subordinate and the superior gave useful feedback that threatened but ultimately maintained a productive relationship.

Tim Jackson was reviewing his section's manpower requirements with his boss. The boss continually interrupted with a string of questions challenging the validity of Tim's figures. As soon as Tim opened his mouth to answer one string of questions, however, the boss would interrupt with another string of questions. This went on for perhaps thirty minutes, during which Tim felt that he was never able to give a good reply. Finally, Tim was so frustrated that he lost his cool, told his boss to be quiet and listen, and explained that if the questions were relevant he should have time to answer them because otherwise it would appear that no valid answers existed.

The boss shut up, turned red and let Tim talk. He still refused to change his decision to cut down the manpower requirements, though.

The next day Tim went to his boss and apologized. The boss responded that after thinking it over he felt that Tim was justified in doing what he did.

There is another lesson that can be learned from this example. If effective communication is important, the context must allow for a degree of freedom of expression. Such a climate is generally not a problem when there is mutual trust or when people agree with one another. However, when there are opposing viewpoints in interviews, meetings, or speeches, openness and freedom are not so easily tolerated. We emphasize *degree of freedom* because there are limits to what a person will tolerate. We've asked many managers if they would be willing to accept *any* feedback a subordinate wanted to give. Almost all had reservations about complete openness, and they expressed widely different latitudes of acceptance. Most indicated that certain kinds of responses were completely acceptable, but some were not. Not every boss, for example, would accept the kind of feedback that Tim Jackson gave, but this one was apparently better off for having accepted it.

5. *Each person is a unique communication filter.* This can be explained in terms of the concept of abstracting. *Abstracting* is the process of focusing on some aspects of message, event, or person while neglecting other characteristics of the same message, event, or person. Each person selects out of his total environment what he wishes to give his attention, and it is this event of selection that is called abstracting. The reason, then, that people may give different interpretations to the same message or event is that they may be focusing on different aspects. (See Figure 3.5.) This selection process is likely to be a habitual rather than a random one. The selected stimuli are then filtered through a mental screen made of the individual's past experiences, language facility, habits of thinking, priorities, purposes, knowledge, attitudes, and communication skills. This is another way of saying that people select and organize what they see and hear in patterns that make sense to them.

Figure 3.5.

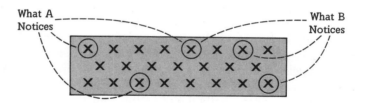

Each communicator comes to the interaction with the same kinds of influences in his filter, but his process of development is certain to have made him different from others in some important ways. The similarities may make communication possible; the differences sometimes lead to breakdowns or the possibility of new learning by each communicator.

Filtering occurs both in the encoding of messages and in the interpretation of them, and it is impossible to get completely outside one's own filter. On the other hand, we are quick to point out that new experiences and new information cause the filter to undergo constant modification. Finally, the recognition that one inevitably filters enables a communicator to expect occasional differences and difficulties and to make some adjustments to account for them.

6. *The message sent is not necessarily the message received.* This is true partly because the sender and receiver have different filters, but it is important to examine further the nature of messages. A receiver can receive many types of messages—handshakes, winks, slaps, memos, letters, speeches, etc. For the moment, however, we are concerned only with verbal messages, which are always made of language organized in some pattern.

One of the most useful ways of examining the nature of messages is to differentiate between message and meaning. A message is formed by manipulating some linguistic code made up of an identifiable group of words and symbols used in accordance with specific grammatical rules. Moreover, there is always a definite physical property about it such as the marks on a page or the sound waves in the air.

Meaning, on the other hand, exists only in the mind. It is the mental association one makes between a symbol or word and its referent. Consequently it has become axiomatic to say that "meanings are in people, not in words." Because these associations or meanings are learned through experience, they are *personal*, and they are constantly undergoing subtle changes. They are personal because to some degree each person has unique experiences that shape his meanings. They undergo changes because new experiences shape the meanings. In other words, none of us ever stops building associations for our language.

This discussion is intended to point out why users of the same language often experience difficulty in sharing their meanings. When this happens, and it frequently does, the communication breakdown is called *bypassing*. Basically, there are two ways in which people are bypassed in their meanings: (1) using different words to mean the same thing without recognizing that they are in fact talking about the same thing and (2) using the same words but having different meanings for them. In the first case, the immediate consequence is an apparent disagreement where none really exists. Perhaps this is what happens when people argue at length and in a very heated fashion, only to conclude that they have been "saying" or meaning essentially the same thing all along.

The second case is probably more prevalent. We often agree at a verbal level but disagree on a living level—same words, different meanings. Complaints about labor-management contracts often occur because one group did not anticipate how the other would interpret its words. And new cases cause the Supreme Court to continually redefine the Constitution. It is rather common to hear someone complain that someone else has kept the "letter of the law" but not its "spirit." In fact, this is apparently what the foreman did in the furnace example at the beginning of the chapter. The following is another real example of the trouble that can be caused by bypassing.

A new laboratory manager was assigned to head the systems engineering laboratory. A senior staff engineer, who had known the new manager only three months, wanted to impress him. Therefore he went into the manager's office and said, "I have some time, since the job I have does not occupy me full time, and I could help you with some new assignment."
The manager answered, "Oh, you have nothing to do?"
The senior systems engineer hastily replied, "Yes, I do, but it doesn't occupy me full time."
The manager then asked, "What are you charging your time to if you have nothing to do?"
At this point the senior systems engineer lost his temper and things went from bad to worse. Finally he was given two weeks to look for another job. Two days later a coworker smoothed over the incident after several hours of discussion with both parties. The senior systems engineer was an excellent engineer, and the laboratory did not want to lose him. But it came dangerously close when an offer to help was interpreted as "nothing to do."

Having already discounted the idea that words themselves have meaning, we must now discount the assumption that a word has only one meaning. Most words, in fact, have many meanings associated with them, and any dictionary is likely to describe several. To further illustrate this point, write your definitions of the following list of words. Have your friends, coworkers, or classmates do the same, and then compare yours with theirs.

Communication	Meaningful work
Profit	Social responsibility
Good grades	Leadership
Adequate pay	Free enterprise
Success	Socialism

This is not just an exercise in semantics. These definitions are important because they determine the way you and others see the world, the way you interpret your work, and the way you behave. The fact that your definitions are likely to differ from those of others simply demonstrates that communicating with someone else may be difficult when you have many meanings for the same words.

Because both the sender and the receiver can bypass and be bypassed, the following three guidelines may be helpful to both: (1) Remember that saying what you mean does not guarantee that you have communicated what you mean. It is particularly easy to forget this with close associates. (2) Ask for feedback and give it freely. It is wise to test whether or not the communicators really understand one another by asking questions or by paraphrasing the messages. (3) Pay attention to contexts. Sometimes other cues help decipher what the sender really means.

7. *The channel influences the interpretation of the message.* Marshall McLuhan's *Understanding Media* even makes the point that the medium *is* the message. In other words, people apparently associate meanings with particular channels; even when the same language is conveyed through different media, the message is somehow changed from one medium to the next. This is why in our model we have the message encircled by the channel. (See Figure 3.6.)

One way the channel influences the interpretations of the message is illustrated in the following example. An employee might well receive a reprimand with a minimum of negative feeling in an interview; he might even view it as being somewhat constructive. But to receive it in a meeting with others present would drastically alter the meaning of the message even if the same words were used. And heaven forbid that it should be inserted in a speech before an audience!

Another way the channel influences the interpretation has to do with the way we abstract. Each person probably has some channels to which he pays attention and some to which he does not. For example, in a university a lot of written messages are circulated among the faculty that are not widely read. Why? Those who don't read the notices have learned not to expect much of that channel. The organizational communicator, then, is always faced with tough questions. What is the best channel available for this particular message? Should time be saved by giving it in a speech to everyone at once? Or should we interview each person individually in order to be sure everyone gets the message and understands it? There are no textbook answers for such questions, and this is one situation in which the communicator's skill as a strategist pays huge dividends.

8. At any given moment, *each communicator has many messages or cues vying for his attention*, not all of them verbal. In some cases a receiver will have a number of different senders trying to get his attention. (See Figure 3.7.) This poses some unique problems for the sender who wants to win over the others. For example, a salesman is frequently in this plight as he tries to make his clients remember him and forget his competitors. What strategies can he use?

Figure 3.6.

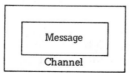

Figure 3.7.

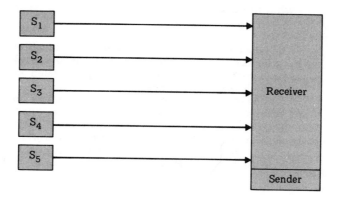

In a similar vein, the speaker before an audience realizes that he, too, has competitors. In fact the receiver is literally bombarded with different kinds of messages other than the verbal one. And these other messages may affect not only the receiver's attention but the way the message is interpreted. Some of these messages are included in the following list:

What is said
How it is said
How the speaker looks
Room temperature
Where the communication takes place
What the receiver wants to hear

Perhaps many more items could be added to this list, but these make the point that at any given time a receiver is consciously and unconsciously assimilating a number of different messages at once. To illustrate how behavior is often interpreted, we could point to a lot of nonverbal research that is trying to analyze what it means when people lean forward or backward, look at the other person or avoid eye contact, or cross their arms and legs in an interview. Not everyone, of course, consciously uses these as message cues, but many apparently do.

Finally, there are cues in the surroundings that some people use as messages. One manager we know says that he can tell what kind of person someone is by looking at his office. According to him, an achievement-oriented person displays his awards, diplomas, and certificates; the people-oriented person displays his pictures of the bowling team, the army group, or some training group of which he was a part; the status, or power-oriented person tends to display things like expensive paintings and maintain an immaculate desk. Whether or not there is any validity to these observations, this manager certainly treats them as messages.

It would be a mistake, however, to consider these additional cues as being unplanned by the sender. The following example leaves no doubt as to what the manager wishes to convey, and he probably will never again have to state it verbally.

When the department head moved into his new office, he took his large metal desk with its conference top with him. When he was asked if he wanted a new chair and desk to go along with the newly decorated office, he said, "Hell, no! This is my lucky chair and desk."

Later one of his colleagues suggested that perhaps he should turn the desk so that when he met with people he could face them without a barrier and be closer to them. His reply was, "This is the way I want it." He did insist, however, on having a large, new, 15-foot conference table with white chairs. The table is boat shaped and will seat 14, but he arranged it so that only 13 can sit at the table. One end can't be used. He remarked, "There is only one head of this table."

JUDGING EFFECTIVENESS OF COMMUNICATION

One of the goals of any communication training is to help people become more effective, and this raises the question, "What is it to be effective?" The answer is not necessarily as simple as we might like. There are three main considerations that should be used in answering it.

First, the qualities of the message and the presentation are often used in judging effectiveness. One could compile quite a list of very desirable qualities such as clarity, timeliness, receiver orientation, interest, ability to attract attention, thoroughness, and consistency. Any critique of a communication situation is likely to revolve around at least a few of these qualities, and in college courses speakers are often graded on the basis of these qualities. In a real sense, however, these qualities are only guidelines that may lead to communication competence; they are not ends in themselves.

Second, effectiveness can be defined in terms of the communicator's purposes. Presumably, all communication takes place in order to achieve some general or particular result, and one view of effectiveness says that the communicator is not effective until he has accomplished the desired result. Earlier we made the point that communication is purposive, and it is enlightening to examine some of the goals people tend to set for themselves. There seem to be at least four consistent patterns:

1) Some people are satisfied if they get the message said or written. Students are often more concerned with fulfilling an assignment to speak for five minutes than with influencing the audience. Managers and politicians sometimes say things just to get them on the record. And the objective for some trainers is simply to fill a time slot; they are not particularly concerned about what they do. In such cases, making sure someone hears them seems to be the limit of their responsibility, and they do not check for comprehension, understanding, or effect.

2) At a different level, communication is said to be effective when someone has not only received the message but also indicates that he understands it the way the sender wanted it understood.

3) Others interpret effectiveness in terms of the receiver not only understanding the message but also agreeing with it. According to their public statements, for example, it seemed inconceivable to some protest groups that others could listen, understand, and still disagree.

4) In some cases, communication is not deemed effective until the receiver understands, agrees, and does what the sender wants done. A parent, for example, may not feel that his or her communication has been effective until the child has obeyed.

Each of us may set different objectives for ourselves at different times, and thus our specific criteria for effectiveness will change. In any case, the compatibility between the communicator's purpose and the effects of the interaction may be one way of judging effectiveness.

The third consideration asks, "When should effectiveness be determined?" Should one use a short-term perspective and judge by the immediate reaction, or should one use a long-term perspective and judge by the ultimate result? Many of the things we now take for granted as being very desirable were once proposed by someone who was castigated for proposing them. Pioneers and change agents are often rejected. In the short run they appear unsuccessful and ineffective; but from a different perspective they appear to have been very effective. The salesman offers another useful example. Is he to be judged ineffective because a client does not respond well to his first overture? And how does he suddenly become effective when a year later he finally gets the client to make a purchase?

Finally, when we take all three of these considerations into account, we have to admit that we probably judge our effectiveness on the basis of all three. We want our communication to have the qualities that others have found lead to success; we want our communication to accomplish our goals; and we want to be considered effective on both a short-term and a long-term basis.

THE CHAPTER IN PERSPECTIVE

Communication occurs at different levels, and each level involves some unique adjustments. The dyadic level focuses on the dynamics that occur when only two people are interacting, as in an interview. The group level involves several people and therefore adds some dimensions that are not present in a dyad. The one-to-many level consists of situations in which a sender has primary responsibility for sending the same message to a given audience. A formal speaker or an editor of a house organ finds himself at this level. The organizational level encompasses all communications that take place between people in an organization. In a sense it encompasses all of the other three levels, but of particular significance here is the fact that the communicators operate in a special kind of interdependence and under some identifiable structural constraints. In the remainder of this book we will examine some special forms of dyadic, group, and one-to-many communications that take place in organizations.

REFERENCES

1. George Gerbner, "Toward a General Model of Communication," *Audio-Visual Communication Review*, 4 (Summer 1956), 173.

2. Lee Thayer, *Communication and Communication Systems* (Homewood, Ill.: Irwin, 1968), pp. 173–176.

3. Christopher Spicer, "The Identification of Communication Competencies Required by Future Businesspersons," paper delivered to the International Communication Association, Chicago, April 1975, p. 14.

4. J. Ruesch, et al., *Non-Verbal Communication* (Berkeley: University of California Press, 1965), p. 4.

PART II

Anspach, Editorial Photocolor Archives

Forsyth, Monkmeyer

PART II
INTERVIEWING

Interviewing is an important part of the communicative life of any organization. There is no manager, no worker who will not at some time or other participate in an interview. For many managers interviewing is a crucial aspect of their jobs. Nearly everyone, of course, has an initial job interview, and when we hear the word *interview* this is what we sometimes think of. But there are many other types, too. An employee seeks information from others in order to do his job; a boss gives instructions to his subordinate; a salesman tries to find out the needs of each client; subordinates receive appraisals, counseling, and discipline from their immediate superiors; the personnel representative seeks out certain people to find out how things are going. Each of these situations is different from the others in important ways, but all of them are interview situations.

An interview is basically a specialized pattern of verbal interaction. It is specialized in that there is a specific purpose for initiating the interaction and there are specific content areas to be explored. The interview differs from ordinary conversation in that we expect more control to be exerted in the interaction, that extraneous matters be excluded, and that the interviewer-interviewee role relationship be maintained.

In this part of the book we want to explore fully but concisely the nature of the interview as a special form of communication. Since there are many types of interview situations, we will impose several limitations on our discussion.

First, even though we recognize the widespread use of group interviewing, we have focused primarily on the more common dyadic or two-person interview. When we go beyond the dyad and add more people, we add new dimensions to the interaction; some of these will be covered in Part III under the discussion of group conferences.

Second, nearly all the literature about interpersonal communication might apply to an examination of the interview, and many theorists like to extend the treatment of interviewing to more informal social settings. We have purposely chosen to avoid extensive reviews of the interpersonal literature and have selected for examination only that which is readily adaptable to the more formal types of interviews. We have done so because we feel that this approach will furnish the most immediate results for the person in an organizational context.

Third, the pervasiveness of interviewing throughout work organizations indicates that there are many different varieties of dyadic interviews—information giving, information seeking, persuasive, counseling, exit, appraisal, selection, discipline, and problem solving. Our purpose here is not to cover all of these but to select three types that are most common and also typify the kinds of interviews that one might encounter. Almost everybody has a *selection interview*, and most managers will have an opportunity to conduct some. The selection process combines information seeking with information giving as the interviewer not only questions the interviewee but also tries to give him information about the organization. The *appraisal interview* is a widespread practice among large organizations, since managers are required to evaluate their subordinates. Depending on the nature of the subordinate, the appraisal may furnish examples of persuasion, discipline, counseling, information seeking, and information giving. The *persuasive interview* is included because it requires some unique considerations. Moreover, organizational communicators commonly face tasks that involve selling ideas and influencing people.

Finally, we have focused on interviewing primarily from the interviewer's perspective. The following behavioral objectives reflect this viewpoint. After reading this section the reader should be able to

1) analyze the interviewing process as a specialized pattern of verbal interaction in terms of purpose, content objectives, kinds of questions, and structure.
2) list alternative ways in which the interviewer maintains control over the interaction.
3) analyze basic problems connected with stating purposes, questioning, probing, and interpreting data, and suggest solutions for these problems.
4) list practical guidelines that can be used in planning and conducting selection, appraisal, and persuasive interviews.

CHAPTER 4
THE INTERVIEWER'S ROLE

Preview

The interviewer has definite responsibilities in planning an interview, conducting it, and measuring the results.

The interviewer's primary role is that of a strategist, and his plans must involve all of the following:

- Clarify the purpose
- Identify content objectives
- Prepare initial questions
- Decide how to structure the interview
- Arrange the setting

Plans are helpful because they represent the interviewer's best thinking about all the alternatives available to him. However, they serve best as guides and not as inflexible rules.

A role can best be defined in terms of the specific behaviors associated with a given position in the organization. In the interview, the interviewer occupies the dominant position for that interaction, and his role is generally characterized in the following ways.

First, the interviewer is the initiator, the strategist, and the planner. The reason for the interview is associated somehow with his position or purposes. Consequently he can and should make whatever plans are necessary for effective interaction. He should, for example, do each of the following *before the interview:*

1) Clarify his purpose for himself.
2) Identify his content objectives.
3) Translate these objectives into preliminary questions.
4) Decide how he will structure the interview.
5) Arrange an appropriate setting for the interaction.

Second, during the interview the interviewer is the controller of the interaction, the tactician. He conducts the interview by adapting in whatever ways are necessary to maximize communication. He is the principal actor, and the interviewee is expected to react to him. One of the most damaging criticisms that can be applied to an interviewer is that he "lost control" of the situation.

Third, during and after the interview the interviewer is the judge, the measurer of results. He determines what topics to discuss, how the information is interpreted, and how it is to be used.

As this discussion role implies, effectiveness as an interviewer calls for considerable expertise in a number of communication skills. However, success in interviewing should not be equated with mastering certain techniques. At its most basic level, the key to conducting a good interview is real sensitivity to other people and to what is taking place between you and them in the interview situation.

CLARIFY THE PURPOSE

In any kind of communication interaction the communicator is probably better off when he can identify exactly what he hopes to accomplish in that situation. The truth is that most of us are not that analytical about our relationships. We talk to family and friends endlessly without thinking of what is being accomplished. And by the time we become adults our patterns of interaction are so ingrained that we do not even consider analysis necessary—that is, until something goes wrong.

The interview, however, should not be a haphazard, purposeless interaction. As we have indicated, part of the interviewer's role is that of planner or strategist; and the basis of any strategy has to be some ultimate purpose. Consequently the most essential thing an interviewer does is to consider the reasons why an interview should be held. The more concretely these purposes can be stated, the more explicitly the interviewer's strategy and behavior can be guided.

Such planning may sound highly mechanical and perhaps even manipulative, but this need not be so. An interview need not be stilted just because some planning has taken place. As a matter of fact, every interviewee is somewhat unpredictable; therefore a part of building strategies is considering alternatives that one can use during the interaction. One student in an interviewing class planned his interviews so tightly around his predictions of how the interviewee would react that his interviews were often completely disrupted when the interviewee behaved unexpectedly. He did this several times, and it never worked well. This was an important learning experience because he discovered for himself the necessity of adapting to whatever occurs in the situation.

Nevertheless, the point needs to be emphasized that until purposes are identified any attempt at planning is relatively useless. Until one knows where one wants to go, one cannot *plan* to go there. In much the same way, the statement of purpose is necessary for evaluating the outcome of the interview. Beginning interviewers often want to judge success or failure in terms of techniques, such as "asking questions correctly" or "motivating the respondent" to talk. These are very important, but they are only means toward some end. The final evaluation of the interview must be framed in terms of some stated or recognized purpose: What did you hope to accomplish?

Throughout this discussion we have referred to the multiple purposes of an interview. And the fact that there is more than one purpose may have several important implications for the interviewer.

Accomplishing several different purposes within the context of one interview may require several different kinds of strategies—perhaps interwoven into an overall plan. For example, in the appraisal interview the interviewer may want to praise the interviewee for the things he does well but also to encourage him to improve in his weak areas. When possible, it may be desirable to rank the purposes in some order of priority. For example, suppose praising is more important than discussing weaknesses for a particular employee. How tragic it is when an interview designed to compliment an employee has a negative impact because 4 minutes were spent telling the person how well he is doing and the remaining 26 minutes focused on the need for improvement!

Purposes may be stated at different levels of generality. It might be well to think of Type 1, Type 2, and Type 3 purposes. Type 1 purposes are the most general, the most abstract. They may, for example, describe how a particular interview fits into a total situation. In a problem or diagnostic situation, one purpose may be "to understand the situation." Similarly, the most general purpose for a selection interview may be "to maintain a satisfied, productive work force."

Type 2 purposes are somewhat more specific, and their labels are often used to differentiate among the types of interviews. They include such purposes as to give information, to get information, to select a candidate for a job, to appraise a subordinate, to discipline, to counsel, to persuade, or to solve a problem. At this level the statement of purpose is characterized by a general description of what is to be accomplished.

Type 3 purposes are derived from the others but may include a list of the most specific things to be done in the interview. The personnel representative, for example, knows that he is going to make a selection, so he may list more specific purposes under that category: to get the candidate to talk about himself or to ascertain the primary motivations of this particular candidate. The appraiser may aim to compliment or to criticize; in some cases his purpose may be to counsel or to establish a helping relationship. And the manager may wish simply to talk about a problem without meting out any discipline.

In summary, the skillful interviewer will recognize that his best preparation comes from knowing as specifically as possible what he wants to accomplish.

IDENTIFY THE CONTENT OBJECTIVES

Once purposes are stated, the next element of strategy is to plan the content of the interview. At this stage the interviewer frames his content objectives, and these, "if properly drawn, define for us the precise kinds of information that will be needed to meet the purpose for which the interview is to be held."[1] Often this step consists of simply making a list of items or categories that the interviewer needs to cover in the interview. In *Interviewing: The Executive's Guide to Selecting the Right Personnel*,[2] Theodore Hariton suggests that all selection interviews cover the following areas: early home background, education, part-time work, professional work career, current off-the-job life, and self-evaluation. Furthermore, he suggests some very specific topics within each of these categories that should be explored.

In most instances, however, such a ready-made list is not available, and the interviewer will have to make up his own. How does he do this? His own analysis of the problem will be helpful; he may want to talk with other people, or he may want to read some literature in order to get a broad understanding of the topic. Suppose, for example, that a manager is interested in discovering why a particular work unit is having some internal friction. It may not be enough to ask a few workers why this is happening. It might be better to come to the interview with a list of specific areas known to be causes of friction in other groups such as the kind of supervision, fringe benefits, personality problems, outside factors, and general work climate. Such a list might have been compiled through both reading and talking with other managers about their experiences.

We do not mean to imply that the only information to be discussed in an interview is that which is planned. In some cases the most productive areas are unanticipated. Moreover, not every interviewer has the prerogative of formulating his own objectives. Situations arise for doctors, lawyers, social workers, and managers in which the client or employee initiates the interview and no planning is possible. In such cases, being a good listener and drawing on one's experiences and composure will allow one to set up one's content objectives as the interview proceeds. Nevertheless, when it is possible to prepare them, a list of content objectives represents one's best thinking about the agenda for the interview. And the beginning interviewer is well advised to write them out in order to ensure that each one is explored.

TRANSLATE THE CONTENT OBJECTIVES INTO PRELIMINARY QUESTIONS

Questions are guides for obtaining information. And despite the fact that an interviewer is much more than an interrogator or inquirer, the asking of questions is probably the single activity most frequently associated with interviewing. In some senses it is an easy activity. Watch an interviewer begin to have difficulties; his easiest and most frequent response is simply to ask more questions, perhaps a little faster. The fact that asking a question is easy, however, does not mean it is easily done well. The following are some considerations that should guide the interviewer as he formulates his questions.

1. *The question determines the subject matter of the response.* Richardson has found it useful to differentiate among (1) objective questions that concern "observable characteristics" or facts rather than opinions, (2) subjective questions that call for feelings and opinions, and (3) indeterminate questions that do not specify whether an objective or a subjective answer is preferable.[3] Both types of information may be useful, but, as in the legal interview, each must be kept in its proper perspective and not confused. This is often difficult because the differences in the way different responses are elicited may be so subtle that they go unnoticed. Asking (1) "What does your coworker do that irritates you?" is not necessarily the same as asking (2) "What is it about his personality that you don't like?" or (3) "What causes the friction with your coworker?" In (1), the interviewer is asking for observable behaviors that can be verified; in (2), he is asking about feelings that may be important but are not verifiable in terms of factual information; in (3), the question does not specify the kind of answer wanted. Yet at first glance an interviewer may *seem* to be asking for the same information in all three questions.

Another reason why these three types of questions should be kept distinct concerns the kind of answer one gets. It is not infrequent that a subjective answer is given to a question that asked for objective information. In such cases the interviewer may need to do some additional coaching as to the kind of information that is appropriate.

2. *The wording of a question either facilitates or inhibits communication.* In order to maximize the likelihood of getting complete and accurate information, three aspects of wording should be considered.

First, the language must be understandable to the respondent. When it is not, two communication problems occur. One stems from the fact that the interviewer cannot really answer questions that he does not understand. The second is a motivation problem. Most of us dislike situations in which we appear ignorant. Not understanding a question may cause enough discomfort so that the respondent clams up, seeks to hide his ignorance by bluffing, or seeks to terminate the interaction altogether.

Most people would never intentionally ask a question that the respondent would not understand; we tend to assume that the words we know are known by others. But we need to be conscious of the difficulties we may have in communicating with each other. Consequently the manager must be exceedingly sensitive to feedback about the understanding of the respondent. One final word of caution is warranted: It is not enough to ask, "Do you understand?"—respondents will rarely say "no."

Second, the wording can load the question in favor of a certain response. For example, if one wishes to know how another person truly feels about exporting grain in a foreign aid program, one probably would be ill advised to ask, "How do you feel about our shipping wheat to the starving people of ———?" The introduction of the words *starving people* is likely to influence the answer, for what kind of person could refuse food to the starving? Similarly, the manager must watch his own language, particularly his evaluative labels. One manager, for example, opened an appraisal interview with the question, "Well, Tom, is there anything that you can't handle, that I can help you with?" Most of us would feel an immediate need to say no, because "can't handle" would be a negative reflection on us. If the question were phrased differently we might even be eager to talk over certain problems and get whatever help the supervisor can provide.

Third, if tabulation of answers is important or if there is some kind of measurement involved, each respondent must be asked the same question in the same way. Interviewers sometimes have a tendency to amplify a question, paraphrasing it to help the respondent. But pollsters, for example, are expressly prohibited from doing this. The reason is that changing words may change the question in some subtle ways.

3. *The scope of the response is prescribed* through the use of open and closed questions, and the determination of scope is a major decision for the interviewer.

The *closed question* restricts the respondent's answers. In this category are multiple-choice questions where the respondent simply selects one of the alternatives, questions that ask only for yes or no, and questions that ask for some kind of identification such as age, sex, or classification in college. For example, "Did you vote in the last election?" is a closed question because the only two appropriate answers are yes or no. Variations in answers such as "I didn't want to," "I couldn't," or "I wish I hadn't" can be interpreted into one of those two categories. Sometimes the alternatives are built right into the question, as in this example: "Do you think your unit can produce more, less, or about the same as last year?"

The decision to use a closed question may be based on several considerations. It "tends to be the most successful when the interviewer's objective is to classify or measure the respondent's answer, when the respondent's level of information is low, or when the respondent is not motivated to talk very much." The answer is "usually less revealing and less threatening than in the case of the open question,"[4] and it also has a real advantage in that it does not take much time.

The open question, on the other hand, does not restrict the answer in any way; it identifies the topic and allows the respondent to answer as he wishes. Ask it of different people and you might get entirely different kinds of answers. The following are some examples of open questions: "Tell me about your work experiences," "What seems to be the cause of the problem?" "What do you think we ought to be doing to improve our productivity?" "How do you feel about our new fringe benefit package?" These open questions are probably most useful when the objectives are to give the interviewer insights into the respondent's situation, to measure his level of information, or to determine his frame of reference in answering a question. They are particularly useful when a respondent is motivated to talk and when the interviewer has lots of time.

These two types of questions have been contrasted not for the purpose of evaluating one as better than the other but to point out that each has some particular advantages that make it complementary to the other. For example, in order to evaluate an organizational training program one may follow "Did you think this course was worthwhile?" with "Why?" The answer to the open question adds a dimension of understanding to the answer to the closed question. Finally, Richardson and Dohrenwend found that "experienced professional interviewers are unable to conduct an interview using only open questions and that some closed questions must be used to sustain the interview."[5]

4. *An indirect question sometimes has advantages over the direct approach.* By far, most of the questions in an interview will fall into the direct category as we ask exactly what we want to know: "How did *you* respond?" or "What did *you* do?" In asking the direct question we assume that the respondent is able and willing to give the information desired by the interviewer. However, there are situations in which this assumption is not correct, and the interviewer may need to use an indirect approach. Two such situations will be discussed here.

The indirect approach may help when the information needed is threatening to the respondent's ego. In attitude surveys, for example, many people will not answer unless they are assured of anonymity. They realize that they may be damaged in some way if their information is revealed. When this suspicion is detected, the interviewer may resort to indirect approaches. Instead of asking, "What do you think of your boss and his style of leadership?" or "What do you think of plant management?" the interviewer might ask, "What do most employees think of their bosses?" or "How do most employees feel about plant management?" The change to the indirect approach allows the respondent to reveal his own ideas without feeling that he is being singled out. Since he answers in terms of "all" employees, he does not feel that he is exposing himself.

Another means of using an indirect question is through a picture story. This method is often used by psychologists and market analysts. Respondents are shown a series of cartoon drawings with the traditional verbal interactions written in small balloons above the heads of the characters. The balloon in the final picture is left blank, and the respondent is asked to fill in the missing response. Not only does this appear to be fun, but it is an indirect means of determining how a person feels about a situation.

The second situation in which an indirect approach may be useful occurs when the interviewer wants information that is not readily available to the respondent. Such situations are encountered in selection interviews all the time. The interviewer hiring people for management positions is interested in personal characteristics such as level of motivation, self-confidence, and moral standards. But an examination of the transcripts of actual interviews reveals that an interviewer will almost never ask, "What is your level of motivation?" "How much confidence do you have in yourself?" or "What are your moral standards?" Instead of such a direct approach, the interviewer gets the interviewee to talk about himself, his education, and his work experiences, and indirectly arrives at some estimation of the respondent's personal characteristics.

At this point it may be well to point out that there are serious concerns about interpretation in these circumstances. Unfortunately, one cannot be absolutely certain that the information revealed in the indirect approach is the same as that which would be revealed if the respondent would answer a direct question. Nevertheless, the indirect approach is useful because it seems to produce data that cannot be obtained in any other way. Moreover, it often happens that talking about a topic indirectly makes the respondent comfortable enough so that he can open up and talk about it directly.

5. *A question may need to be placed in some sort of verbal context* for the interviewee. Interviewers frequently need to give the reasons for asking a question or to explain why a particular topic is germane to the interview. For example, a manager may want to uncover the reason for a drop in job performance; he may ask if anything is wrong at home. Some interviewees would resent such an invasion of privacy unless the interviewer carefully explained his reasons for asking the question. It is also helpful to show how questions are related to one another. Such explanations are basically attempts to motivate the interviewee to respond more freely, and we must remind ourselves over and over that an interview is not just a grilling of the respondent.

STRUCTURE THE INTERVIEW

The actual anatomy of an interview can be dissected only after it has taken place. Unlike a speech, it cannot be completely outlined in advance. Katz and Kahn describe a social system as a "structuring of events or happenings rather than of physical parts . . . it therefore has no structure apart from its functioning."[6] Similarly, an interview is similarly a structuring of events over which the interviewer has only partial control.

Traditionally communication events have been analyzed in terms of an introduction, a body, and a conclusion. However, the primary aspects of structure that are most amenable to planning occur in the body. Therefore only the body of the interview is discussed in this chapter; the introduction and conclusion are discussed as tactics in the next chapter.

The body is the main part of the interview; it is where the main purposes of the interview are achieved. When the interviewer plans his content objectives and lists his preliminary questions, he is actually planning the body of his interview. The next stage is to put these topics and questions into some order or structure. In doing so, he will need to assess his priorities and give some thought to the planned sequence of questions for a given topic and to his overall organizational style.

PLANNED SEQUENCE It is highly unlikely that an interviewer will get all he wants to know about a topic from one question. Therefore it is wise to make a list of questions. This will then need to be set into some order. The two general patterns are the funnel and the inverted funnel. Each is useful within the unique conditions of different interviews, and to some extent each can be prepared in advance. Generally, these patterns apply to the development of a particular topic within the interview and not necessarily to the interview as a whole.

In the *funnel* sequence the questions go from the general to the specific. Each succeeding question is related to the preceding one but has a narrower focus. The following questions are arranged in a funnel sequence:

1) **What do you think are the most important problems facing our organization?**
2) **Of those you mentioned, which do you feel is the *most* important? Why?**
3) **How does this problem affect you in your job?**
4) **In the past, several solutions have been proposed as remedies for this problem. Suppose we were to try to solve it by _____. How would this affect you?**

In this example the interviewer begins the sequence by getting information about a number of problems and ends it by getting a reaction to one proposed solution for one problem. (See Figure 4.1.)

The funnel sequence can be arranged before the interview, and it may be advisable to do so under the following circumstances: (1) When a comprehensive view of one's experiences or feelings is desired, asking the most general question first may eliminate the need to ask many specific questions. Therefore the funnel sequence will save time and energy. For example, the first question in the preceding list made it unnecessary to ask, "Do you think —— is an important problem?" about a number of topics. (2) In order to discover the respondent's perspective, an initial general question will avoid limiting the interviewer to a particular frame of reference. Again, the first question did not identify what the interviewer considered to be problems, and it may well be that the interviewee's concept of what is a problem would be quite different from that of the interviewer. (3) Sometimes the interviewer knows that there are many unknown aspects about an event or topic. If he were to start asking specific questions, these unanticipated responses would be lost. Consequently the initial question is designed to let the interviewee fill in some of these details. In the preceding example the interviewer might know some of the important problems, but the generality of the question allows him to discover whether or not

Figure 4.1. Funnel sequence.

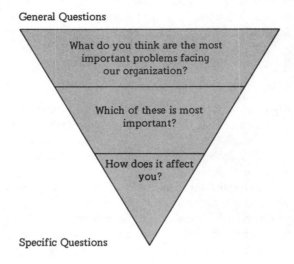

General Questions

What do you think are the most important problems facing our organization?

Which of these is most important?

How does it affect you?

Specific Questions

there are some important problems that he has overlooked. At the same time, he learns a great deal about this particular employee's criteria for "importance."

Whereas the funnel sequence goes from the general to the specific, the *inverted funnel* starts with specific questions and proceeds to more general ones, with each new question having a wider scope. Figure 4.2 illustrates an inverted funnel sequence. The inverted funnel sequence is particularly useful in motivating a reluctant respondent. Sometimes an interviewee feels inadequate or threatened when he is asked to discuss a general topic or to evaluate some general practice. However, it has been found that starting off with a discussion of concrete behavior or specific instances tends to "warm him up" or get him involved so that he feels more comfortable answering the general question. A low-level supervisor, for example, might balk at the idea of discussing the general merits of appraisal interviewing, but a few specific questions might prove to him that he does have some experiences and ideas that are worth sharing.

The inverted funnel sequence may also be helpful when the facts of a situation need to be established before the general discussion can take place. This is particularly true when the respondent knows the facts but the interviewer does not. In order to investigate some friction between people in the organization, a manager used the following questions:

1) Exactly what happened between Bill and John?
2) Has this friction been an ongoing problem?
3) How long has this been building up?
4) Do they seem to have the same problems with other workers?

Figure 4.2. Inverted funnel sequence.

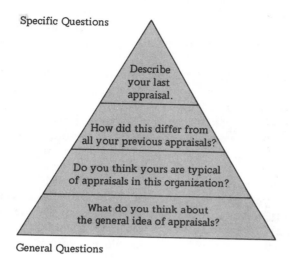

Specific Questions

Describe
your last
appraisal.

How did this differ from
all your previous appraisals?

Do you think yours are typical
of appraisals in this organization?

What do you think about
the general idea of appraisals?

General Questions

In this example the manager not only needed to get the facts, but the sequence was designed to give him a perspective from which to evaluate the incident.

ORGANIZA-TIONAL STYLE   *Style* refers to the amount of predetermination in structuring the interview. In general, the style the interviewer chooses determines how closely he wants to control the interview and how much flexibility he is willing to allow the respondent in initiating discussion. Professional interviewers vary their styles to fit the circumstances, but they tend to use one of three basic types: scheduled, unscheduled, and modified scheduled. A *schedule* refers to the list of questions used by the interviewer in guiding the interview. It is seen by the interviewer but not by the interviewee.

In *scheduled interviews*, preliminary questions are prepared in advance and are listed in order on a page that the interviewer will use during the interview. Public opinion and research interviews are among the most tightly scheduled. These interviews are standardized so that each question is repeated exactly the same way and in the same order for all respondents.

There are several advantages in having a schedule. It can give a sense of order to the interview; discussion occurs in a well-thought-out sequence. Moreover, it is an important aid to the novice interviewer. A schedule provides a kind of insurance that allows him to be more comfortable in the interaction. He does not need to worry about where he is going in the interview because the schedule tells him. Furthermore, the schedule is required when there is measurement or comparison involved, because a certain constancy from one interview to another is needed. In a survey of employee attitudes, each employee needs to respond to the same questions and talk about the same topics; to do otherwise is to make any final generalizations suspect. Similarly, a recruiter might use a schedule to make sure he gets the same kind of information from all candidates so that he is in a better position to make comparisons. Finally, any time several interviewers are trying to get the same information from different respondents they need to share the same schedule.

A schedule restricts the interviewer's flexibility somewhat, and it may make it difficult for him to adapt to the unique aspects of a respondent. Nevertheless, the schedule need not be seen as a liability. The interviewer should control the schedule rather than become its slave; when greater flexibility is mandatory, he may choose to modify it or even to disregard it.

In contrast to the scheduled interview, the *unscheduled interview* is relatively unstructured. The interviewer knows his central purposes, but he does not prepare a list of questions or topics in advance. Typically, he initiates the discussion and lets the respondent's answers lead him into new areas. Moreover, it may be unimportant to him that the same kinds of materials be covered for each respondent.

The lack of a schedule gives the interviewer maximum flexibility, and many professionals prefer it. It seems to be most useful in situations in which some counseling takes place or in which the objective is to have the interviewee determine what is discussed in the interview. To a certain extent this is what is done in the management-by-objectives situation.

On the other hand, unstructured situations are sometimes deceptively simple in their appeal, particularly for the interviewing novice. An undisciplined interviewer who tries to remain completely unscheduled will often find that he does not accomplish his objectives. A review of a number of transcripts showed that beginners often became so interested in a particular topic that they forgot to pursue other, very important ones. This is not always detrimental, but it often is. Metzner claims that the unscheduled approach is a liability, particularly for a personnel recruiter:

If the interviewer follows no specific plan, he probably will not cover the same areas in each interview. One applicant may then be evaluated in terms of the number of credits amassed in his major field and another on the kind of movie he usually attends.[7]

A compromise between the completely scheduled and the completely unscheduled interview is an interview that uses a *modified schedule*. It tends to combine the best of the previous two styles. The overall purposes are stated, and a partial list of topics and questions is made. The interviewer often keeps the list before him and checks items off as they are covered. Frequently the specific order of discussion does not make any difference, but it is important that each item be discussed. In such cases the interviewer may welcome the respondent's additions to the agenda as long as his own priorities get discussed. Therefore the respondent is given freedom without the interviewer relinquishing any real control.

Any interviewer has all three of these stylistic options for any interview he conducts. However, the following illustration is given to indicate some of the relative merits of each. Assume that the person is to survey the organization to find out how satisfied the workers are and also to find out what kinds of things contribute to their satisfaction and dissatisfaction. This might be done in three stages.

Stage 1 includes a pilot study in which twenty people are interviewed without any kind of schedule. The overall objective of this stage is to identify as many categories and examples of satisfaction and dissatisfaction as we can. We simply want some insight into how people think about their jobs.

Once this is completed, a composite list of items from the interviews is made. Suppose we find four things about which people tend to be satisfied and five things about which they are dissatisfied. We now train our interviewers to use this list of nine items as a modified schedule for stage 2. Again they are instructed that the objective is to find out what workers find satisfying or dissatisfying about their jobs, but they must make sure each of these nine areas is explored. They are also instructed not to initiate discussion of any of the nine areas until after they have asked the initial open question about what the worker finds satisfying or dissatisfying. At this point we may choose to do the entire survey using such a modified schedule, or we may decide that our results would be better if we got the responses from every worker in a way that would be easier to measure. If we decide on the latter, we go to stage 3.

We now feel reasonably certain that we have compiled a comprehensive list, so we decide to do the survey with a tightly scheduled interview. A standard introduction is prepared to orient the respondent, who is asked to do two things: (1) indicate on a 1–7 scale how satisfied he is with his job and with each of the specific items on the list, and (2) explain why he is satisfied or dissatisfied with it. The first response is to a closed question, and the answer can be quantified. The second response can be used for getting an in-depth understanding of worker satisfactions.

ARRANGE THE INTERVIEW SETTING

Effective communication involves much more than just the exchange of verbal messages, and one of the most important variables is the context or setting in which the interview takes place. In the first place, *timing* is of vital importance. The interviewer should select a time that is mutually beneficial to both the interviewee and the interviewer. As the person in control of the situation, the interviewer can usually plan his own schedule;

but where circumstances permit, it is desirable to check ahead with the subordinate to find out when it would be convenient for him or her. This is not just a courtesy; it can also be good communication strategy in that a subordinate will usually be more attuned to the purposes of the interview if he has had some time to prepare psychologically. Whenever subordinates are pulled away from their jobs unexpectedly, they frequently are so anxious to get back that they either resent being pulled away or have difficulty attending to the interview as much as the interviewer would want. In addition, the interviewer should arrange for enough time to be allocated to the interview so that neither person feels rushed.

Place is important to the context also. The overriding consideration should be one of privacy. This may involve not only selecting a place that is somewhat isolated but also involve asking a secretary to hold all calls during the period of the interview. Some managers have found that they can best eliminate distractions by conducting the interview in some place other than their work area or office. This may have the added advantage of reducing the status barrier some employees feel when they are called into the boss' office.

THE CHAPTER IN PERSPECTIVE

As the strategist, the interviewer draws the blueprints and lays the groundwork in anticipation of conducting a good interview. At this stage he is the dominant person, and his planning must necessarily be aimed toward controlling the interview in terms of clarifying the purpose, identifying the content objectives, framing the preliminary questions, structuring the interview, and arranging the setting. In terms of the models in Chapter 3, we might picture the interviewer as shown in Figure 4.3.

Communication blueprints, however, have to be rather general or tentative because we have learned that in most communication situations a person cannot predict the formula that is going to guarantee success. A recruiter, for example, may use basically the same plan for every interview he or she conducts, but no two of them are likely to be identical. There will be similarities, of course, but each new interviewee is unique in some ways, and the interviewer will have to adapt to him in some im-

Figure 4.3. Interviewer.

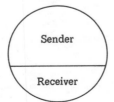

portant ways. Many interviews wind up being quite different from what the interviewer anticipated. In summary, planning is absolutely necessary, but so is flexibility in implementing those plans.

As this discussion of the interviewer's role implies, effectiveness as an interviewer calls for considerable expertise in a numbr of communication skills. Success in interviewing, however, should not be equated with mastering certain techniques. At its most basic level, the key to conducting a good interview is real sensitivity to other people and to what is taking place between interviewer and respondent in the interview situation. That is why the next chapter considers the interviewer's role in terms of tactics.

REFERENCES

1. Robert L. Kahn and Charles F. Cannell, *The Dynamics of Interviewing* (New York: Wiley, 1963), p. 93.

2. Theodore Hariton, *Interviewing: The Executive's Guide to Selecting the Right Personnel* (New York: Hastings House, 1970).

3. Stephen A. Richardson et al., *Interviewing: Its Forms and Functions* (New York: Basic Books, 1965), pp. 212.

4. Kahn and Cannell, pp. 132–138.

5. Richardson et al., pp. 149–150.

6. Daniel Katz and R. L. Kahn, *Social Psychology of Organizations* (New York: Wiley, 1966), p. 31.

7. Norma R. Metzner, "Interviewing Scientists and Engineers for Employment in Federal Service," prepared for the Office of Naval Research, n.d.

CHAPTER 5
CONDUCTING THE INTERVIEW

Preview

Conducting the interview calls for the interviewer to be a tactician who adapts to the specific interviewee and does what is necessary to maximize communication.

The introduction of the interviewer should give an adequate orientation and set the proper atmosphere for the interview.

Motivating the respondent requires a knowledge of basic communication inhibitors and facilitators.

Skillful probing is one of the most important keys to a successful interview.

Concluding the interview is a time for orienting the interviewee toward what is to follow.

Bias is a problem that can show up in almost any aspect of the interview.

The preceding chapter focused on the interviewer as planner and strategist, but that is only the beginning of his role. The objective of this chapter is to describe the role of the interviewer in the actual conduct of the interview. In this context he is a tactician, the person in charge of the interaction, the person who has the responsibility for maximizing communication between the two individuals, and the person who has to adapt to all kinds of problems during the interaction.

TACTICS

A *tactic* is defined as the pattern in which an interviewer adapts his communication skills and techniques to the necessities of the situation in order to accomplish his purposes. While it may fit into an overall plan, a tactical decision stems from a spontaneous assessment of what is needed at a particular moment in the interaction. This assessment must take into account the probable impact of the tactic on both the *content* of the interview and the *relationship* between interviewer and interviewee. The interdependence of these two factors will be demonstrated over and over by the fact that the relationship between interviewer and interviewee often determines whether or not the interviewer can achieve his content objectives.

Four of the most visible areas in which the interviewer must make tactical decisions are (1) beginning the interview, (2) motivating the respondent, (3) probing the content, and (4) concluding the interview. An overview is given of some of the basic concerns in each area; but because of the nature of a tactical decision, sensitivity to people and to the communication process itself takes the place of rules.

BEGINNING THE INTERVIEW	The introduction sets the atmosphere for the entire interaction and is therefore crucial to a successful interview. The aim of the introduction is to establish a certain kind of relationship between the people involved rather than substantive content. However, the most successful introduction will accomplish two objectives: It will build rapport between the interviewer and the interviewee, and it will give both some orientation as to what is going to be accomplished in the interview. In order to accomplish both goals, the interviewer may plan three specific behaviors.

1) A *realistic* greeting is in order. The greeting is a prelude to business, a time when each person can get his bearings in relation to the other. Frequently it is a time for exchanging pleasantries designed to make the interviewee feel at ease. On the other hand, there are times in discipline or appraisal interviews when the interviewee sees the exchange of pleasantries as a delaying tactic; instead of putting the interviewee at ease, they make him more anxious—he's wondering, "When is he going to drop the bomb?" The same anxiety often occurs when an employee is called in to see his superior without knowing what the boss wants. In such cases it may be more realistic to get to the point very quickly.

2) As part of his orientation, the interviewee should be told the purpose of the interview and how the information is going to be used. If this information is made explicit, the interviewee is in a position to react honestly, without playing guessing games that make him wary about giving information and perhaps cause him to introduce bias into the interview. Letting him know who will see the information and how it is going to be used also has an ethical dimension because it gives him the prerogative of deciding whether or not certain information should be revealed.

There are some exceptions to this rule in the research or marketing interview. It is supposed that if one were to tell the interviewees the exact purpose of the interview the results would be biased. The interviewers, in such cases, ought to consider the ethics involved and at least offer the interviewee a debriefing that not only tells him the purpose of the interview but explains why he could not be told beforehand.

3) The interviewee should be given some indication of the role he is to play in the interaction. Since the interviewer is generally in the dominant position, it is up to him to give some indication of what behaviors he expects of the interviewee. A recruiter might do this by saying, "Mary, I'd like to start off by asking you a few questions about yourself. And then later on I'll give you a chance to ask me any questions you might have." Such a simple statement gives the interviewee an idea of what is expected of her. In a counseling situation the interviewer might need to spend a lot of time convincing the respondent that it is the interviewee and not the interviewer who is going to determine the topics to be discussed and that it is the interviewee who is going to make any decisions that are made. Finally, a superior may enter the appraisal interview determined to persuade the subordinate to take a certain action. Consequently he may indicate that the interviewee should "hear me through"; in this way the subordinate knows very quickly that major interruptions are not expected.

MOTIVATING THE RESPONDENT

Motivation theory attempts to explain all human behavior in terms of the individual's drives and his physiological and psychological needs. One of its most basic principles is that *all behavior is caused* by an attempt or drive to fill some conscious or unconscious need. A second principle is that a person has many different needs and is therefore motivated by a number of things at different times. There have been a number of attempts to group the most basic motivations a person experiences. Krech and Crutchfield,[1] for example, grouped them into survival, security, satisfaction, and stimulation. Perhaps the most famous, however, is the list compiled by Maslow,[2] who added a new dimension by trying to group individual needs in a hierarchical order. Figure 5.1 depicts each of the needs in its appropriate rank, with the physiological needs the most basic.

Figure 5.1. Maslow's hierarchy of needs.

A third important principle is that every individual is motivated somewhat differently than any other person. For example, both the interviewer and the interviewee bring to their interview their own set of motivations, their own reasons for behaving as they do. Differences in motivation constitute yet another reason why interviewers must use different tactics with different interviewees.

Although we could analyze the motivations of both the interviewer and the interviewee, our focus in this section is on the respondent and how he is influenced by the interviewer. In a real sense the degree of success one has as an interviewer depends on one's abilities to predict and to influence the actions of the respondent within the immediate context of the interview.

First, it is necessary to distinguish between the *extrinsic* and *intrinsic* dimensions of motivation. The extrinsic dimension deals with factors outside the interview itself. Examples include the raise or promotion that a boss promises his subordinate in an appraisal if he will just do what is expected of him. Or it may include the threat of punishment that pervades the disciplinary interview. There can be no doubt that these are powerful motivators and have a profound persuasive influence on the respondent. These are the kinds of motivations that the interviewer will use to suit his purposes.

Our major purpose now, however, is to examine intrinsic motivations. When we speak of "motivating the respondent," we have to ask, "Motivating him to do what?" The answer is, "Motivating him to participate fully and freely in the interview." In other words, we are talking about the kind of influence the interviewer has over the way the respondent participates in the interview. Because not all of this influence is either conscious or intentional, the following discussion examines motivation from the standpoint of communication inhibitors and facilitators.

Inhibitors One of the best ways of learning about respondent motivations is to examine the recurrent problems that seem to restrict willingness to respond. It is well to keep in mind that some of these things are operating at an unconscious level for both the interviewer and the respondent. An awareness of their potential existence, however, should enable the interviewer to make better tactical choices in adapting to his respondents.

1. *Timidity is a frequent inhibitor.* All of us find ourselves at times somewhat intimidated by the status or position of someone else. This is particularly prevalent in a work situation, where subordinates shrink from full and free interaction with their superiors. When asked their opinions, they may be very guarded, brief, and tense. We must admit that this is the way some superiors like the situation because they find it useful to them. But for those who want to minimize the impact of timidity, there are some tactics that are helpful. Basically, the interviewer must build an atmosphere that encourages mutual interaction and trust. Achieving such an atmosphere may require concentrated effort over a long period, for

these are not things that can be switched off and on. Moreover, it must be recognized that the atmosphere within the interview will nearly always be a reflection of the atmosphere outside the interview situation. And if one wishes to reduce the impact of timidity on the interview, one must also try to change the kinds of things that produce it outside the interview situation.

2. *A problem of etiquette may also serve as an inhibitor to communication.* Gordon defines such a problem as the barrier operating "when the answer to the interviewer's question contains information perceived by the respondent as inappropriate to give to the type of person doing the interviewing."[3] Consequently the respondent's answer is changed or filtered to avoid shocking or embarrassing the interviewer. This, of course, is one of those situations in which the nature of the relationship determines the kind of content introduced into the interview.

In the work situation problems of etiquette may stem from role differences or perceived differences in values. Social workers have found that clients who have children are often reluctant to admit that they have not been married. Apparently they are trying to avoid shocking the social worker with the information that they have not lived up to a social norm that they feel the social worker probably approves of.

One of the most frequent tactics used by superiors in discussing problems with their subordinates is to ask, "What would you do in my shoes?" Sometimes it works beautifully in that the subordinate suddenly has to adopt a much wider perspective. At other times, however, the subordinate who has vigorously told his coworkers what he would do if he were the boss suddenly feels that it would be a breach of etiquette to level with his boss.

It is significant that in problems of etiquette the interviewer is generally unaware of what is happening. Therefore it is hard to deal with this problem. The answer lies in the establishment of a fairly open relationship between the two and the ability to listen to the other person without registering shock or embarrassment.

3. *A negative relationship between interviewer and interviewee is one of the greatest hazards to communication.* Generally, we do not like to interact with people with whom our experiences have been unpleasant. It is particularly hard to listen to such a person. Tension becomes heightened, and it is hard to be objective. This is true socially, and it also applies to work situations. In such a case the interviewer should give careful thought to the possibility of having someone else conduct the interview. If this is not feasible, perhaps one of the best tactics to use in the interview is to spend some time talking about the relationship before getting to the main content of the interview.

4. *When a person's ego is threatened,* the most universal behavior is to react defensively in order to protect his self-esteem. He may try to change topics, or, thinking the best defense is a good offense, he may suddenly

become quite aggressive. This may happen to either the interviewer or the interviewee; in either case, communication is somewhat impaired.

Most of us have experienced a threat to our egos, and it makes us uncomfortable. When the personnel representative, for example, asks the candidate to describe his strengths, he tends to talk and talk—modestly, of course. But when he asks the candidate to describe weaknesses, as recruiters often do, the candidate will think and think, hem and haw, and maybe come up with something relatively innocuous and safe. Disciplinary, appraisal, and problem-solving interviews are particularly susceptible to this problem. Adults find it difficult to listen dispassionately to someone describing a weakness or problem, blaming them as the cause, and perhaps threatening some sort of reprisal.

Because of its very nature, ego threat will probably never be abolished, but there are some tactics that may help lessen its inhibiting impact on the interview. First, the person and the situation should be kept in perspective. A lot of things over which the person has no control will influence his performance in the organization; so it may be desirable to examine the situation and not just the person. For example, a manager in a large packing company is doomed to failure because of a contract signed by his corporate headquarters without the plant manager's knowledge or participation; yet some of his bosses have already begun to evaluate the manager negatively, and it is likely that some will hold him completely responsible for the plant's inability to produce at a profit.

Second, recognize strong points. No person is a total failure; he will have enjoyed some success in some aspect of his job. By the same token, anyone can be placed in situations where he would fail. Consequently an interviewer might try to reduce ego threat by accenting the positive aspects of the respondent and his situation.

5. *A crucial motivation problem occurs when the interviewee rejects the goals of the interviewer.* Any salesman knows that people do not come to him to be persuaded to buy what he has to sell. In fact, most of them probably do not want to buy. His purpose is to create a need. In the organizational context there are a lot of interviews designed to sell an idea, a change, a promotion, a product, or a person. Whereas the interviewer wants to sell, in many of these interviews the avowed purpose of the respondent will be to avoid buying. We have conducted a number of attitude surveys in organizations, in which the goal was to find out how people feel about their jobs. In almost all of these surveys a number of respondents resisted the interview because they felt that it was a useless activity, that nothing would ever come of it, that the managers were just being nosy, or that the interview was an imposition because it took them away from their work.

In such cases, what tactics are available to the interviewer to influence the respondents to participate? A thorough explanation of the goal wins many. The promise of having an interviewer listen to them wins others. And listening must not be considered just a ploy to manipulate the respondent; the truth is that the interviewer may profit a great deal from knowing why the respondent rejects his goals. Finally, a respondent often responds positively to an interview because of the warmth of the atmosphere and of the person conducting the interview.

6. So far we have talked about problems that inhibit a respondent's *willingness* to participate fully and freely in the interview. Loss of memory, however, is a serious problem that stems from a person's *inability* to respond. Forgetting is probably one of the greatest inhibitors to good communication. Some interviewers have helped respondents with their memory by being persistent but patient. Absolutely the worst tactic is to demand immediate recall as if the respondent were forgetting deliberately. One of the best tactics is to *probe* carefully and patiently what the respondent does remember. By listening carefully the interviewer may be able to sort out needed details, the right time sequence, or a pattern of events. While the questioning may be quite pointed, the overall tactic should be to establish a helping relationship and give the respondent time. Rushing him will generally aggravate the loss of memory.

Facilitators The six problems we have just discussed certainly do not include all of the motivation problems an interviewer will face. But they are common ones for which he or she should be on the alert. In analyzing each of these problems, we actually suggested some means of facilitating the full and free communication desired by the interviewer. If we analyze those suggestions we find that they revolve around four main tactics that the interviewer has at his disposal to motivate the respondent and facilitate communication: (1) orientation, (2) recognition, (3) catharsis, and (4) an atmosphere of freedom.

Because it is difficult to know how to behave in ambiguous situations, the *orientation* the interviewer gives his respondent is a motivator, and it is one of his best means of influencing the communicative behavior of the respondent. In discussing the introduction, we stated that early in the interview the respondent should receive an orientation as to the purpose of the interview. But orientation does not end with the introduction. The reason for asking some questions may have to be explained later, and it may be necessary to demonstrate the relevance of some of the materials discussed to the purposes of the interview before the interviewee will respond. These are forms of orientation. Moreover, as digressions creep into the interview the respondent may need to be reoriented. Consequently orientation is a motivator that may facilitate communication at any time in the interaction.

According to Maslow's hierarchy, the desire for *recognition* as a human being worthy of some respect and dignity is one of our most powerful needs. No matter who we are, we are involved with ourselves and want to feel valuable. The interviewer should be mindful of this need and should search for ways of fulfilling it. In the selection interview, for example, the candidate automatically gets a lot of recognition because the interview is likely to focus on his accomplishments. After the candidate is hired, however, he is likely to feel a lack of recognition. At least this is indicated by some of our research. In surveys of two large companies we found that the kind of information most wanted by people at all levels was personal feedback about how well they were doing in their jobs. And they were not necessarily looking for a pat on the back; to some, even criticism is better than being ignored. Of course most employees recognize that they are more likely to get attention when things go wrong. This makes it even more important that some positive recognition be given. Even during a disciplinary interview it might be highly desirable to recognize and support the successes a person has had even while reprimanding him for certain specific actions. Such recognition will facilitate participation in the interview and perhaps make even the bad news palatable.

People also have a great need for *catharsis*. There is a kind of emotional release that comes from getting things off our chests and out of our systems. And it may be necessary that the negative energy be spent before there can be a return to positive communicative interaction. It is important that interviewers recognize the cathartic effect of some interviews, particularly those initiated by the subordinate. What is required of the interviewer in such cases is a period of listening—not necessarily agreement, but *very active* listening. Carl Rogers describes listening as one of our greatest but least used motivators:

Listening brings about changes in people's attitudes toward themselves and others, and also brings about changes in their basic values and personal philosophy. People who have been listened to in this new and special way become more emotionally mature, more open to their experiences, less defensive, more democratic, and less authoritarian.[4]

Finally, the kind of *atmosphere* that allows listening and catharsis is characterized by a degree of openness and freedom. The nature of role relationships and group pressures prevents most of us from feeling completely free, but we recognize easily when the restraints get too heavy. Whatever the kind of interview, the interviewer has much to gain from establishing an interactive atmosphere, one that encourages the interviewee to respond. For example, if the purpose is to persuade the interviewee, it is useful to know how the interviewee feels and what some of his major objections are. If the purpose is to get information, the interviewee will need to feel that he can answer honestly. If the purpose is to appraise the person or to solve a problem, it may be highly desirable to get the interviewee's true perspective.

In a sense atmosphere refers to the kind of rules or guidelines that each permits the other to follow in an interaction. Therefore it is the most important determinant of whether communication is facilitated or inhibited.

PROBING   The single most important skill for an interviewer is the ability to probe well; this ability differentiates more than almost anything else the skilled interviewer from the unskilled one. In spite of the fact that the interviewer may plan diligently some of the principal questions to be asked in the interview, he probably will not be satisfied with the answers he gets. This means he will have to pursue the topic with additional questions that have not been planned; such follow-up questions are called *probes*.

Ironically, many interviewers, especially beginners, concentrate so much on the questions they want to ask that they do not really listen to the answers. It seems that the important thing to them is to get a verbal response—*any* verbal response. Consequently a lot of their questions go unanswered as they move on to a different topic or question. The skillful interviewer, however, knows that his objectives are not met until he gets an *appropriate* response. Therefore he not only listens carefully but evaluates the acceptability of the answer before responding. His evaluation tells him the way in which the answer is deficient, when to probe, and how to probe. Basically, the different kinds of probes fall into two categories: directive and nondirective.

Directive   The direct style is to be very specific about what you want to know. Be-
probing   cause there are many reasons why a particular answer may be considered less than satisfactory, the probe may take many different forms. We shall consider four: (1) repetition, (2) clarification, (3) amplification, and (4) confrontation.

REPETITION. Respondents frequently give answers that are either completely irrelevant or somewhat tangential to the question asked. In some circumstances they may not answer the question at all. When this happens, one of the options open to the interviewer is to repeat the question, with or without some kind of amplification. This is the option chosen by the personnel manager when an irate employee burst into his office one morning.

Employee: I want to be transferred . . . work somewhere else.
Manager: Why?
Employee: I don't want to work there.
Manager: Won't you tell me why?
Employee: (mumbles a few words)
Manager: I'm sorry. I didn't hear what you said.
Employee: I'll quit if I have to go back there to work.
Manager: Won't you tell me what's wrong? Why do you want to be transferred?

Ideally, the manager would eventually have gotten the respondent to explain what the difficulty was; as it turned out, however, the probe was unsuccessful, and the employee actually quit without explaining. Nevertheless, this example illustrates the use of repetitive probing while demonstrating that good interviewing technique does not always get the desired result.

AMPLIFICATION. Some answers are on target but are simply incomplete. They do not go far enough. In these instances the interviewer's tactic is to probe in ways that will increase the scope of the answer by supplying more details. One recruiter even planned the areas in which he would probe. He liked to have the candidates start by describing their educational experiences. If they did not include things he wanted to know in their answers, he would ask them questions about why they chose their particular schools, how much they had to study, how they selected their majors, and what their plans were for additional education. Another way of asking for amplification is illustrated by the following medical interview.

Doctor: You say your knee hurts? Tell me more about it.
Patient: Well, sometimes it hurts so bad that I can hardly stand up, and it swells a little bit, too.
Doctor: When it hurts, can you describe the pain?
Patient: It burns constantly, and sometimes it feels as if someone were sticking tiny needles into it. When that happens, I just have to sit down.
Doctor: Does it hurt all the time? Or are there just certain times when it bothers you?
Patient: I'm always aware that something is wrong with it, but I wouldn't say that it really hurts all the time. It comes and goes, . . . except it never really completely goes.

In this example the physician has to probe rather specifically to collect some details about the hurt knee.

CLARIFICATION. Because a respondent knows exactly what he means by an answer, he may feel that he should keep his answer short because the interviewer will understand it the same way. But one of the lessons we learn early about communication is that meanings are in people, not words. And we really do not necessarily understand answers the same way others do. In fact, interviewers are often guilty of bias in interpretation because they assume that they knew exactly what an interviewee meant by some remark and do not check to see if it is really what the interviewee meant.

It would be a good habit for interviewers to develop a pattern of probing for clarification even when they are pretty certain of what is meant. This would help prevent a lot of communication breakdowns. The following example is taken from a selection interview, and it illustrates how an interviewer can probe to clarify an answer.

Interviewer: What do you think, Mike, is the most important thing that you want in your job?

Mike: I think you've got to construct a model, like you just said. And it would be very nice if you could put everything in the model and apply a present value factoring and just come out with a number for every aspect of the job. But you can't. You can't really say. I think probably the factor that I weigh the most is growth of myself in the company and growth of the company, and growth of the industry that the company is in.

Interviewer: When you talk about personal growth in the company, what exactly do you mean?

Mike: I mean growing in the way you function in the organization. Sometimes you learn how to do new things; sometimes you just learn to do what you're doing better. I think you should at least strive for the optimum whether you can reach it or not.

Interviewer: When you talk about the organization's growth, are you talking about growth in terms of sales or growth in terms of profitability in relation to sales, or growth in terms of both of these to a substantial degree?

Mike: Well, I think you have to talk about both of those factors. If a company just increased its sales at 10 percent a year and doesn't increase profitability at all, then there is no gain there.

Interviewer: Then that really isn't a profitable company?

Mike: No.

Interviewer: I mean it's not really a growth company?

Mike: No.

Interviewer: But could it be a growth company, Mike, if it had experienced no increase in sales and yet increased its last year's profitability by 10 percent?

Mike: In the long run it couldn't be a growth company either. A company that is profitable is looking for new areas in which to invest. And through these investments it gains; it does increase its sales. You can't just sit there and stagnate.

Notice how thoroughly the interviewer probes Mike's meaning for the word *growth*. He even uses a specific example to test how Mike would classify a company as a growth organization. Not all situations call for such detailed probing, but it is useful to know how to do it when it is needed.

CONFRONTATION. Occasionally an interviewee will give an answer that appears to contradict something he has already said. Obviously these instances should be probed, and it is possible to do so without using an accusing or indicting manner. The problem may be a simple misunderstanding of one of the answers, or it may be that further explanation can clarify the apparent contradiction. Nevertheless, there are times when for some reason the interviewee will actually contradict himself, and this is a useful area to probe. The following example is taken from an appraisal interview between a manager and his subordinate, who is himself the supervisor of an office secretarial pool.

Manager: Sometimes people kinda jam up on you at the end of the day, huh?

Subordinate: Yeah, they do and, well, I suppose when, uh, when things jam up that way you can't make everybody happy.

Manager: Sometimes they gripe to you, do they?

Subordinate: Well I, uh, I don't like to, uh, say that, that anybody gripes really. I, I'm not complaining.

Manager: I didn't mean that. I thought you, uh, indicated a few minutes ago that, uh, every once in a while they complain.

Subordinate: Well as a matter of fact you can't please everybody. I guess that's what it comes down to. I don't want to point the finger at anybody as complaining. Let's just say you can't make everybody happy.

In this particular case the manager confronts his subordinate with what appears to be a contradiction. Apparently people do vent their gripes, but the subordinate feels that it is necessary to preserve the image that people do not complain. The subordinate never does admit the contradiction, but by failing to do so he tells his manager a lot about himself and his needs.

In summary, then, it is necessary to become sensitive to the areas that need direct probing and to do so in a manner that motivates the respondent to participate until an adequate answer has been given. There is a danger that direct probes can appear to be a legalistic grilling of the respondent, but the manner of the interviewer should be such as to convince the respondent that he is not trying to put him "on the spot."

Nondirective probing   While direct probes pinpoint exactly what the interviewer wants to know, there are many situations in which the interviewer will find advantage in just keeping the respondent talking. There are a number of ways of doing this without interrupting with a question, and these are called nondirective probes. These probes are unique in that they usually work outside the respondent's level of consciousness. In other words, he is not really aware of them. Four of the most common nondirective techniques are the following: (1) pause or silence, (2) neutral phrases, (3) reflective or mirror statements, and (4) internal summaries.

PAUSE. A pause, or period of silence, is often the most effective way of encouraging communication. Most people have very little tolerance for silence in any interpersonal situation. When two total strangers ride in an elevator together they either exchange pleasantries or are likely to feel very uncomfortable. The novice interviewer is generally so uncomfortable with silence that he tosses in a new question whenever the respondent stops talking. The rationale for using silence as a nondirective probe is the tension created by a momentary pause. If the interviewer can train himself to be comfortable with pauses, the interviewee's tension will cause him to keep talking about his answer. It is one of the most useful ways of getting the respondent to amplify his answer. A pause has another advantage, too. Most of us need time to think about our answers.

NEUTRAL PHRASES. There are a lot of phrases that people in our society habitually use in responding to another person. Our conversations are filled with "uh-huh," "I see," "yes," "go on," and "ummmmmm." These phrases really do not interrupt the speaker at all; in fact, they are generally given, like a nod of the head, during the other persons comments. The overall impact of these habitual responses makes them particularly useful to the interviewer. They are a means of participating noticeably in the verbal interaction without necessarily giving direction to the person doing the talking. They indicate that the interviewee is receiving the interviewer's attention, and he seems to be more comfortable in a situation where he gets this kind of feedback. Finally, they act as probes because they encourage the talker to keep talking.

REFLECTIVE STATEMENTS. The interviewer can probe nondirectively simply by reflecting back to the respondent exactly what he has already said. Almost invariably the respondent will keep talking and perhaps amplify his answer. The reflective statement is particularly useful in getting the respondent to clarify part of his answer.

The following excerpt is taken from an interview in which a corporate industrial relations representative was interviewing a plant manager about the need in the company for supervisory training.

Interviewer: Do you think the corporate headquarters ought to offer more training for plant personnel?

Respondent: Yes, I do. Very definitely. It would be a good idea . . . particularly at this time.

Interviewer: At this time?

Respondent: Well, yes, particularly at this time. We've grown a lot, and nobody seems to know where we're going. It's been my experience that aside from the new theories and ideas you pick up in training sessions, you benefit a great deal from the interactions with people from other parts of the company. You find out how they operate, how they react to certain kinds of problems. You also get to feeling more a part of the company.

Interviewer: More a part of the company?

Respondent: Well, you know, you get to know people. You make friends. It makes it easier to move around in the company. And you get a sense of who you're working with and what the company is doing, where it's going.

Interviewer: Then you think the side benefits of the training are as important as the training itself.

Respondent: In this case, I really do. And I wish we could convince top management of this. There are a lot of needs that aren't getting filled.

INTERNAL SUMMARIES. Periodically it is useful for the interviewer to attempt to summarize what has been covered in the interview and to try to restate what the interviewee has been saying. Such summaries serve two valuable functions. First, like the reflective statement, they motivate the interviewee by showing that the interviewer has been listening. Second, they give the interviewee the opportunity to correct any misinterpretations the interviewer has made.

If we were to keep listening to the example just described, we might very well hear the interviewee use such a summary.

Interviewer: Well, you seem to be saying that the company *should* concentrate more on supervisory training, and that it should do so, first, because people learn new ideas, and second, because these classes are an important internal communication channel.

Respondent: Ummmmmmm. I really hadn't thought of it before as a communication channel, but I guess, as I talked about it, that's really what I was talking about. It all depends on who does the training and who is invited to attend. Maybe that's something the big boys ought to consider, because we certainly need better communications.

The results of using this summary statement showed that it was a successful nondirective probe. It was a restatement of the respondent's ideas that apparently got the respondent to think about his statements in new ways and also elicited some new comments about the company's internal communications.

CONCLUDING THE INTERVIEW

When the content objectives of the interview have been accomplished, there is no reason to continue the interaction, and it is the interviewer's responsibility to bring the interview to a close. It is generally impossible to plan conclusions exactly, since they must be based on the prior interaction and, therefore, must be somewhat spontaneous. Nevertheless, there are several functions that the best conclusions will serve.

1. In terms of content, *a review of what has been discussed and accomplished in the interaction is often vital.* Perhaps the overall purpose should be restated so that it can be demonstrated where the interviewer and respondent are in relation to it. In this way the total content of the interview is put into some perspective so that there are no loose ends left hanging. In other words, both the interviewer and the respondent are aware of the purpose and know exactly where they have been, and the two do not leave each other wondering "what all this was for."

2. Like the introduction, *the conclusion is a time for orientation.* In most cases the end of the interview interaction does not mean the end of the

relationship. Consequently the conclusion is a transition period, and the interviewee needs to be told what to expect of the relationship in the future. In some cases additional interviews are planned. For example, in an appraisal interview a boss may want to look into something more and then "get back to" the subordinate. In the case of the employment interview, the conclusion is a time for setting expectations about when the respondent can have some answer about the possibility of his employment. The following example is a conclusion taken from an actual interview.

Interviewer: All right. Well, here's the way I would like to leave it with you, Mike. I see our time has more than gone by now. What I'd like to do is this. I'd like to take this now and review it with our financial division in terms of your interest in their corporate accounting area. I'll be in touch with you within the next week and a half so that you'll know definitely what our decision will be. And I'll just say that it will be in written form from me and it will be very straightforward. I'll either say that we've reviewed your form and we don't feel that your background is adaptable to our job and therefore there is no further interest. Or, the more positive approach, I'd be saying we definitely are interested and we want you to propose several available dates and we want you to come into Chicago at our expense for interviews with our department. And at that point you would have four or five interviews with members of our financial division. And a decision would be made that night, whether we are going to send an offer or not. So we'll follow on that basis and you'll hear from me in written form within a week and a half. OK?

3. An appropriate ending to many interviews would be to exchange pleasantries again or to thank the respondent for his time and cooperation. Even when the respondent has had no choice but to participate in the interview or when the interaction has been heated or negative, it is still appropriate to express appreciation to the respondent for his participation. Such a statement may be vital in setting up the desired atmosphere for the next interview between the two.

OVERCOMING PROBLEMS OF BIAS

Bias is the distortion of truth that results from unwanted influences in the interview, and every aspect of the interaction is vulnerable to bias. Because these biasing influences often operate without our being aware of them, it is very important that the interviewer begin consciously to analyze his behaviors in order to reduce their potential for bias. Two of the most important areas for analysis are errors in asking questions and errors in interpreting results.

ERRORS IN ASKING QUESTIONS

1. *A leading or loaded question biases the answer* because it indicates to the respondent the answer wanted or expected by the interviewer. There are many times when people use them intentionally. One of the best examples is the gas station attendant who never asks you, "How much gas do you want?" but generally tries to influence your answer by asking, "Fill it up?" However, we are concerned here with the unintentional and perhaps unconscious use of leading questions because they introduce unwanted influences. And if there is a genuine desire to avoid implying the answers to our questions, then we need to be aware of the most common ways in which we do this.

Probably the most frequent means of loading a question toward a given answer is through *word choice*. For example, compare the impact of the following two questions:

A. How do you feel about the government's increasingly antibusiness stance in regard to profits?
B. How do you feel about the government's passing more and more laws to regulate business transactions and profits?

Question A seems to call for a conclusion—that the interviewer might well believe—that is more emotionally laden than the conclusion called for by question B.

A second means of loading a question is through *antecedent comments*. Some interviewers inadvertently tell the respondent what answer is desired by their comments before they ask the question. The following example illustrates how this can shape the respondent's answers.

Interviewer: This job calls for a lot of paper work. You do enjoy paper work, don't you?

Any respondent who needs a job desperately or wants this particular job will feel compelled to answer yes. A less biased approach would involve finding out how the respondent feels about paper work before explaining that it is a necessary part of this particular job.

Sometimes questions become loaded because they are *linked with a particular person or goal.*

Interviewer: The president of the company has been talking to a lot of groups in the company, urging them to moderate their views on environmental protection. He says we're moving too fast and we're hurting the company economically and may lose some jobs. How do you feel about environmental protection?

In this case some respondents would give an honest reaction. But many would answer on the basis of a reaction to the president, not the issue. If they like him, they will agree with his opinion; if they dislike him, they will probably react negatively. There is also a phrase here, "lose some jobs," that may pose an inherent threat to some people. Thus we can see a number of potential influences in this question besides the issue of environmental protection.

A fourth way of leading a respondent may be the *omission of some category.* "Are you a Republican or a Democrat?" for example, leaves out the choice of answering as an independent or a member of a minority party. Similarly, value judgments sometimes creep into our questions, forcing the respondent into either a good or a bad stance. An interviewer once asked about a candidate for a job with the following question: "Would you say that he tends to be basically gregarious or aloof?" Not only are these not the only two choices in describing a person, but the statement that someone is aloof would probably be taken negatively. A more neutral way of asking for this information might be, "Describe his working relationships with others."

2. *A mistake many interviewers make is to bombard the interviewee with questions.* Sometimes he may ask many questions at once, leaving the interviewee confused as to which one he should answer. Most of the time, however, this occurs because the interviewer apparently is not pleased with the way he stated the question and keeps refining it as he asks it.

3. *Phrasing two questions as one* is a subtle error that we often overlook. The reporter who asks, "How do you feel about the defeat of the bond issue and the failure to make Midvale a more progressive city?" is doing just that. Defeating a bond issue is one proposition; making a city more progressive may well be another. Similarly, the supervisor who asks, "How can we make our employees happier so they will produce more?" may be doing the same thing. Studies have shown low correlations between a person's satisfaction and his level of production. Consequently the interviewer may need to divide the question, asking how he can make employees happier and also how he can make them more productive.

ERRORS IN INTERPRE- TATION   Interpretation of results is often left out of discussions of interviewing techniques. After all, it is supposed to happen after the interview has taken place, and people have grown accustomed to doing their interpreting more or less automatically. We think it needs more thought, however, because errors in interpretation are one of the principal ways bias is introduced into the interviewing situation. There are three primary causes of misinterpretation: (1) failure to probe, (2) unwarranted assumptions, and (3) errors in recording.

Much has already been said about the necessity of probing, but it needs to be emphasized again and again that a verbal response is not necessarily an adequate answer to a question. When important things are left out, the interviewer is likely to fill in the gaps by inferring what the respondent might have said or meant but did not say. Because these inferences are often wrong, important information should be probed explicitly.

The famous Kinsey report on the sexual experiences of American males provides an illustration of an error in interpretation due to unwarranted assumptions. A team of researchers offered the following criticisms of its assumptions. First, it assumed that a person had had every kind of sexual experience unless he protested. The critics argued that some males probably felt pressure to say they had had some of those experiences even if they had not. To deny them might be a threat to one's masculine image. Second, the assumption that these males were typical of the general population was questioned. The critics noted that all the respondents were volunteers and wondered if a person is typical if he volunteers to talk about such an intimate aspect of his life.

The Kinsey example represents one type of assumption that can be made. The important point is that our assumptions do guide our interpretations of people and of situations, and these assumptions need to be analyzed periodically to be certain that they permit us to make valid assessments.

Errors in recording also contribute to misinterpretations. There is no best means of recording answers. Each individual must discover what works best for him. Maybe after an examination of the potential pitfalls of each he can make a better choice.

Some people prefer to take notes during an interview. In many cases this works well; the taking of notes probably cuts down on the number of mistakes. In others, the time it takes to write things down tends to inhibit the verbal interaction between interviewer and respondent. Sometimes the respondent becomes curious and wants to see what is being written down, too.

Many people like to wait until the interview is completely finished and then write a summary of their reactions. This, too, has the advantage of immediacy. The interviewer should be careful not to wait too long after the interview, however. Some recruiters get rushed and may wait until after two or three interviews to write down their reactions. In such cases some kind of "halo effect" may begin to operate.

A third way of recording is to use a tape recorder to tape the conversation. For example, an industrial relations supervisor once taped interviews so he could make a thorough analysis of the sentiments expressed. This, of course, gives the greatest accuracy in terms of keeping a record. It suffers from a time disadvantage, however, in that it takes just as much time to listen to the interview as it did to conduct it. Some people object to the use of the tape recorder on the grounds that it inhibits the respondent; it may, but our experience leads us to believe most people grow accustomed to it very quickly and soon forget it. In the aftermath of Watergate, however, one needs to be certain that the respondent knows the interview is being taped and knows how these tapes are to be used.

THE CHAPTER IN PERSPECTIVE

Every interviewer wants to conduct a successful interview, and a word about evaluating performance is terribly important here. Sometimes we find ourselves aghast because difficulties or problems occurred in the interview or because some techniques did not get the desired results. These difficulties need to be kept in perspective, however, because it is impossible to avoid every potential problem. Sometimes in the pressures of a particular interview one's best judgment is just not good enough—even for the most skilled interviewer. Therefore it is not the occurrence of a problem that is ultimately important but, rather, how well the interviewer handles it and rebounds from it. He may goof terribly, but if he makes a skillful recovery his objectives can still be fulfilled at the conclusion of the interview; and that is the criterion on which success or failure must be judged. In other words, one's success as an interviewer ultimately rests on one's tactical abilities in adapting to the situation. In this chapter we have discussed the five tactical areas that are most vital. The successful interviewer will be able to (1) establish the most desirable climate in beginning the interview, (2) motivate the respondent by reducing the inhibitors to communication and maximizing the facilitators, (3) probe answers skillfully, (4) overcome problems of bias wherever they occur in the interview, and (5) bring the interview to a close so that both the interviewer and the interviewee know what to expect as a result of the interview. These five skills will be useful in any kind of organizational interview.

REFERENCES

1. William V. Haney, *Communication and Organizational Behavior* (Homewood, Ill.: Irwin, 1973), p. 141.
2. Ibid., p. 144.
3. Raymond L. Gordon, *Interviewing* (Homewood, Ill.: Dorsey Press, 1969), p. 76.
4. Carl Rogers and R. E. Farson, "Active Listening," in Haney, p. 81.

CHAPTER 6
SELECTION INTERVIEWS

Preview

Selection interviews are useful supplements to other aspects of the place-ment process because they offer some unique opportunities for com-munication.

The basic purpose is to find out what kind of person the candidate is.

The information covered revolves around past experiences and future expectations, but often the perspective a candidate seems to have is more important than the specific details.

Selection interviews seem to follow a basic structural pattern that in-vestigates the candidate first and then explores aspects of the job.

Interviewees come to the interview with their own purposes, and they should make thoughtful plans for the interview.

The selection interview has received more attention than any other kind because almost everyone participates in at least one while hunting for a job. Despite their universal use, however, such interviews are not without critics. Some even argue that selection interviews are not useful because they have been shown to be too subjective to be reliable or valid. It is true that they are subjective, as most of our social and communicative re-lationships are. But being subjective is not synonymous with being useless.

The fact remains that most organizations will not consider hiring some-one without a job interview. In recognition of the interview's subjectivity, however, information from the interview is weighed along with informa-tion from application forms, academic records, resumes, tests, and letters of recommendation. Nevertheless, the interview performs an important function because interviewers and interviewees alike feel that the inter-view allows them to accomplish things that could not be accomplished in any other way. Some of the interview's main contributions are the fol-lowing:[1]

1) The interview offers an opportunity to exchange information about the candi-date that might not be answered otherwise. Being able to probe also gives more depth to the information. Moreover, a face-to-face encounter is desirable be-cause if the candidate is hired he or she will enter a face-to-face work rela-tionship.

2) On the basis of the interview, judgments can be made about the candidate's personality, appearance, compatibility with others, and ability to communicate orally.

3) The interview offers an opportunity to exchange information about the company and the job, eliminating the ambiguity and generalities of brochures. The company becomes more personalized through the interviewer, and the interviewee has an opportunity to ask specific questions about the organization.

KNOW YOUR PURPOSES

According to our survey of college recruiters, the primary objective of the interview is to find out what kind of person the candidate is. The recruiters were interested in getting some estimate of the candidate as a whole. In order to accomplish this purpose, interviewers set out to get the interviewee to talk about almost anything because they would be able to get an impression of him regardless of the focus of his remarks. Nevertheless, most recruiters have a list of content objectives.

A second general purpose of the interview is to represent the company well. In some cases this may mean trying to sell the candidate on the company; but even if it becomes apparent that the candidate is not going to be hired, the interviewer still wants to leave him with a favorable impression.

SET CONTENT OBJECTIVES

The specific content objectives will vary considerably, depending on the kind of job being filled. Nevertheless, for management and staff positions there is an amazing kind of similarity among the kinds of content explored. Most personnel interviewers prescribe that, as a minimum, each of the following should be explored: (1) early home life, (2) academic experiences, (3) work history, (4) current home situation, and (5) long-range ambitions. It is often stated that the best predictor of what a person will do in the future is what he has done in the past. Theodore Hariton puts it this way: "To analyze a person, you should know what the forces were that have been brought to bear on him.[2] We analyzed the content of twenty interviews and discovered that the following topics were explored most frequently.[3]

A. Information about the Candidate
  1. Job expectations
  2. Academic background
  3. Knowledge of the company
  4. Scholastic record
  5. Work experience

6. Geographic preference
7. Knowledge of the job he is being interviewed for
8. Marital status
9. Family background
10. Long-range goals
11. Extracurricular activities
12. Acquaintances within the company
13. Salary expectations
14. Strengths and weaknesses

B. Information about the Job
1. General organizational orientation
2. Specific job area
3. Management development and promotion policy
4. Advantages of the company
5. Economic growth
6. Company image

C. Information about the Interviewer
1. His job
2. His background

These lists indicate not only what people look for in candidates but also how much variety exists in what people look for even within the same organization. We also surveyed a number of recruiters representing many organizations to find out what they thought were the most important characteristics of candidates. The top fifteen are listed here in order of importance:

1) **Enthusiasm and motivation**
2) **Ability to communicate orally**
3) **Emotional stability**
4) **Aggressiveness and initiative**
5) **Self-confidence**
6) **Moral standards**
7) **Leadership potential**
8) **Pleasant personality**
9) **Writing skills**
10) **Poise during the interview**
11) **Interest in people**
12) **Good personal appearance**
13) **Good scholastic record**
14) **Preparation for the interview**
15) **Formulated long-range goals and objectives**

These are a lot of judgments to be made in a thirty-minute interview, but interviewers do it—and do it with confidence. Moreover, they make their decisions on the basis of five or six of the content areas identified earlier.

But as the preceding list shows, their main interest is in the personal characteristics of the interviewee. Our content analysis also revealed that almost two-thirds of the time in the interview was spent discussing the candidate.

Content objectives form the basis for the kinds of decisions that are made about each candidate. The following sample interview summary forms indicate what the interviewers who use them are examining. Notice the different kinds of responses called for by each. One requires a numerical rating; the other simply asks that a check be placed in the appropriate box.

FORM 1

Interviewer's Evaluation Work Sheet	Superior	Good	Average	Fair	Poor	Observations
Communication—expresses self well; attentive listener						
Initiative—applies self, works enthusiastically and conscientiously						
Perseverance—persistence; completes tasks in spite of difficulties						
Loyalty—puts work interests before his own; willing to do more than just his own share						
Confidence—self-reliance, ability to handle situations without excessive help						
Sociability—relations with others; able to deal with people						
Leadership—inspires confidence; others accept his aid and direction; promotability						
Competitiveness—desire to excel; does his best at whatever he undertakes						
Motivation—industrious; needs and desires (security, money, recognition, ambition)						
Maturity—common sense; good judgment; self-discipline; realistic						
Appearance—dress; grooming; physical features						
Manner—poise; how he handles himself						
Personality—personal qualities, temperament, disposition						
Intelligence—ability to grasp the point quickly, reason logically						
Overall rating						

FORM 2

Interview Write-Up by
Theodore Hariton[4]

Name:
Job Considered for:

Early Home Life

Education and Training	1	2	3	4	5
	Favorable				Unfavorable

Work Experience	1	2	3	4	5
	Favorable				Unfavorable

Current Off-the-Job-Life

Personal Characteristics

Abilities and Skills (1–5)

———— Mental ability   ———— Communication skills
———— Mental flexibility   ———— Practical judgment
———— Incisiveness   ———— Ability to plan, organize,
                                               and follow up

Motivation and Interests (1–5)

———— Willingness to work hard,   ———— Interest in people
       Self-discipline   ———— Breadth of interests
———— Initiative on job   ———— Realism of goals and aspirations
———— Drive to improve self and get
       ahead

Personality and social effectiveness (1–5)

———— Self-confidence   ———— Team worker
———— Personal adjustment   ———— Social effectiveness and
———— Character   persuasive skills
                                         ———— Leadership and supervisory
                                               skills

Assets		Liabilities			
Overall rating	1	2	3	4	5
Overall summary:					

Another way of identifying what criteria are used in judging candidates is to ask the interviewers. Robert Martin asked two groups of supervisors at Hughes Aircraft to identify those they thought were most important in evaluating potential employees. The top ten for each group are listed here:[5]

A
General intelligence
Ability to communicate
Maturely directed energy
Ambition

B
Basic capacity for job
References
Productivity
Motivation

A	B
Specific professional competence	Compatibility
Integrity	Experience
Attitudes/personality	Communication
Creativity	Salary
Growth potential	Sincerity
References	Personal background

Finally, the importance of being able to communicate orally should receive specific attention here. It ranked second in the preceding list, and it was the most frequent answer to the open-ended question, "What do you think are the most important things that help you size up an interviewee?" Apparently communicative ability has a general influence on the interviewer's decisions and appraisal.

TRANSLATE OBJECTIVES INTO QUESTIONS

Four observations can be made about questions in selection interviews. First, open-ended questions are dominant. They are used to give the lead to the candidate and have him or her do most of the talking.

Second, the questions reflect the overall objective of revealing some personal information that goes far beyond just the factual data the candidate might put on a resumé or in a questionnaire. The following are some actual questions that are frequently used:[6]

1) What are your strengths? weaknesses?
2) Why do you think people succeed or fail?
3) Why did you choose your particular school? Would you make the same choice now?
4) Why are you interested in my company?
5) What are your career goals for the next 5 or 10 years?
6) What would you do differently if you could start over?

In asking such questions the interviewer is not looking for a particular answer. What seems to be important is the kind of *perspective* the candidate has toward his work, his school, his goals, and himself.

Third, not all questions are phrased in the interrogative form. There are variations such as "Tell me about yourself" or "Describe your work experiences."

Fourth, the kinds of questions asked frequently make the interviewee nervous or tense. Few people like to discuss their weaknesses; many do not know what they want to be doing 5 or 10 years from now; and it may be difficult to explain logically just why one wants to work for a particular organization or in a particular job. These questions do not make it easy for the candidate, but they do give the interviewer a lot of data about him.

STRUCTURE THE INTERVIEW

The question of how much to structure a selection interview is an important one, and to a certain extent each reader will have to discover what works best for him or her. Some interviewers attempt to tailor each interview to the candidate, but research by Mayfield suggests that highly structured interviews lead to greater interview reliability.[7]

Generally, the structure used by most professional interviewers follows this organizational pattern. After a short greeting, they go directly into a discussion of the candidate. On the average, this takes up about two-thirds of the interview. The interviewer then describes the company and the job, allows the candidate to ask questions, and concludes the interview.

The greeting should be brief and businesslike but pleasant enough to motivate the interviewee to want to interact. The interviewer should explain to the candidate how he wants to proceed, and start the questioning.

The body of the interview should be controlled in a directive manner. Whether or not one uses a schedule, the same general areas need to be explored for each candidate considered for the same job. Whenever a candidate hedges on questions, as many do on questions of salary or long-term plans, probe but give him time to think.

Discussions of the company should allow the candidate to ask questions that suit his own needs for information. The interviewer needs to have a broad grasp of the company so he can represent both the company and the particular job well. If he does not have the answer, he should promise to get it for the candidate.

The closing should be pleasant and instructive. The candidate should be thanked for his time; and since most selection interviews call for some follow-up, the candidate should be told exactly what to expect.

SUGGESTIONS FOR THE INTERVIEWER

As we suggested in the previous chapter, the interviewer has a lot of power over the interview, but he still must adapt to the interviewee. Consequently one can improve one's own interviewing techniques if one knows some of the chief criticisms of interviewers by interviewees looking for jobs. The authors asked 152 students the question, "What are the most frequent complaints that you make or hear about interviewers?" The following answers are listed according to the frequency with which they were mentioned.[8]

1) Many felt that interviewers had a general deficiency of information about specific jobs and about job opportunities with the company.
2) Interviewees frequently resented some of the questions asked. Questions about long-range ambitions and personal strengths and weaknesses were found to be the most objectionable.

3) Interviewees were particularly resentful if the interviewer seemed to lack interest in the applicant. A number of interviewees complained that their interviews suffered from poor rapport because the interviewer gave a standardized spiel or was overly cold and formal.

With these complaints in mind, the following suggestions are designed to help interviewers make their selection interviews work better for them.

1) **Prepare thoroughly.**
2) **Use multiple interviews.** Talk to a candidate more than once or have several people interview him. Comparison of impressions can be useful in forming the best estimate of the candidate.
3) **Analyze your biases and be aware of them,** and try to have a consistent yardstick for all candidates.
4) **Double-check your initial impressions to make sure they are valid.**
5) **Be an active listener and show a real interest in the interviewee.**
6) **Probe.** We assume that complete information qualifies one to make a better decision.
7) **Take time at the end of the interview to record your impressions while they are fresh.**
8) **Follow through on promises made to the candidate. Be efficient.**

SUGGESTIONS FOR THE INTERVIEWEE

When you are the interviewee, remember that you are a vital link in the communicative interaction. You have a lot at stake. You are not just looking for a job; you are looking for a job at which you can be fairly satisfied, and you are looking for an organization with which you are compatible. In other words, you are evaluating the job and the organization at the same time that the interviewer is evaluating you. Your role in the interview will be dictated largely by the interviewer, but the following suggestions are designed to make you more effective in accomplishing your purposes.

A good starting point is an examination of some of the most frequent complaints that interviewers make about interviewees.[9]

1) One of the most frequent complaints revolves around unrealistic attitudes. Selection interviewers complain that the applicants expect too much too soon, overestimate their own worth, or are unrealistic about the amount of work required for success.
2) Another complaint is that the applicant has vague interests and goals or has not formulated any definite career objectives.
3) A low information level about a particular kind of job or industry indicates lack of preparation for the interview.
4) A frequent complaint is that interviewees simply do not communicate very well. More specifically, interviewers often feel that an applicant cannot speak up or express his or her ideas.
5) Finally, a number of complaints center on personal facts such as unkempt appearance or nervousness.

Naturally, if an interviewer makes any of these complaints about you it is going to affect his evaluation. Therefore the following checklist may be useful in planning your own participation in an interview.

1. *Prepare thoroughly for the interview.* This will involve a bit of research, but it is well worth the time it takes. First, you will need to know something about the organization. There are several sources available that will give you vital information. The *College Placement Directory*, Thomas' *Register of American Manufacturers*, Standard and Poor's *Corporation Records*, and *Fortune*'s review of the top 500 companies in the United States are all professional publications that can be quite informative. You might also secure valuable information before the interview simply by writing to the organization's personnel or public relations department.

Second, you will need to know something about the kind of job for which you are applying. In order to get this information, you might talk with a counselor or with someone already working in that kind of job. These people can not only tell you about the job but also give you some idea of the salary range you can expect.

2. *Prepare a resume.* In many cases interviewers will request that a resume be sent before the interview. Even so, they sometimes forget what is on the resume. Consequently it is to your advantage to have one with you. Moreover, preparing a resume is useful in that it gets you to think about your best qualifications; your answers to the interviewer's questions may be a bit quicker and more articulate as a result.

3. *Analyze potential questions* and think (even practice) how you might answer them. For example, earlier in this chapter we identifed certain areas that are almost certain to be explored. It might be very helpful if you tried to articulate aloud to yourself or a friend why you want this particular job, what your career objectives are, or what your greatest strengths are.

4. *Be honest and frank.* A lot of interviewees try to second-guess the interviewer in answering a question. However, if you keep in mind that you want the job only if it meets some of your needs, you will realize that your answers need to be forthright if you are going to find the right fit between you and a job. But don't be too quick to answer. Take the time to give some thought to your answer.

5. *Follow the interviewer's lead.* In most cases he will indicate what he expects of you in the interview.

6. Realize that your *nonverbal behavior will affect the interviewer* as much as your verbal answers. Two of the best things you can do in this regard are to maintain eye contact with him and to be enthusiastic and energetic in responding to him.

7. *Sell yourself.* You are in competition with others for the job, and it is up to you to make the best case for yourself that can be made. This is particularly important in applying for managerial jobs because the interviewer will be looking for people who are confident and promotable.

THE CHAPTER IN PERSPECTIVE

The selection interview is a type of information-getting interview that most people will encounter a number of times. But the interviewer and the interviewee have a tremendous stake in the outcome, and that is why they each need to give a lot of thought to their planning. For the interviewer, it is important that he know his purposes, set his content objectives, prepare the kind of questions he wants answered, and plan some overall structure for the interview. During the interview it is imperative that he demonstrate his interest in the interviewee and the interviewing process. Similarly, the interviewee has a key role in the interview. He, too, can come to the interview thoroughly prepared with information about the organization and questions he wishes to have answered. Even more important, however, is the fact that he must come to the interview prepared to sell himself as the best person for that particular job.

In this chapter we have examined in depth some of the unique features of the selection interview. We would like to end the chapter by stressing that the initial screening is only the first selection interview one may have in a particular organization; each time one comes up for a promotion a similar process may be involved. Finally, a transcript of an actual employment interview is given so that the reader may analyze it in terms of the principles and suggestions described in this chapter.

REFERENCES

1. Cal W. Downs, "What the Selection Interview Accomplishes," *Personnel Administration* (May 1968): 10–12.

2. Theodore Hariton, *Interview* (New York: Hastings House, 1970), p. 23.

3. Cal W. Downs, "A Content Analysis of Twenty Selection Interviews," *Personnel Administration and Public Personnel Review* (September 1972): 25.

4. Hariton, pp. 93–94.

5. Robert Martin, "Toward More Productive Interviews," *Personnel Journal*, 50 (1971): 359–363.

6. Cal W. Downs, "Perceptions of the Interview," *Personnel Administration* (May 1969): 12.

7. E. C. Mayfield, "The Selection Interview—A Reevaluation of Published Research," *Personnel Psychology*, 17 (1964): 239–260.

8. Cal W. Downs, "Perceptions of the Interview," p. 12.

9. Ibid., p. 21.

10. Interview taped by permission. All names have been changed.

SELECTION INTERVIEW[10]

I. Well, to introduce myself first, Allen, I'm Robert Smith. I'm with ATTCO in Akron, Ohio, which is our corporate office; and I work in the area of management and development. So I'm here today to talk to the M.B.A.s and I've seen four or five so far. You're the first one after lunch. Let's start off, Allen, and have you tell me, very briefly, the kind of job that you'd most like to have if you could write your own job description.

R. Well, I think I'm most interested in long-range planning. I've gotten very good grades in accounting, and I'm getting my masters in business administration; my main area of concentration is math, and I'm most interested in long-range planning—weighing the opportunity costs of various investments and opportunities and picking the ones that have the highest present value to the firm.

I. Now this is in line primarily with the financial planning type of thing?

R. Financial planning; I wouldn't be very good in technical planning because I don't have a technical background, so I would have to be in the area of financial planning.

I. Now I would like to hear a little bit about how this interest has been established and developed, since I think it's very important to see the basic background that has led to this decision. Let's start first of all with your work at Illinois. Why did you start taking an academic program in accounting? What was your interest there? How did you get interested in that?

R. Well, possibly by chance. I started out as a chemistry major and I didn't handle the math with the proficiency with which I would have had to handle it to do anything in chemistry, beyond the bachelors level. Because chemistry today is a branch of physics and physics is a branch of mathematics. So you have to have the math. And I sort of started; I took one chem course while I was in the college of liberal arts and sciences and I found it wasn't distasteful. I couldn't say it was enjoyable at the time. Then I could see that accounting was a very useful field. The common trend is analytical. It gives you an analytical outlook on the firm itself. I have also taken quite a few liberal arts courses, many more than I had to have in the college of business administration. I have a language requirement fulfilled in German. I've had related courses in sociology, psychology, and political science. My last quarter in school I took a survey course in Shakespeare because I feel that this helps development as a person. That I can better understand the world this way. So, how is this related to long-range planning . . . I think you've got to have a broad overview if you're going to plan for the long time. Well, I've tried to give myself as broad an overview as I could. Now, getting to finance . . . I didn't have much exposure to finance until I was a junior, the second semester of the junior year. I had some exposure to finance and then in the senior year I had exposure to finance. I find that finance is much more demanding than accounting. At least that's my opinion. In that finance deals with the projection of the future and you're shaping your own destiny; while with accounting you're working with figures that are past. To me they are dead. They can point the way. But I think that with finance, on the other hand, you are able to shape the future rather than to just see the past.

I. All right, well now, why did you decide that it was important that you come to the graduate school of business in order to get an M.B.A.?

R. Well, I've always been interested in progressing as far as I could in anything. In education in particular. I was relatively young when I graduated. I just turned 21 and I'll just turn 22 when I graduate from R.U. I don't think education hurts at all and I think whatever knowledge I get makes me a better person. It helps me understand the world and it helps me perform whatever duties I'd have in a firm better. I was interested in finance and I didn't feel that I had the background that I would have needed or would have wanted in finance. And R.U. had a reputation as having a very good finance department, so I chose R.U.

I. All right, now I see the absence of any related work experience here. What kinds of jobs have you held either during the summer or during vacation periods? Have you held any jobs of any significance related to the field?

R. Well, of no significance at all. As I said, I am relatively young, and then part of the time was spent going to summer school, too.

I. What does your father do, Allen?

R. My father is a contractor.

I. Is it his own? Is it his own company?

R. No . . .

I. How big a family do you come from?

R. I've got two younger brothers.

I. Two brothers. You say they are both younger?

R. Right, I've got one brother that's going to graduate school in Illinois in August, who is a psychology major. Then I've got another brother who's a freshman in high school.

I. All right. Well now, Allen, at this point in your interviewing—I'm assuming you've taken interviews with different companies—what kinds of jobs have these companies ended up talking to you about at the end of the interview?

R. Well, some of them have recommended long-range planning and others have suggested the area of controllership. And I've sort of gotten the opinion that it's not actually the job that you are placed in initially that really matters. It's the job that you put yourself into that matters. I realize this much more now than when I started interviewing.

I. Has this been an interesting experience for you? Do you feel that you're learning an awful lot from this experience as an interviewing process?

R. Definitely. The interviews as they go on become much better.

I. All right, now just let me pick up where you started, Allen. And see if I can mold you into our program.

[At this point the interviewer described the company in detail and some job possibilities for Allen.]

It's always very hard and you see I could ask you this question, Allen, I could say, How, in the final analysis, after talking to people on the campus about their firms and then later visiting their plan operations and taking in extensive interviews with four or five people, how are you going to finally evaluate those companies that are of most interest to you and how are you going to make your final job selection? And I would assume that you would answer by saying that you are going to base it not only on the caliber of people you talked to but on their description of the job that you would start on, and be seeing evidence of mobility and movement through the organization. And I would assume that you'd be interested in some background of the company and their profitability over the years and their growth and diversification. And I assume that there would be lots of things that would finally enter into your decision. And certainly salary and location and fringe benefits and those things would enter someplace in your plan. But what do you think, Allen, is really the most important thing you're going to want to find in a job?

R. Well, I think you've got to construct a model, like you just said, whether it's an overt model or a covert model, whether you sit down and weigh everything analytically or whether a picture forms in your mind and you make a judgment out of the way you view your surroundings and your contacts. It would be very nice and easy if you could put everything in a model and apply a present value factoring and just come out with a number and the company that had the highest number would be the one that you chose. But it's not that easy. You can't really say. I think probably the factor that I weigh the most is growth, both growth of the individual in the company and growth of the company and growth of the industry that the company is in. And then the surroundings and the people that you have to work with probably. Well, maybe that is . . . equal. If the surroundings aren't pleasant and the people you work with don't help you in performing your task, the function you will perform in the firm, then you can't do a job in working, you fall short of the optimum. And I think you should at least strive for the optimum whether you can reach it or not.

I. When you talk about growth, Allen, are you talking about growth in terms of sales or growth in terms of profitability in relation to sales, or growth in terms of both of these factors to a substantial degree?

R. Well, I think you have to talk about both of these factors. If a company just increases its sales at 10 percent a year and doesn't increase profitability at all, then there's no real gain there.

I. And that really isn't a profitable company, is it?

R. No.

I. I mean it's not really a growth company?

R. No.

I. But could it be a growth company, Allen, if it had experienced no increase in sales and yet increased its last year's profitability by 10 percent?

R. In the long run it couldn't be a growth company either. It . . . they're masked. A company that is profitable is looking for new areas in which to invest. And through these investments it gains, it does increase its sales. You can't just sit there and stagnate.

I. All right. What kind of company do you think would best fit these criteria for you, Allen? Would you say that you are going to be hopeful of finding a company that has a 10 percent growth per year in terms of both sales and profits? Is this your idea of a growth company?

R. I think it's the future outlook. I'd hate to put a number on growth. It depends on the industry too. Some companies grow at 30 percent a year and when they hit 20 percent major disaster strikes. And other companies grow very well at 10 percent a year and . . . or 5 percent a year. If you take the earnings function and you discount it to infinity I think most companies would be equal. They'd have infinite profitability. You know, how large is infinity? A company that's growing or a company that you can grow in where you can assume responsibility would be the type of company I think I would like to work with.

I. All right, what are the relative merits in your mind of taking a position with a banking firm or an investment or stock brokerage firm versus a manufacturing enterprise or industry like ATTCO?

R. Well, my opinion of banks is not very high. I think banks are a little bit stodgy. And that they haven't . . . well, in some areas they have progressed, but in other areas they just aren't as dynamic as the manufacturing companies have been. Investment—I wouldn't be a customer's man in a brokerage firm. I can see myself doing analyses in a brokerage firm. I would enjoy that much more. It depends on the brokerage firm and you can't really say. So far, with my contact with all three areas I think that a manufacturing company presents the most challenge.

I. Just some general questions now, Allen, relative to your academic background. What was your cumulative grade point average at the University of Illinois?

R. Well, it was about 3.7 out of a 5. However, if you don't count my first year when I was in chemistry it goes up to a little bit over 4, I find. If you just count the last three years.

I. All right. And what about your grades here so far at the university?

R. My grades have been sporadic here. It ranges just above a C. However . . .

I. Which is what, about a 2?

R. About a 2.25 out of 4.

I. Which courses have you done best in . . . so far?

R. I do best in statistics; I do best in accounting and administration.

I. And in what?

R. The second administration course. I can't think of the title of it. I'm under the four-quarter program.

I. All right. What do you think, Allen. What is your greatest asset, or the greatest thing you have to offer a company as a salable product? In other words, what I'm saying, in relation to all of the other M.B.A.s that you associate with here at the university, in what ways do you seem to think, in your personal evaluation or self-analysis, how do you stand out, how are you better than they?

R. Well, maybe it's my outlook. I think it's the way that I judge factors. I seem to, in an unconscious manner, am able to apply an analytical outlook. I think this is the greatest thing I have to offer. Besides my technical training. Actually, my technical training is competent, very competent . . .

I. You mean in the accounting and finance?

R. In the accounting and finance areas. I have had, well, many finance courses. I'm taking a finance course now. In the initial finance courses I had waivers from Illinois.

I. What's your greatest weakness, in your opinion, as an individual so far? The greatest thing that a company will have to be concerned about in considering you for employment?

R. I at times have a little difficulty in adjusting. It can take me a couple of months before I'll feel . . .

I. Adjusting to people, conditions? Adjusting . . .

R. Adjusting to outside influences. I work up to an optimum. It takes a couple of months until I feel comfortable after changing conditions.

I. A bit of a slow starter but once you get under way you can do a commendable job.

R. Yes.

I. Particularly in your area?

R. I feel . . . yes.

I. All right. Let's talk a little bit now about this business of location. I place a lot of emphasis, a lot of importance on location. You're primarily a Chicago boy, or have operated within the state of Illinois, at least. What problems do you foresee in relocating in Akron, Ohio, as a permanent base of operation?

R. Well, I don't know much about Akron; I'd like to find out something about it. I . . .

I. You've been to Ohio before?

R. I've never been . . . I've traveled west of the Mississippi.

I. But never east, huh?

R. Well, Florida. But not the East Coast, no. I don't see any intrinsic difficulty in moving to Ohio. I don't, beyond . . . living in a big city. I think all cities over a couple of hundred thousand people are about the same.

I. Now, specifically, of the areas that I have mentioned very, very briefly is there one that seems to be of most interest to you?

R. Capital budgeting. However, I would like to say that when you asked for the ideal job, it's very hard to give you an ideal job. Not having had work experience on the level that you're asking me to give you an ideal job for. It is very difficult.

I. Well, this is understandable, Allen, because I can appreciate that it's very difficult for you, having come from primarily an academic background, to relate to me the kind of job you want and have it fit into my company and specifically to jobs we have available. So I can appreciate your position and of course it's equally difficult for me to sit across the table from you and find out exactly what you're best at, and to take those words that you used and put them into something that seems to be significant in our company. But the purpose of our being here is to at least do some prescreening and to try to do that if we can. Let's go into this now. You say capital budgeting is the one that sounds of most interest to you. When we are talking about capital budgeting, we have a budget department in the auditing and controlling division. And this group is going to be responsible for setting up some plans for where we're going to get our money to do our business, where we're going to generate our capital. And it's going to be not only in the domestic operations but in the international as well. As you probably know, we're a company that's diversifying quite rapidly in terms of products and locations. So this whole business of investment and financing and budgeting is very, very important to us and we're taking a long look at that and we're putting some more strength into those areas because we're just not staffed right now sufficiently to handle the needs in this growing end of our business. I must say that wherever you start in our company, Allen, it's going to be understood that that's only a starting point and you may only be on that first assignment for a year or a year and a half. And then we hope that there is sufficient mobility and flexibility in our operations to be able to move you to another assignment where you can adapt and adjust and make a definite contribution and continue to grow and develop within the company. So we're looking primarily for high-potential, very promotable people that can grow within the company, working within several different aspects of our operations into a general management kind of position. And we're doing this through all of our M.B.A. programs regardless of where we start them at. But I can assuredly say, as I said before, that you are going to start in Akron, Ohio. You'd start in a number of studies related to capital budgeting for the corporation on both a domestic and an international basis. And it would be very conceivable that you could move from there into a cost position, from there into a tax department, from there into a pensions and insurance area, for example, from there into something connected with our treasury, or on our financial staff, or with some of our key controllers, or you could even move internationally or domestically as a chief accountant or controller of a small subsidiary operation. So there would be lots of possibilities for improvement; this is only a starting point. Well, now that we've covered that as a possibility, let me throw it open to you now, Allen. Do you have any questions to ask me that would be pertinent to our situation here?

R. Well, I realize that it's very difficult for you both to judge my abilities and for me to see a job opportunity that exactly fits into my scheme of thinking. Actually, I realize that you can really conceptualize what you want. At least I can't conceptualize what I want until I can actually get into a company and be working in it. It's difficult, as you said. I don't think you can really judge a person's capabilities until he has worked and done something within the firm. It's very difficult to say, well, you come from such a background and here's where it fits because no one really knows where he fits until he's done something and proven himself, can realize what you said previously.

I. So as long as it's a large metropolitan area, you don't think you'll have any trouble with adjusting?

R. No.

I. And the fact that you're 350 or 375 miles from family and friends won't necessarily be too much of a problem. You don't think so?

R. I don't think so, no.

I. All right. Well, what questions do you have now to ask me, Allen? That we haven't covered? I think I've asked most that I want. And I'll turn it over to you now.

R. Well, I'd like to find something out about Akron. How big is it?

I. Akron is a town of about 325,000. It's a rubber industry town, of course. It's all located there. It's called the Rubber Capital of the World, with Firestone, Goodyear, Goodrich, and General Tire all having their corporate offices there. It's about 35 miles south of Cleveland. Or about an hour's drive from Cleveland proper. It's a town that is very active in golf and winter sports, and they have a lot of fine restaurants and dine-and-dance places. But principally it's a rubber industry town and it centers in between Canton, Ohio, and Cleveland. And it's about 370 miles from right here.

R. In other words, it's not far from a very large metropolitan area. Cleveland is very close.

I. Right.

R. And all the recreational and educational and cultural facilities of Cleveland, would you say, are at hand?

I. That's right. In many cases we think Akron has some things to offer that the large metropolitan Cleveland area doesn't have. So in many ways that's a plus in our favor, we think.

R. Aside from that, I don't have any questions.

I. All right. Well, here's the way I'd like to leave it with you, Allen. I see our time has more than gone by now. What I'd like to do is this. I'd like to take this now and review it with our financial division in terms of your interest with their corporate accounting area, their corporate capital budgeting areas. I'll be in touch with you within the next week and a half so that you'll know definitely what our decision will be. And I'll just say that it will be in a written form from me and it will be very straightforward. I'll either say that we've reviewed your form and we don't feel that your background is adaptable to our job and therefore there is no further interest. Or, the more positive approach, I'd be saying we definitely are interested and we want you to propose several available dates and we want you to come into Akron at our expense for interviews with our department. And at that point you would have four or five interviews with members of our financial division. And a decision would be made that night, whether we are going to send an offer or not. So we'll follow up on that basis and you'll hear from me in written form within a week and a half. OK?

R. Fine.

I. Fine, Allen, enjoyed talking to you. Thanks for coming here and best of luck to you.

CHAPTER 7
APPRAISAL INTERVIEWS

Preview

Appraisal interviews are important because most employees want to know how their job performance is being rated.

The basic content objectives should include:

• Job description
• Evaluation of past performance
• Future goals

Motivating the respondent requires a balance between positive reinforcement and negative criticism.

Different structures can be used to adapt to a particular interviewee.

The appraisal interview taps the communication skills of an interviewer more than any other kind of interview.

Most people want to know how they are doing in their job and where they stand in the organization. Surveys have shown that this kind of personal feedback is desired at every level in the organization. It is absolutely necessary for people who are self-motivated achievers, for they like to keep score and need to have some evaluation of their performance in order to measure improvement. Because the upper managers of some organizations feel that the effective use of appraisals is the main characteristic that differentiates successful managers from less successful ones, the appraisal serves a vital role in management development as well as organizational effectiveness.

The appraisal process varies among organizations, but it commonly includes the following stages: (1) Preliminary discussions are held among several superiors for the purpose of evaluating the performance of a given subordinate; (2) these discussions are summarized in a report; and (3) the subordinate's immediate supervisor meets with him to discuss the report. During the final stage the employee himself has an opportunity to make some input to the evaluation. In fact, in management by objectives the objectives set by the employee and his supervisor would be the criteria by which his performance is evaluated.

Ideally, an employee should get feedback throughout the year, but in practice the appraisal interview is a special time set aside for talking over job problems and future plans more broadly than is possible in the normal course of work relationships.

The appraisal interview is now used widely in business, the military, government, and even in public school systems. Its popularity has made it the object of much analysis, and there are many who view it critically. The most frequent criticisms are that the interviewer is playing god, the interviewees are unresponsive, the judgments involved are subjective, and causes and effects are confused. There can be no doubt that some appraisals are badly done and that some of the criticism is warranted. Nevertheless, people apparently do want this kind of information; it has worked well in many organizations: Mayfield has found that "90 percent of the people who have been interviewed express satisfaction with the procedure."[1]

KNOW THE PURPOSES

The overall purpose of the appraisal is to perpetuate the organization by providing it with more effective workers and managers. It also is a channel of information because it gives workers the information they want. Consequently the appraisal is doubly useful in that it has been shown to answer individual needs as well as benefiting the organization.

At a more specific level, a given appraisal may have any number of purposes. The following list suggests some of the most common:

1) To give feedback that lets the employee know where he stands
2) To praise good work
3) To improve superior-subordinate relations
4) To communicate the need for improvement
5) To give the employee a sense of participation in his job
6) To counsel and provide help
7) To discover what employees are thinking
8) To recognize and reward contributions
9) To let a person know what is expected of him
10) To assess the employee's future in the organization
11) To serve as a record for that individual
12) To set objectives for future performance
13) To warn or threaten
14) To get things "off one's chest"
15) To persuade the employee to go in certain directions

Not all of these are likely to be combined in any one interview, but several of them might. Whenever the appraisal involves combinations of purposes, care must be taken to ensure that each is put in an appropriate balance with the others. The phrasing of purposes can make subtle differences in the interviewer's communicative behavior, too, so care must be taken that he states the purpose as well as he can. Finally, the more thoroughly an interviewer has thought through his purpose and the more concretely he has stated it, the more likely he is to attain it.

SET CONTENT OBJECTIVES

The list of purposes just given suggests three general content areas that should be explored in an appraisal: (1) job definition, (2) evaluation of past performance, and (3) goals or targets for the future. Although we may talk about these separately, they really are inextricably bound together. Performance ought to be measured in terms of goals, which, in turn, are set in reference to the job description. Any appraisal that does not cover these three areas is probably deficient.

JOB DEFINITION

Defining a job often sounds easy and may even seem to be a waste of interview time. After all, a person who has held a particular job for a long time ought to know that job. But that is true only if we assume that the job does not change and expectations are always the same. Experience leads us to believe that these are bad assumptions. Most jobs do change, and most superiors progressively revise their expectations of their employees in order to meet the demands of the organization. Consequently a periodic review of every job description is important.

First, the job should be viewed in the overall context of the organization. It is important that the employee know how his job contributes to the broad organizational picture. Moreover, he should be kept abreast of changes within the total company that affect his work unit and perhaps redefine his job in important ways. Second, the employee's own job responsibilities should be reviewed. Job descriptions are rarely static; they grow or die as interactions change or as individuals expand or reduce them. This review is also important because it has been shown that a worker and his boss frequently differ on an average of 25 percent of their expectations of the responsibilities and goals for the job. Therefore it is imperative that job responsibilities be mutually defined if appraisals are going to be effective.

PAST PERFORMANCE

What is appraised is really up to the interviewer. His position in the organization gives him a great advantage in this sense. However, successful appraisals seem to follow certain guidelines.

First, the evaluation should be based on criteria that have been, or can be, explained to the interviewer. It is best to avoid surprises.

Second, the performance review should be job related and as objective as possible. The diagram in Figure 7.1 helps explain this point.

Some people feel that it would be ideal if the performance review could

	Job Related	Non job Related
Objective	A	B
Subjective	C	D

Figure 7.1

deal exclusively with Box A, where everything is objective (measurable) and job related. As much as possible, this area should be explored thoroughly. But it is also necessary to explore Box C. Although work relationships, compatibility, measuring up to one's potential, and matters of dress are highly subjective, in some cases they may be related to one's effectiveness on the job. For example, the higher one moves up the organization, the more crucial are his abilities to work with others, but it is difficult to measure these in an objective way. Furthermore, relationships are subjective, and the superior and subordinate may profit from a discussion of their interactions. As much as possible, appraisals should not include the areas covered by boxes B and D.

Third, the evaluation should stay with recent performance. Generally, a definite period is specified because there may be a rule that an appraisal be conducted once or twice a year. Some bosses, however, have difficulty forgetting things that happened long ago so that their current evaluations are colored by the past. When this happens, the evaluation is unrealistic and unfair to the employee.

Finally, all elements of performance should be kept in proper balance. It is easy to fall into the trap of spending 5 minutes complimenting the interviewee and 45 minutes criticizing him. There seems to be a definite tendency for many of us to focus primarily on problems anyway, and a supervisor is particularly sensitive to job deficiencies because these are the things that create problems for him. Spending most of the time on problems may cause the total impact on the employee to be negative even though some of the things he does well are far more important than the areas in which he needs to improve. This type of distortion of reality is often present in appraisals.

SETTING TARGETS

The setting of targets or goals is not subject to a great deal of prior planning. Targets tend to grow out of the discussion of prior performance and should be mutually derived by the interviewee and the interviewer. In practice, some supervisors even insist that targets be initiated by the subordinate and then reviewed by the two of them together. If the original targets are not acceptable, then the subordinate is asked to think about them and make a new list of objectives. This implies, of course, that the interviewer must think out in advance the nature of potential targets that would be acceptable to him.

As a means of illustrating some guidelines for setting targets, the following examples have been compiled from reports of actual appraisals:

1) A production supervisor set himself the goal of reducing waste on line 7 by 5 percent by June 30.
2) A plant industrial engineer set himself the target of finishing a 5-year cost comparison on a plant shutdown.
3) A training supervisor set a goal to complete a new training program on management by objectives by April 1.
4) A student resolved to make a 3-point grade average at the end of the semester.
5) An industrial relations manager proposed to investigate the use of S & H Green Stamps to generate ideas on the company's suggestion system by the end of the year.
6) A supervisor set himself the target of having all his own employees set targets for themselves within 2 months.

By examining these goals we can perhaps identify several characteristics that can guide us in setting meaningful goals. First, any aspect of the job can be explored as a potential target. Some involve changes in the job itself, some involve relationships with others, and some involve the product. Another way of classifying aspects of the job is to say that some involve control over routine matters, some involve creative ideas, and still others focus on crucial problems.

Second, the number of targets should be limited to the most important and most meaningful aspects of the job. It is impractical to concentrate on everything the individual does. Perhaps one should follow the old 80/20 rule: Take on the 20 percent of the problems that give the largest return.

Third, these targets are described specifically, and their completion can be measured. They contrast in this regard to very abstract or general resolutions "to improve" or "to work on my human relations." In such cases the goals are not concrete enough to measure.

Fourth, a time period is planned for each target. This should be realistic, but it is important that it be set. Many of us work best when deadlines confront us.

Finally, targets seem to offer some challenge to the worker. Set by himself, they permit him to participate in making his job more interesting; perhaps more important, they require that he think about his own growth process.

PRESENT THE CONTENT OBJECTIVES

Whereas the selection interview is basically an information-gathering interview, the appraisal interview is designed to discuss problems. And it requires that a presentation be made about each of the content objectives. These presentations may be followed by questions that probe the interviewee's reactions and assessment of the situation. The whole process requires great sensitivity to the other person. The following guidelines are designed to help the interviewer achieve a degree of excellence in his use of communication skills.

1) **Consider feelings as well as facts.** People are very involved with themselves, and an appraisal has great potential for emotional involvement. Our self-image is our most important psychological construct, and we will do almost anything to protect it. At the same time, we must remember that the interviewer's desire to avoid the unpleasant frequently leads to error in conducting appraisals. His history of interactions with the subordinate should make the supervisor a good judge of what can be said with good effect.

2) **Welcome the respondent's reactions and his differing perceptions.** None of us sees ourselves as others see us, and we have already pointed out that others do not see our jobs as we see them. These different perceptions should be regarded as opportunities to grow by both the interviewer and the interviewee.

3) **Concentrate on improvement, not perfection.** A demand for perfection is destined to be thwarted; a demand for improvement can be rewarded over and over again.

4) **Be problem oriented rather than solution oriented.** When confronted with a problem, some people start searching for an answer before they know what the problem really is. Proper analysis of the problem is a prerequisite to a good solution.

5) **Be situation oriented rather than person oriented.** Look for elements in the situation that affect performance, and do not be too eager to point to an individual as the cause of a problem. The tendency to try to assign blame in every situation is not a healthy characteristic for a manager.

6) **Be positive.** Assume that most people can change their performance and their attitudes over time and with a little assistance. Have a little faith in the subordinate.

STRUCTURE THE INTERVIEW

THE INTRODUCTION How one starts an appraisal depends in part on the objective one has for it and on one's own personal style. However, consideration should be given to several aspects. The initial greeting and preliminary remarks should allow for a warm-up period in which the two become acclimated to one another in the appraisal setting. The reason for the interview should be stated in such a way that it establishes the supportive nature of the relationship. Sometimes organizations require that an appraisal be conducted at certain times, and a common opening is, "Well, it's that time again. . . ." This telegraphs the apparent reluctance of the interviewer to begin and often minimizes the overall worth of the interview. It does nothing to establish a supportive climate or to motivate the respondent.

THE BODY In *The Appraisal Interview* Norman Maier has given one of the best analyses of three different styles of appraisal interviewing: (1) tell and sell, (2) tell and listen, and (3) problem solving.[2] Each of these is characterized in the following discussion.

The objectives of the *tell and sell* approach are to communicate an evaluation to the employee and to persuade him to accept the evaluation and follow a prescribed plan for improvement. The role of the interviewer is that of a salesman or persuader, and he generally does most of the talking. Both positive and negative incentives are offered to convince the subordinate to accept the plan. In some cases he is promised a raise or promotion; in others he is warned and threatened. This approach tends to work well for young employees, those who are very loyal, and those who have a high regard for the interviewer. The potential dangers are that only one side is explored and that defensive or hostile feelings are aroused.

The objectives of the *tell and listen* approach are to communicate an evaluation to the subordinate and get his reaction to it. Here the role of the interviewer is that of an active listener, and typically the pattern of interaction goes like this. The interviewer does most of the talking in the beginning; the middle of the interview is dominated by the subordinate as he gives his reactions and analyses; and the interviewer takes over again at the end in order to summarize and focus their thinking. The advantage of this approach is that it gives the interviewer a lot of feedback that can help him understand the subordinate's job performance in ways he has not understood it before. The risk is that a plan of action may not be developed easily, and the interviewer may still need to resort to persuasion at the end.

The *problem-solving* approach is more unstructured than the others, because the interviewer tries to avoid the role of judge or evaluator. He chooses not to initiate the discussion of problems but hopes they will come up after he has developed an atmosphere in which the interviewee will feel free to describe them and perhaps ask for help. This approach relies a great deal on the intrinsic motivation of the subordinate within the interview itself. When subordinates respond well, it is a highly desirable approach. However, when they lack ideas or are unwilling to level about problem areas, it may be so deficient that the interviewer will have to resort to another approach. It also suffers from the fact that a subordinate may not always be aware of some of the larger perspectives needed to evaluate his own performance.

All three of these approaches have merit, and no one of them will work equally well with all subordinates. Although a supervisor may identify the style he prefers, he will be wise to have the kind of flexibility that will allow him to resort to another style when his own approach is not working.

THE CONCLUSION   The conclusion of the appraisal is as important as the beginning. It needs to summarize the discussion, identify the main points, restate the main goals, and conclude with some orientation as to what is going to take place as a result of the interview. The interviewee always needs to know how information is going to be used. To be most effective, appraisals should be held periodically. When they are, and when some continuity can be planned, the conclusion of one appraisal really serves as a statement of the agenda for the next.

THE CHAPTER IN PERSPECTIVE

The appraisal interview taps nearly all of the interviewer's communication skills; in addition to giving and getting information, he will need to evaluate the respondent, counsel him, perhaps discipline him, and at the same time motivate him to perform better. Because of this, the principles and suggestions covered in this chapter would be generalizable to many other interview situations.

From the interviewer's standpoint there are two important guidelines that should be implemented. The appraisal should be as concrete as possible, and whenever possible the employee should be made aware of the exact criteria on which he is being evaluated. Also, it is necessary to let the interviewee vent some of his own emotions during the interview in such a way as to permit the interviewer to maintain control over the situation.

As in the preceding chapter, a transcript of an actual appraisal is provided here. The reader can profitably analyze this interview in terms of the following questions: How specific is the interviewer? What kind of power struggle goes on in the interview? What procedures does the interviewer use to maintain his control?

REFERENCES

1. Harold Mayfield, "In Defense of Performance Appraisal," *Harvard Business Review*, 38 (March 1960): 82.
2. Norman R. F. Maier, *The Appraisal Interview* (New York: Wiley, 1963), pp. 21–32.
3. Transcribed from a role-played situation.

APPRAISAL INTERVIEW[3]

Supervisor: OK, Jim; how's it going today?

Jim: Oh, not too bad.

Supervisor: OK, the reason I called you in today, Jim, is to discuss something I think could be extremely important to both of us, but particularly to you. Last week I was required by the bosses to put in a recommendation for promotion to help somebody foreman another section of the plant. You were one of the three people from the section that I considered for the promotion; so what I wanted to do was discuss with you exactly what considerations I had in the recommendation I did make and then go over some of the things, which because of my analysis, and what I had to sit down and really think about you and the other two people concerned, I'd like to share with you and get your reactions to them.

Jim: Who were the other two?

Supervisor: OK, there was you and John and Bob. Now, here's the way I'd like to run it if we could. Just bear with me. What I'd like to do first of all is to give you the recommendation I made, the considerations I had in the recommendation, and specifically, my appraisal of you, the appraisal I had to make during the time I was considering you for the recommendation for the promotion. After that, I'd like to give you the opportunity to give me your reactions to the appraisal I've made of you during that time. And lastly we'll discuss it if you so desire.

OK, first of all, I did end up recommending John Adams for the promotion to foreman. Now, there were some other things outside of this particular job that had an effect on my recommendation. As you know, the company policy is that every so often a certain percentage of the employees are recommended for promotion based on their ability to go beyond the position in which they are going to be placed. Well, this was one of those promotions. The bosses told me specifically that in this promotion they wanted somebody recommended who could now, at the present time, go two or three rungs higher in the company.

Jim: On this recommendation that you made—you were the only one who had input into that. Is that right?

Supervisor: That's right, but let me finish . . .

Jim: You recommended this guy Adams.

Supervisor: Yes, I recommended John. But let me finish first. I'll give you a chance afterwards, Jim, because I want to get your reactions, too . . . Now, the biggest factor was the one I just told you: the fact that the company wanted someone who had the opportunity and the ability to go much higher in the company—at least two or three rungs or even four rungs higher on the ladder. OK, now in my appraisal of you, Jim, this is what I want to discuss. I don't want to discuss my appraisal of Bob or of John or of anybody else; but I want to discuss with you my appraisal of you, as a result of the thought I had to put into it during the time I was considering you for the recommendation.

You've got many strengths. In fact, I've got no doubt in my mind, whatsoever, that you could hold down the job as foreman. I know you can do it. You've done it here whenever I'm absent, and you've done a damned fine job. So that wasn't the main concern. You're the best worker in the whole section—you know that, I know that; everybody else knows it—you have the respect of the other people in the section, you're very competent, you've got a lot of initiative, and another good point is that whenever we get new people in you do an outstanding job of training people. In fact, as you know, you've been one of the mainstays who trained John and other people in the section. But there are some things that work to your disadvantage, I feel, in this particular promotion because of the requirement to consider your ability to go higher than the foreman job; and let me just outline these for you.

The first one was—well, actually there are three of them that tie in together. One is an argumentativeness, another one is a lack of tact, and a third one is a lack of cooperation, sometimes. Now, you don't have these deficiencies at all times. I'll be the first to say that. But there are times when you are very argumentative about how to do a job, a particular job, the way you feel it's right, and you don't want to listen to anybody else. During that same time you sometimes show a lack of tact. You don't even want to consider what anybody else has to say because you feel strongly that you're right, and you stick by your guns, and maybe justifiably so. And then other times there's a lack of cooperation with me and with other people in the group. Now, this has nothing to do with your ability to do your job, Jim. You do it well; but I feel that they have a big effect when you're talking about going up to the higher ranks, rungs of responsibility here in the company. And the other thing—probably the thing that worked to your biggest disadvantage, in this particular promotion at this particular time—was because of the requirements placed on me. Right now you have the same academic abilities and inabilities that you had five years ago when I came here and probably 12 years ago when you first came to the company. And it's something that is a serious drawback for promotion above and beyond foreman. It's a little bit of a drawback, I might add, even to the promotion to the job of foreman, but particularly beyond that level. OK, Jim, I've had my say. Now what I'd like to do is get your reactions.

Jim: There's no way I can go along with the crap I've just heard. That's just terrible. I take it that since you recommended Adams—does that mean he's going to get the job?

Supervisor: Yes, it has already been accepted by the bosses. I might add that no official announcement has yet been made, so I'd like you to keep this under your hat until such time as they do make the announcement, which will be very shortly.

Jim: I don't know. It just kinda gripes me the way this whole thing was conducted.

Supervisor: OK, what specifically?

Jim: You know. Just the way I perceive what you're trying to do. There's just too much politics in it. I don't think this decision was made on the basis of merit.

Supervisor: What do you classify as merit?

Jim: I think you have to consider the relationship between the foreman and the worker. The people that are going to work under him. And not the relationship between that man and his superiors. And I think that's the whole reason that Adams got the promotion, that he's in real tight with his superiors. He does a lot of apple polishing.

Supervisor: For the job of foreman, there's a lot of truth to that, Jim. But as I said, for this particular promotion at this particular time the bosses wanted someone who could not only hold down the job as foreman but had the ability to go up higher in the organization. That was their main concern. And you know as well as I do that the company's policy is in-the-organization promotions.

Jim: Yeah, but I don't . . .

Supervisor: And there are a certain percentage of those promotions that they wanted to have people in them who could go higher. And right now, Jim, you just don't have that ability. I'm not saying you can't develop it, because you have many strengths—many strengths. But right now, Jim, you just don't have it.

Now, if you'd like to discuss it, there are some recommendations that if you followed, I think you could definitely develop that. Because you've got the ability, the potential to improve substantially. 'Cause right now, as I've said, you're the best worker I've got in the section, Jim. There's no doubt about it. You know how to train other people. You showed that.

Jim: That seems like important abilities for a foreman to have.

Supervisor: Well, that's very right. That's very right. But there are other capabilities, Jim, that are more important as far as going up the ladder.

Jim: Yeah, but what about the guy who doesn't really care to go up the ladder? What's wrong with just being a foreman?

Supervisor: Well, OK, if there's a guy that only wants to be a foreman and doesn't really want to go beyond that, there will most likely be other opportunities for promotion to the job of foreman. Unfortunately, at this particular time—this is the first time we've had an opening in a long time, as you know—that's not what they wanted. They didn't want somebody who would just be a good foreman. Whether you or I agree or disagree with that, those are the requirements that were placed on me at this time. They wanted somebody selected this time who had the ability to go beyond foreman, so they weren't concerned just with the capability to be a good foreman. If that were the only consideration, Jim, I tell you right now, I would've put you in for the recommendation.

Jim: Yes, but that doesn't do me any good.

Supervisor: Well, I realize that, Jim. I feel sorry about it. But I didn't have much choice on it either. They were very specific in exactly what they wanted this time. But I know that you've done a good job, and I know that you could be a good foreman. There's no doubt in my mind. You're a good foreman whenever I leave, when I'm absent for some reason, and you sit in. In fact, I wouldn't be surprised if you turned out to be a better foreman than me. You've got the ability to be a foreman.

Jim: Yeah, but what's so bad about that is you never get the chance.

Supervisor: Well, I don't have a crystal ball, Jim, I . . .

Jim: This isn't the first time this has happened. I've been passed over before and I can just see that this is nowhere for me.

Supervisor: When were you passed over for a promotion before?

Jim: Oh, gee. I think it was a long time before you came here. It was just a lead man's job and I was just a regular worker, and that didn't go over, and there was your position that came open before you were hired into it, and I didn't get that either. And now this job's come up in another department where I thought there might have been a chance, but . . . it's not that; the thing that really ticks me off is this deal with Adams! No way. He wasn't the best qualified. The other guy, Bob, I really think he got the screws. I really must disagree with you. . . . It's all I can do to keep from picking up this desk and throwing it!

Supervisor: That's your right, Jim. You don't have to agree with me. I'm the one who had to make the decision. I'm the one . . . that's the way it is. But, uh, I'm more concerned with your reactions to what you want to do. Are you the type of individual you mentioned before? Would you like to be a foreman, and that's about as high as you'd like to go? Or do you think you'd like to go higher in the company?

Jim: I don't think I want to get too much higher, no.

Supervisor: So you're concerned with going as high as foremanship.

Jim: Yeah, I'd like to get there.

Supervisor: Well, would you like to get from me my recommendation of what I think you could do to make yourself even more competitive? for that job?

Jim: Well, I think maybe later. I'm too upset. This has come as too much of a shock. I probably could have seen it coming, but now that it's happened, I don't think . . . I don't know, I just kind of need to clear my mind.

Supervisor: OK, I'll tell you what, Jim. You seem to be very upset about it, and so we probably wouldn't get anyplace discussing it right now anyway, so if you'd like to come in some other time, when you feel a little more clearheaded, and get your ducks lined up and get what you want to say exactly, without getting too involved with it . . .

Jim: One of the deals is, that I can't figure out—I've always had a lot of respect for you, and when you threw this thing at me, I, well it really blows my mind, and I really wonder what this company's coming to. This is going to be a morale problem down at the shop. It's going to set the place afire. I think maybe you've lost contact with me.

Supervisor: You say you don't think Adams is a good man for the job?

Jim: No. He doesn't have the rapport that's necessary for the job. Ever since he's come here, ever since I've trained him he's used my ideas to go up to the bigwigs and tell them about it, and he's gotten the credit for it. And the only thing he's been concerned with since he's been here is getting in close with the supervisors. And he's not nearly as friendly as he used to be. You know, . . . what I'm saying is that you made the decision, you're going to have to live with it. But you're going to lose a lot of ground with the people that you count on to do the work. And I've been here long enough so that I know that. I'm not saying that, hell, I didn't get the job—fine. I didn't get it. But what you've done is going to . . . I don't know if you could ever get back in good with them.

Supervisor: Well, I'll have to face that. If that's the way you feel, fine. You see, I had a litttle different perception of Adams. I didn't really desire to discuss Adams, because I was more concerned about you. If that's what's mainly concerning you, though. . . .

Jim: Yeah, but what concerns me personally is that, you know, is that my career has just been cut. Drastically. And that affects me, and I think what I need to know, if I'm going to stay with this company, is how people above me are going to evaluate me in competition with my peers. Because this is what's happening.

Supervisor: Well, Jim, as I said before, the main thing I was concerned about this time, in this particular promotion, was not exclusively and solely the ability of the individual to be a good foreman. Because at this particular time, the bosses specified that they wanted somebody who, right now, has the ability to go at least three or four rungs higher on the ladder.

Jim: There's a difference between ability and connections. See, he's got the connections. He went to Cornell with the boss and all this other mess. He's going to go high just because he's who he is. Not because of what he can do.

Supervisor: Well, I disagree with you, Jim. You may ha e some personality difficulties with him; he may have some difficulties getting along with some of the other workers. That's very likely. But he's a bright individual, he has a lot of initiative; whether or not he has all the ideas himself or whether he utilizes ideas of other people, he still has the ability to get along in a group, and to present his ideas and to present them well. Now, if you could develop some of that ability yourself, Jim, if you go back, for example, to give you a very specific example, refresh some of your academic background, upgrade it so that when you get in with a group of people like you would if you were going to be a foreman, and be up higher than that, you'd be able to express yourself without any difficulty, without any problems in expressing yourself in using grammar. That has nothing to do with your job ability and your job performance now, but when you start going up in the ladder, Jim, it really does. And it's things like that which aren't very tangible maybe, which maybe don't affect your ability to do the job right now, but they do have an effect on promotions within the company. Now, as good or bad as you may think that is, Jim, that's just one of the ways the bosses work. That's one of the things they look for within the company.

Jim: Well, maybe I had better find a more compatible company, where maybe I could get along a little better. Because I'm not the kind of a guy who goes along with all this PR bit and getting along good with my superiors. I just want to do my job the best I can.

Supervisor: Well, there's not that much PR.

Jim: I mean, that's what you're talking about. Express myself, and get along with everybody, I mean . . .

Supervisor: You get along with everybody you work with. You get along with most of the other people, but there're just some times, Jim, when those four things I pointed out work to your disadvantage. And this is one of those times. If you're going to be a foreman, or are going to be promoted up higher in the company, you've got to have a certain amount of tact, understanding, ability to get along with others of equal rank, that you're supposed to work with. You can't go around if you're going to be a boss and just cajole and threaten and tell everybody else that he's full of bull. You can do that for only so long and then you're just going to fall apart. And I don't think you'll find it any different anyplace else, Jim. But you don't need to go someplace else; you've already proven yourself here. It's just unfortunate that at this time I couldn't have recommended you for the foremanship, which I would have liked to have done, because of the other requirements placed on this particular job. If they had just asked me for somebody who could be a damned fine foreman, right now, to do the job, you would have been my first choice. No doubt about it.

Well, I guess there's not too much more we can say right now, Jim. If you'd like to, we can get together and discuss this at a later date. I didn't really expect that you'd buy everything I said and I realize that it was my decision, my appraisal, and that's about the way it stands. But I was very concerned about sharing this appraisal with you at this time, because I think it's a unique opportunity. This may be something I should have done previously. But we haven't had any appraisal requirements here, there haven't been any opportunities for promotion in a long time, as you know, and this time I really had to sit down and think things through, and evaluate people, and place weight and merit on different things to be considered for promotion, and I thought I owed it to you, as well as to the other two individuals concerned, to have a heart-to-heart talk with you. Now, what I'd like you to do is give it some thought, give it some serious thought, and then we can get together and discuss it again. How's that sound? . . . Or do you have something else on your mind? . . . OK, I tell you what. Why don't we get together in a couple more days? Because what I'd like to do is to continue a little bit further, if you're up to it, and give you some recommendations that I think would help you. But I don't think you're up to it right now.

CHAPTER 8
PERSUASIVE INTERVIEWS

Preview

Persuasion in dyadic relationships is a major activity in organizations; it involves the selling of ideas as well as the selling of products.

Persuasion requires the formulation of very specific strategies:

- Know exactly what you want the interviewee to do.
- Analyze the interviewee's potential reactions.
- Pick a time and setting when the interviewee will be most receptive.

The telephone company needed a better way to keep track of equipment used in installing telephones. In the past the installers had written out all the equipment used on a report form; these forms were then sent to the office for someone else to compile. This was a costly procedure because it took several people to keep track of the equipment. After discussing this problem management decided that it would be more efficient to have the installers carry computer cards with them; instead of writing out descriptions of the equipment used, they would punch the same information directly on the card. These cards could then be fed directly into the computer. The result would be a saving in time, energy, and cost. It was decided that this new procedure would be tested by one group of installers before the company tried to make it a permanent policy.

Supervisor Jack Bonham called in one of his foremen for an interview to explain the new procedure and try to get him to give it a fair trial. The supervisor could have forced the foreman to try it, but he felt that persuasion was a better tactic. The interesting thing about a "fair trial" is that there are few ways of checking on it. If the foreman doesn't like the idea, he can make sure it will fail. Therefore the supervisor must do all he can in the interview to ensure that the foreman understands the process and accepts the idea of trying it.

While we generally associate persuasion with public speaking and with salesmanship, there are many other communication situations in organizations like the telephone company that have as their main objective the persuasion of one person by another. It happens in sales interviews, in tell and sell appraisals, in initiating new ideas, in creating new programs, and in determining goals for the future. Some of these are formal interviews, but many occur informally and rather spontaneously. After a conference, for example, a member will often "buttonhole" a neutral or swing vote to try to convince him of the "right" way to vote.

There are two ways of getting people to change their minds or accept new ideas. One is coercion; the other is persuasion. Coercion involves the use of force. Persuasion involves a voluntary change of mind based on new insights, new information, or the promise that certain needs and desires will be fulfilled. Both are used extensively in organizations, but it is wiser to get people to accept ideas voluntarily. Consequently the persuasive interview plays a major role in the communication life of nearly all organizations.

STATE THE PURPOSE

The overall purpose may be simply to persuade the interviewee to accept the idea, change his behavior, or help management accomplish some goal. In stating the purpose, it is useful to be as concrete as possible. State exactly what you want the other person to believe or exactly what you want him to do. Probably most of us have been in persuasive situations where the ultimate intent of the persuader was too ambiguous for either person to know what was really expected.

There is an interesting interpersonal dimension to persuasion that should be considered here. Persuasion is not necessarily something you do to someone else: "Indeed, it is not far from the literal truth to say that every time a person is persuaded, he *persuades himself*."[1] In other words, a person is not persuaded until he arrives at the desired conclusion on the basis of his *own* reasons, not someone else's.

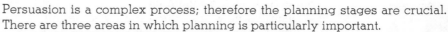

IDENTIFY CONTENT OBJECTIVES

Persuasion is a complex process; therefore the planning stages are crucial. There are three areas in which planning is particularly important.

1. *Analyze the person to be persuaded.* The interviewer needs to anticipate as much as possible. This may include learning something about the interviewee's experiences and personal history, his motives and assumptions, and particularly his value orientations, that is, what he thinks is really important. Two of the best pieces of information to have are (1) how the interviewee generally reacts to proposals of this nature and (2) the nature of the relationship between the interviewer and the interviewee. While we often say that the ideal in persuasion is the acceptance of an idea on its own merits, we know that people very frequently accept or reject an idea because of the person associated with it. In addition, it may be

very important to know the interviewee's attitude toward decision making in the organization. Some people like to be told what to do; others like to be asked. These two types must be approached quite differently.

2. *Have a thorough knowledge of the topic or problem.* It is good to know not only the basic rationale for the idea but also the possible criticisms and negative reactions. Learning all this may take valuable time, but it could prove well worth while. A vague development of an idea may arouse unnecessary suspicions or irrelevant objections; besides, the respondent will want answers to his questions. Moreover, thorough knowledge of the topic will permit anticipation of, and preparation for, some of the chief objections that might be raised.

A good way to be certain that you know the topic thoroughly is to use the Dewey reflective thinking pattern:

Define the problem.
Analyze the problem.
Suggest alternative solutions.
Identify criteria for a solution.
Choose a solution.

How a problem is defined often dictates the kinds of solutions found. For example, some consultants nearly always view organizational problems in terms of *people.* Consequently they try to solve the problem by means of training programs or the hiring of new people. Other consultants looking at the same problem in the same organization might define it in terms of *structure.* Therefore they suggest that the organization be changed but not the people. This shows that different people have different orientations toward the same problem, and you need to be able to give your own rationale for defining the problem as you do.

3. *Pick a time and setting conducive to the discussion of ideas.* Whenever possible, it is desirable to schedule appointments ahead of time because many workers feel pressure and irritation when taken off the job unexpectedly. Moreover, scheduling ahead may permit a choice among physical conditions. In the telephone company example, the word *computer* would be frightening to a lot of employees. In anticipation of this problem, the supervisor might schedule the interview for a time when he can show the foreman some cards and perhaps even walk him through the entire process.

STRUCTURE THE INTERVIEW

THE INTRODUCTION The role of the introduction in the persuasive interview is much the same as in other types of interviews. First, it should be designed to build rapport. One way of doing this is to stress the things the interviewer and interviewee have in common. Second, the introduction should give some orientation to the respondent. There will be some differences in how this should be done, depending on the type of interview. The salesman, for example, might well begin an interview by identifying the company he represents and describing its products. But in handling an important problem a supervisor might choose to identify the problem area in the introduction and save the statement of his real persuasive intent—that is, the solution—until later.

THE BODY   The body is the time for exploring the main content objectives that have been planned. In revealing these, however, it is wise to remember that

> good persuasive interviews are not speeches delivered to an audience of one; they are conversations involving the persuadee as an active participant and characterized by all the qualities of good communication, including listening and efforts to understand the persuadee and to protect his ego.[2]

In other words, there should be give and take. The most productive interviews are those in which both people have opportunities to probe the ideas and share their reactions. Remembering that a person usually persuades himself, it might be useful to consider that sometimes the greatest persuasion is taking place when the interviewee is doing the talking rather than the interviewer.

Finally, it is in the body of the interview that most of the communication barriers must be overcome. Dr. Jesse Nirenberg has listed the six human tendencies that work against a meeting of minds as follows:

1) **Resistance to change.** People do not want to exchange the ideas they already hold for new ones, particularly if their ideas are based on long-held attitudes.
2) **Distraction by personal concerns.** Every talker is competing with the inner thoughts and feelings that tend to draw the listener away from the subject at hand.
3) **Talking before thinking.** People start talking before their ideas are clearly formed, so they keep changing the direction of their thoughts.
4) **Wishful hearing.** People hear what they want to hear rather than what is actually being said.
5) **Jumping to conclusions.** Both the speaker and the listener make unwarranted assumptions about what the other person knows or accepts.
6) **Habitual secretiveness.** People withhold information because of a vague feeling that the less another person knows about their thoughts the better.[3]

While these tendencies are certainly not limited to the interview situation, the following suggestions are designed to help overcome some of these barriers in the dyadic context.

1) **Adapt to the interviewee.** Find ways of connecting your new information and ideas to what he or she already knows.
2) **Welcome his questions and his reactions.** They will help you tailor your communication to him. But it is important that *you* select the time when he begins to give them. Premature interruptions can cause great problems because dis-

cussion begins before the completed idea has been given. Consequently the discussion cannot be as productive as it might be because some important considerations will be left out.

3) Demonstrate your understanding of the other person's position. When you do, he will probably feel that you are willing to be objective, and this may influence his reaction toward you.

4) Keep your materials clear and simply stated. Focus on one or two issues at a time, and maintain order throughout the discussion.

5) Deal with emotional interference. Many persuasive situations arouse strong emotions that sometimes interfere with rational processes.

There are several things to be kept in mind when emotional interference occurs. For one thing, emotions cannot be displaced by logic. When the respondent begins to show strong emotion, perhaps the best tactic is to stop your presentation and get him to talk. In doing so, he is likely to reduce the emotional tension building up inside him. You can then demonstrate some understanding of his feelings and resume your presentation.

It is also necessary to recognize that not all emotional interference originates with the respondent. Interviewers also are emotionally involved with their ideas and will find themselves feeling tension, anger, and fear. When this happens, it is best to admit it to yourself. The *feeling* of an emotion is not controllable, but a person can control whether or not he *acts* on it. In cases where you find yourself having difficulty controlling your behavior, perhaps the wisest tactic is to continue the interview at another time.

THE CHAPTER IN PERSPECTIVE

Persuasion is a commonplace activity in any organization that takes many forms. In this book we write about it not only in terms of the dyadic interview but also in terms of persuasion in conferences and persuasive speeches. Nevertheless, there are some special observations to be made about persuasion in the dyadic context.

It is perhaps more important in the persuasive interview than in the other types covered to know exactly what one hopes to accomplish. In addition, persuasive strategies may need to be planned in more detail, and the interview may need to be more structured than for some of the other types. Finally, accomplishing the persuasive purpose calls for the closest analysis of and adaptation to the interviewee. In selection and appraisal interviews the interviewer may ultimately rely on his status or position in the organization to accomplish his ends, but if he does this in the persuasive interview he is changing his strategy from persuasion to coercion.

No transcript is provided here for analysis, but the reader is encouraged to go back to the case study described at the beginning of this chapter and plan the persuasive strategies that might be used in convincing the foreman to give the new program a fair trial.

REFERENCES

1. R. S. Goyer, W. Charles Redding, and John T. Rickey, *Interviewing Principles and Techniques* (Dubuque, Iowa: Kendall/Hunt, 1968), p. 50.

2. C. J. Stewart and W. B. Cash, *Interviewing: Principles and Practices* (Dubuque, Iowa: Brown, 1974), p. 135.

3. Jesse S. Nirenberg, "Persuasive Communication—When You Consult with People," training handout of the Cornell University Extension Division, p. 1.

PART III

Chwatsky, Editorial Photocolor Archives

Forsyth, Monkmeyer

PART II
GROUP CONFERENCES

As an organization becomes increasingly complex, the need for group decision making becomes correspondingly greater. The establishment of the National Security Council, for example, is illustrative of the demands caused by increased size and complexity of government on the national level. So many different departments and agencies of the federal government became involved in national security, and were so interdependent, that some coordinating body had to be created where information and viewpoints could be exchanged and mutual problems solved.

The place of discussion, quite obviously, extends far beyond the confines of the federal government. Wherever two or more people share the responsibility of determining policy, solving problems, or making decisions, there is a need for group discussion. In business and industry, for example, many important decisions can no longer be made by a single, all-powerful individual. These matters are now commonly decided collectively at executive meetings.

The needs of a democratic society and the demands of increasingly complex organizations have combined in this age to make discussion more important than at any other time. Discussion, like space travel and nuclear energy, must be accepted as a necessary aspect of modern life. And it, as in the case of these other phenomena, must be managed and controlled in ways that will be helpful rather than harmful.

In the following four chapters we have attempted to encapsulate the information and ideas most essential to the intelligent management and control of group discussion. We begin in Chapter 9 with a survey of the strengths and weaknesses of discussion, move on in Chapter 10 to analyze the principal factors involved in the dynamics of groups at work, and conclude in Chapters 11 and 12 with a series of practical suggestions for effective participation and leadership in groups.

When the reader has finished this part of the book, he should be able to:

1) discuss the advantages and disadvantages of the group method.
2) identify vital attributes of group anatomy.
3) demonstrate good group leadership techniques.
4) participate effectively in a group discussion.
5) analyze what is happening in group interaction.

CHAPTER 9

WHAT GROUP DISCUSSION CAN DO (AND WHAT IT CAN'T)

Preview

The conference is one of management's most fundamental tools. Sensitivity to group potential is thus vital to the organizational communicator.

Shortcomings of group conferences:

- Groups take time.
- Groups diffuse responsibility.
- Groups cause conformity.

Advantages of group conferences:

- Groups produce better decisions.
- Groups produce stronger commitment.
- Groups increase understanding.

After receiving a disappointing report from a committee he had appointed, an administrator friend of ours remarked in disgust, "If I had told those guys to design me a horse, they would probably have come up with something that looked like a camel." It was similar feeling, no doubt, that prompted a New York business executive to express his disdain in the following poetic form:

Search all your parks in all your cities . . .
  You'll find no statues to committees!

THE TROUBLE WITH COMMITTEES

Clearly, attitudes like these are not uncommon among people charged with the responsibility for making important decisions. Turning decision making over to a group looks like a complete contradiction of the qualities—independence, decisiveness, sound judgment—that good managers are supposed to possess. And reactions like this are not altogether unjustified; group action does pose a number of significant problems.

To begin with, there are some jobs that groups are simply not cut out to handle. It is, for example, a total waste of time to assign to a committee a question that can be answered by an expert on the basis of scientific demonstration. A former student of one of the authors—a man who was a grade school principal during the day and took courses toward an advanced degree at night—illustrated this point perfectly in a report. During a science project in one of his second-grade classes, in which the students were studying squirrels, one of the 7-year-olds wondered out loud whether the baby squirrel they had in class was a boy or a girl. After pondering the issue for a few minutes, one budding scientist offered the suggestion that they have a class discussion about it and then take a vote.

A second type of task in which group effort is almost always destined to failure is in the area of creative work such as report writing. Although it is certainly true that a committee can provide guidance concerning the content of a report and can even make useful suggestions for improving the document once it is drafted, the actual writing of the report should be left to a single individual working alone. The only exception to this rule that would normally apply is that on some occasions various parts of a report may be composed by different people, leaving to someone else the editorial tasks of synthesizing and coordinating. This book is itself an example of such a project; although it was authored by three different people, the task was divided into parts, with each author writing his own section. Meetings were used to plan and to share ideas. Anyone who has had the misfortune of trying group writing understands that the specific job of putting ideas into words and words onto paper is just not conducive to group action. As self-evident as this observation might appear, however, it is astonishing how often groups will attempt a cooperative composition when assigned the task of writing a report. The inevitable result is almost constant disagreement and bickering over problems such as style and punctuation. One solution is illustrated by the following incident:

During a staff meeting of four people with the department head, I saw that the group was trying to write out policy for several problems and was having a frustrating time doing it. I proposed that we change the purpose of our meeting to the identification of problems that we each wanted to work on. Then we were to assign each problem to an individual to develop further. Next the individual was to report back to the group, which would review the accumulated data. And finally the group would assign one individual to finalize the written statement. It was effective in that it shortened our meetings and made them much more tolerable.

In addition to acknowledging the fact that there are some jobs that groups just don't do very well, one must also concede that there are certain aspects of group endeavor that may, depending on individual circumstances, be undesirable.

**GROUPS
TAKE TIME**

Almost any kind of group decision making is going to take more time than if the decision is made by an individual acting alone. In addition, in most cases the larger the group, the more time it will take. For this reason anyone who contemplates using, or being a part of, a discussion group must understand that "taking time" and "wasting time" are not necessarily the same thing. Blaming a committee for taking time, therefore, is roughly like blaming a cat for chasing birds; it is simply the nature of the beast. This problem was presented vividly to one of the authors a few years ago while he was serving in the Navy as the pilot of a large patrol bomber. During a review of emergency procedures one day the crew was instructed that in the event of an emergency such as a fire the pilot would activate a loud horn as a signal to the crew to bail out. In reacting to this message, one young college graduate who had recently joined the squadron as an enlisted man expressed the opinion that since certain kinds of fires might be controllable through in-flight procedures it would be a good idea for the pilot to consult with such experts as the first mechanic and the airframes specialist before ordering such irrevocable action as abandonment of the aircraft. The idea might have seemed more credible were it not for the fact that just a couple of months earlier, before the questioner had appeared on the scene, one of the squadron's aircraft had crashed in the mountains behind San Diego as a result of an engine fire, with both pilot and copilot losing their lives. The navigator reported later that just before he jumped, the copilot, who was right behind him, had announced that he was going back up to the cockpit to "talk it over" with the pilot.

Peter Drucker, a noted author and business consultant, points to the same problem with a different story.

My first grade arithmetic primer asked, "If it takes two ditch diggers two days to dig a ditch, how long would it take four ditch diggers?" In the first grade, the correct answer is "One day." In executives' work, however, the right answer is probably "Four days," if not "Forever."

Drucker proceeds to point out that a common managerial time waster is poor organization. "Its symptom," he says,

is an excess of meetings. One cannot meet and work at the same time. Organizations will always require meetings because the knowledge and experience needed in specific situations are never available in one head; they have to be pieced together out of the knowledge and experience of several people. But whenever a time log shows the fatty degeneration of meetings—whenever, for instance, people find themselves in meetings a quarter of the time or more—the system needs to be corrected.[1]

Clearly, there are occasions when there is no time (or insufficient time) for talk. In such cases, even if a thorough discussion might possibly result in a *better* decision, the responsible administrator must make the decision alone. To assign a decision-making task to a group and then complain that the process is time-consuming is an indictment not of group action but of the complainant himself.

GROUPS DIFFUSE RE-SPONSIBILITY

Many executives feel it is important that some one individual be account-able for every act that is performed or every decision that is made. To those who feel this way the idea of group decision making is repugnant. There is no question that group action tends to diffuse rather than focus responsibility. Because responsibility is shared, some individual group members may be inclined to put forth less than their best effort. They reason that as long as they cannot be blamed for the group's failure (if that is the outcome) it would be silly to work very hard. To the extent that individual members feel this way, the group's effectiveness will un-questionably be reduced.

Not only is there the possibility that group action will allow the unmoti-vated and unproductive member to escape undetected, but it may also reduce or destroy the motivation and productivity of the good worker. If there is little opportunity for individual recognition and reward, it is un-derstandable why some otherwise productive workers will reduce their efforts. On the other hand, even if the good worker decides to continue making a strong effort and as a result the group becomes productive, the long-term effect can be undesirable. This occurs when productive group members become discouraged and demoralized by a system that rewards the slacker and the incompetent to the same extent that it recognizes the talented and hardworking members of the group. An example of this problem was presented to one of the authors recently by a student at the university where he teaches. Professors in the graduate communication program at this school seemingly made much more extensive use of group projects and reports than the undergarduate institution from which this young woman had recently graduated. She was determined to continue her record of academic excellence during her graduate education, but frequently felt cheated by a system in which she was required to work extra hard to make up for the deficiencies of poorer students who hap-pened to be in her group while they reaped all the benefits of her labors. Those who have experienced this situation probably find somewhat un-satisfactory the explanation that the loafers are "only hurting themselves" by not working to their full capacity.

Even though it is well to recognize the hazards created by the tendency of group action to diffuse responsibility, it would be a mistake to use this as a basis for condemning all use of groups. For one thing, there are ways (which we shall discuss in Chapters 11 and 12) to avoid or minimize this problem. Beyond that, however, it is well to recognize that the diffusion of responsibility can sometimes be a great advantage. By way of illustra-tion, a department head has told us of an incident in which he was able to utilize this characteristic of groups. As it happened, a recently retired senior employee of the organization had requested that he be allowed to continue working on a part-time basis. Because of the interpersonal rela-tionships involved, the department head was inclined to agree to the re-quest even though he knew it would establish an undesirable precedent—

one, in fact, that he would be unable to honor in the case of several other employees who were nearing retirement. As a way out of the dilemma, the problem was taken to the department's executive committee for discussion. Even though every member of this group was a friend and former colleague of the man making the request, the group found it easy to reach a decision to deny continuing employment. The reason, of course, was that no single member of the group needed to assume responsibility for the decision. At the same time, the man whose request was denied could not blame any one individual for the action. As a consequence, not only was a good decision reached but interpersonal relationships were also largely maintained. The same general advantage of diffused responsibility applies to a whole range of group activities, including those with such critical functions as juries and firing squads.

GROUPS CAUSE CONFORMITY It takes very little insight to understand that in most groups the individual members are not all equal. Sometimes members, by virtue of being bosses, celebrities, or officials of one type or another, bring status from outside the group. At other times members who may have no particular status outside the group earn a special place for themselves on the basis of their intelligence, knowledge, or verbal skills. But no matter how group members achieve status, those who have it are in a position to exercise more than ordinary influence over the rest of the group—to cause other members to conform to their way of thinking.

Pressures to conform, however, exist in groups even when no member appears to have any special status. There is simply a tendency in most of us, no matter how much we may try to resist it, to go along with the crowd. The extent to which this is true was well illustrated a number of years ago in a classic study by psychologist Solomon Asch.[2] What Asch did was to show a group of college students a series of three lines, all clearly of different lengths, and a fourth line that was the same length as one of the other three. Each member of the group was then asked to decide which of the first three lines matched the length of the fourth line and announce his decision. The task would normally have been an easy one, but Asch had previously instructed all but one member of each group to intentionally select the wrong line. The result was that fully one-third of the time the one uninstructed group member was willing to forsake his own clear sense perception in order to be in agreement with the majority. This was true even in groups as small as four people, where the odds were only three against one. If group members will abandon their judgments concerning tasks where there is a clearly defined, objective standard, one can imagine how much more readily they will do so in the face of the more subjective policy matters with which groups are usually called upon to deal.

It is this strong tendency for individuals to conform while in group situations that led behavioral scientist Irving Janis to issue his well-known warning against the dangers of "groupthink." After studying a series of group-made decisions at the highest levels of government, such as those that led to the Bay of Pigs invasion of Cuba during the Kennedy administration and the increasing escalation of bombing levels in Vietnam while Lyndon Johnson was President, Janis concluded: "In each case study, I was surprised to discover the extent to which each group displayed the typical phenomena of social conformity that are regularly encountered in studies of group dynamics among ordinary citizens."[3] The problem, as Janis analyzes it, is that after they have been together for a period of time group members begin subconsciously to value their respect and liking for each other more than they value critical thinking. They "become motivated to avoid being too harsh in their judgments of their leaders' or colleagues' ideas. They adopt a soft line of criticism, even in their own thinking. At their meeting, all the members are amiable and seek complete concurrence on every important issue, with no bickering or conflict to spoil the cozy, 'we feeling' atmosphere."[4]

Whether it results from deference to those with special status or from deep-seated needs to maintain harmony, it is evident that significant pressure toward conformity exists in most, if not all, group situations. When this occurs it inevitably follows that critical thinking and sharp decision making will suffer.

When one considers the problem of conformity along with the time-consuming and responsibility-diffusing qualities of group discussion, it is not surprising that a substantial number of executives and administrators are suspicious—even hostile—toward the committee approach to decision making and tend to avoid it whenever possible.

DISCUSSION IS INEVITABLE

As must be obvious by now, it is not the intention of this chapter to argue that group discussion is the best approach to all problems. Quite the contrary. Our advice to those who have the responsibility for decision making within organizations is to avoid groups whenever there is a better way to approach the problem. However, having thus declared ourselves, we will now maintain that not only can group discussion do some things extremely well, but it is often impossible to avoid, regardless of its strengths and weaknesses.

One of the characteristics of life in the United States, and in many other countries as well, during the latter part of the twentieth century is that whatever vestiges of the feudal system still remain are disappearing fast. People will no longer bow to the opinions, directives, or edicts of someone else simply because the other person wears the label "president," "supervisor," "director," or "foreman." Authority, regardless of its power or position, will not endure for long these days without the consent of those subject to that authority. In the true spirit of what college students of the late 1960s referred to as "participatory democracy," people simply insist that they have an important say in matters that affect their lives. The days of the autocratic, iron-fisted leader are, in other words, either gone or going fast, and anyone in a position of authority who doesn't realize this is headed for big trouble. This surging democratic impulse is one of the principal reasons why, in the contemporary organization, group discussion is inevitable. Discussion is the most effective means of sharing ideas and participating in decision making.

A second reason why discussion is inevitable in today's world is that our organizations have become so large and complex. The former head of a department in an insurance company provided a vivid example of this problem; a revolt by his subordinates provided the motivation for him to resign his administrative position. During the years he had served as head, the department had simply grown away from him without his knowing it. In the early days, when there were only three or four people in the entire department, he had assumed (accurately in most cases) that he knew how everyone felt and that he could confidently make decisions based on that knowledge. As the firm grew, however, and his staff doubled and redoubled in size, this was no longer the case. Yet the department head continued as in the old days, falsely confident that his empathy with his staff remained unimpaired. When the uprising finally occurred, it came as a total shock. What happened to this insurance department has happened in government, education, religion, and other kinds of organizations across the continent. In all too many cases organizations have simply become too large for the manager to be able to depend on informal, personal contacts as the basis for reliable information. In these cases discussion groups composed of representatives of the various facets of the organization become one of the very few viable means whereby management can send and receive information.

In addition to their virtual inevitability within organizational structures, one can argue that discussion groups are an essential aspect of society in general. As educator Herbert Thelen has so eloquently phrased it,

The face-to-face group working on a problem is the meeting ground of individual personality and society. It is in the group that personality is modified and socialized; and it is through the workings of groups that society is changed and adapted to its times. These two processes are not separate; they are merely two aspects of the same phenomenon. Moreover, they are necessary to each other: without social purpose shared with others there would be no basis for the give-and-take through which the individual develops his capabilities, and without the differences among individual personalities there would be no basis for the creation of new and better solutions to the problems of living.[5]

THE ADVANTAGES OF DISCUSSION

It is one thing to say that discussion is inevitable and quite another thing to argue its desirability. In this case we shall do both. As we have just finished pointing out, it is virtually impossible to avoid the use of discussion groups in the modern organization; fortunately, the use of discussion can also often be highly advantageous. Among the many outcomes of group interaction, certainly some of the most important and desirable are the following: better decisions, stronger commitment, and increased understanding of others.

BETTER DECISIONS Even Irving Janis, who has so convincingly warned of the dangers of "groupthink," concedes that "a group whose members have properly defined roles, with traditions concerning the procedures to follow in pursuing a critical inquiry, probably is capable of making better decisions than any individual group member working alone."[6] Of course one cannot help but note the number of qualifications Janis ties to his endorsement of group decision making. Such qualification is expedient, for there are a variety of circumstances that will influence the ability of any given group to make decisions. It is vital for any administrator responsible for deciding how problems will be approached to know what these circumstances are and how they function.

Some of the most significant variables in determining group effectiveness grow out of the nature of the task. Some tasks, as mentioned earlier, are simply not amenable to group action because they require no division of labor. If, to return to our previous example, the problem is writing a report, there is probably no point to having ten people stand around kibitzing while one person does the writing. Determining the *content* of the report, on the other hand, might very well be the kind of task that could be better handled by a group.

Even in problems susceptible to group action, however, one must distinguish between the synthetic and the interacting group. In *synthetic* groups, several people will contribute to the task's resolution, but they will not work together. A company executive, for example, might choose to have each of several subordinates write an analysis of the company's slumping sales, leaving for himself or herself the task of integrating the results, rather than calling the individuals together for face-to-face discussion of the problem.

In other instances, it is evident that problem solving is best served by an interacting group. The reason is obvious: Discussion has the potential to stimulate creativity by allowing participants to benefit from and build on the ideas of others. At the same time, it offers an opportunity to test and critically evaluate those ideas. Whether or not these potential advantages of the interacting group will be realized depends in large measure, of course, on the attitudes and skills of individual group members. Although these attitudes and skills are obviously important and will be given detailed treatment in Chapter 11, it should nevertheless be noted that even when the variable of differences among individuals is disregarded, interacting groups have unique advantages when it comes to problem solving.

One of the more interesting and convincing studies of group problem solving was reported by Taylor and Faust in 1952. In a modification of the "Twenty Questions" parlor game, the experimenters contrasted the ability of individuals, two-person groups, and four-person groups to solve problems. What they discovered, as indicated in the following tables, was that groups were superior to individuals in both the number of questions and the amount of time it took to arrive at a solution.

	Questions required to solve the problem			
	Day 1	Day 2	Day 3	Day 4
Individuals	25	20	19	19
Groups (both 2 and 4 people)	20	16	15	14
	Minutes required to solve the problem			
	Day 1	Day 2	Day 3	Day 4
Individuals	8	7	4½	5
2 Person Groups	7	5	3	3
4 Person Groups	6½	4	3	2

The only way group effort compared disadvantageously with individual performance in the Taylor and Faust study was in the minutes per person required to reach a solution. The average time in man-minutes expended per problem over the four-day period was as follows: individuals—5.06; two-person groups—7.40; four-person groups—12.60.[7]

Although the "Twenty Questions" study does demonstrate the superiority of groups over individuals in the area of problem solving, it does not (as you may already have noted) prove that groups make better decisions. Individuals acting alone were also able to solve the problems—it just took more time and effort. This limitation, however, is more likely due to the limitations of our research methods than to any inherent deficiency in the group approach to decision making. In the "real" world, in contrast to the laboratory, we do not know in advance the "right" answers to the problems we face. When a company is trying to determine whether a product price cut will ultimately result in increased profits, or a university faculty needs to know if a curriculum revision will produce better education, or a United Fund committee ponders the fairest way of distributing money, or an executive merely tries to judge which of several applicants will make the best secretary, there is simply no way of divining an ideal or perfect solution by which to measure the success of the various problem-solving efforts. Perhaps later, from the perspective of hindsight, some sort of judgment of relative success can be made, but even then it is often impossible to know for sure whether some other decision would have been better.

Even though our scientific investigations of approaches to decision making, owing to the complexity of the problem, have been something less than perfect, they have produced information that is relevant to the issue. The following two studies, for example, which dealt with problems such as riddles to which the solution, although improbable, was obvious to everyone in the group once it was discovered, both found that group effort was superior to individual effort. Tuckman and Lorge, after comparing the work of individuals with that of groups on a fairly complex task, reached the obvious but useful conclusion that there is a "greater probability of getting a good solution from a group of five than from any one individual."[8] In another study individuals were asked to reproduce a story that had been read to them. First they worked alone, then in groups, and finally once more alone. The result was that "group recall was superior to the average initial individual recall, the initial individual recall of the persons with the best memories, and the average final individual recall."[9]

Even though, as we have attempted to demonstrate, there are many qualifications that must be attached to any conclusion concerning the best way to approach problem solving, the conclusion reached by four social scientists after an exhaustive review of the appropriate literature does seem warranted: "In general, in the evaluation of the relative quality of the products produced by groups in contrast to the products produced by individuals, the group is superior."[10] This conclusion, we submit, becomes even more valid as the problems addressed increasingly depend on value judgments and critical thinking for their solutions.

STRONGER COMMITMENT

Indifference and alienation appear to have reached near-epidemic proportions in contemporary society. Within organizations these characteristics often show up in the form of absenteeism, inefficiency, pilferage, and even such extreme behavior as sabotage. As such, they constitute a problem with which anyone involved with the management of organizations—from business enterprises to social and political action groups—must be concerned. The fact, therefore, that increased commitment is a frequent result of group activity may in itself be sufficent justification for the use of discussion groups within organizations.

Although a person may join or be appointed to a group because he or she has some special competence or interest that relates to the group's activities, it is also true that the person who becomes affiliated with a group, for whatever reason, tends to develop an interest in the activities of that group. This principle of human behavior has been used to advantage by any number of successful managers. A case in point was provided by the father of one of the authors—a clergyman—who regularly used his appointive powers to induce peripheral members of his congregation to become active participants. In one particular case, a talented woman who had for years been only a nominal member of the church became an energetic supporter after being appointed an adviser to the congregation's youth club—a position she initially accepted with great reluctance. Illustrating the same point, but in a quite different context, one of our students has conducted a study that demonstrates that small "consciousness-raising" groups have played a major role in the success of the contemporary women's movement. As she puts it, these groups have served "the vital purpose of gathering members and solidifying commitment to the movement."[11]

Two general factors contribute to this kind of outcome. The first of these occurs, not through active participation in the group (although this, too, is important), but simply as a result of being *publicly identified with the group*. What happens, as explained by the approach to human behavior known as dissonance theory, is that it is not uncommon, for any of a variety of reasons, for people to find themselves in a position of doing or saying something in front of others that is contrary to their private beliefs or attitudes. Since most of us find such a position psychologically uncomfortable, we will usually try in some way to reconcile the conflict. Because, however, our behavior has been witnessed by others while our attitudes and beliefs are known only to ourselves, it is easier to adjust attitudes in the direction of behavior than the other way around. That, therefore, is what we tend to do.

The process hypothesized by dissonance theory has been illustrated through experimental studies on numerous occasions. In one of the earliest of these studies two experimenters, Janis and King, asked a number of college students to give speeches, as convincingly as they were able, on subjects contrary to their personal beliefs. The listeners for these presentations had also been selected on the basis of their opposition to the points of view expressed in the speeches. On the basis of tests given before and after the presentations, Janis and King were able to determine that those who gave the speeches changed their attitudes in the direction advocated by the speech more than those who merely listened to the arguments. This difference was attributed to the fact that the speakers had *publicly* identified themselves with the positions advocated in their speeches.[12]

The relationship between stating a position in a speech and affiliating with a small group should be apparent. Both entail a "public" identification with an idea, a cause, or an organization, and to that extent both tend to produce in the individual involved an increased sense of commitment to that idea, cause, or organization.

The fact of affiliation, however, is only one of the ways in which group participation leads to a stronger sense of commitment; perhaps even more important in this regard is the influence that results from interactions *within* the group. Because we will, in the next chapter, examine in some detail the cohesiveness and norms produced by group interaction, it is sufficient to point out now that the same process that, as indicated earlier, may lead to the undesirable consequences of "groupthink" may also result in the sometimes desirable outcome of increased commitment.

INCREASED UNDER-STANDING In addition to their capacity to produce better decisions and stronger commitment, small-group discussions also hold great promise as vehicles for increasing our understanding of both ourselves and others. Even though some task-oriented individuals would like to think that personal feelings should be of no consequence in formal decision-making groups, the fact of the matter is that social-emotional considerations play a prominent role in *all* small groups, regardless of their purposes, and must be recognized and accommodated if the group is to be successful.

There is abundant evidence that people in groups cannot function effectively if they are not relatively comfortable in their interpersonal relationships with other members of the group. One particularly interesting study in this regard was conducted by Ewart Smith for the U.S. Navy in 1956. Smith formed three groups of equal size and gave each a series of problems to solve. The first group served as the "control." To the second group he added two extra members, who were instructed that no matter what happened they were to remain absolutely silent throughout the proceedings. The third group also had two extra members who were instructed to remain silent; but in this case, just before the problem-solving activity was to begin, Smith gave each person a list of various roles that members might take (arbitrator, attentive supporter, listener, etc.) and asked him to check the category he thought best described himself. The two silent members indicated that they would act as listeners. Smith then collected the cards and read the results to the group. In so doing, he provided some explanation to the rest of the group members of the roles the silent members would play. The results of the experiment indicated that the group in which all members conformed to "normal" behavioral patterns and the group in which "abnormal" (silent) behavior was explained were significantly more effective in accomplishing their tasks than the group in which the abnormal behavior of two members was not understood.[13]

After analyzing 124 task-oriented discussions during a study conducted several years ago, one of the authors discovered that the members of groups in general, like Smith's experimental groups, demonstrate considerable concern for the social-emotional aspects of their activity. In the cases studied, only about 60 percent of the meeting time was devoted to the substantive issues of the group tasks, while 32 percent was spent on questions of procedure (how the members would go about working together) and 8 percent was consumed by matters of personal interest to the participants that had no direct bearing on the job at hand. In other words, even though the groups in this study had all been created specifically for the purpose of performing some task, the members spent almost half of their time talking not about that task but, rather, about their relationships to one another.

Because of the number and the potential complexity of the interactions involved in small-group discussion, such activity offers a nearly ideal laboratory for the study of interpersonal dynamics. Group members, therefore, if they are willing to take advantage of the opportunity, are in a position to learn a great deal not only about the behavior of others but about their own behavior as well.

THE CHAPTER IN PERSPECTIVE

Group conferences are integral to almost all organizations. The individual executive can hardly escape committee meetings, informal work-related discussions, or formal group conferences. Harold P. Zelko has aptly observed that "the conference is here to stay as one of management's most fundamental tools of communication. . . . Supervisors at all levels of management will find themselves attending more and more conferences in this age of teamwork and the application of democratic group process to business."[14] Recognizing the existence of groups and assuming that the first vital decision for any manager concerning groups is when to use and when not to use the conference method, this chapter initially sets forth some thoughts about what group discussion can do and what it cannot do.

In the first place, groups are unable to handle all tasks efficiently. Initial drafts of reports are best written by one person, with the committee polishing the final draft, and scientific demonstrations and dissemination of information can best be handled by a single speaker. Other undesirable characteristics often associated with groups are that they take more time than an individual acting alone; that they diffuse responsibility, often resulting in inefficiency; and that they cause conformity.

Yet in today's world group discussion is inevitable. Living in the age of "participatory democracy," people want to be part of the decision-making process. Discussion is viewed as an essential aspect of a democratic society. Moreover, organizations tend to be so large and complex today that it is hard to conduct the necessary business without some committees and group interaction. Staff meetings, for example, seem absolutely essential from time to time.

Without question, in some instances, for certain tasks, and with effective leadership and participation, group conferences are beneficial. As a general rule one can expect better decisions to come from groups than from individuals. In addition, the group process tends to generate stronger employee commitment and increased employee understanding of problems and policies.

Morale, although hard to define, is important to any organization. One often takes little notice of good morale, but it is hard to be unaware of bad morale. The increased association and communication that group conferences require among members can increase organizational morale. Mutual trust and cooperativeness usually result from these associations, and greater efficiency often occurs. Employee participation can develop the kind of commitment that enhances the work effort and increases productivity—the final objective of any organization. With these thoughts in mind, the next chapter will dissect the anatomy of a group.

REFERENCES

1. Peter Drucker, "How to Manage Your Time," *Harper's Magazine* (December 1966).

2. S. E. Asch, "Effects of Group Pressure Upon the Modification and Distortion of Judgments," in Eleanor E. Maccoby et al., eds., *Readings in Social Psychology* (New York: Holt, Rinehart & Winston, 1958), pp. 174–183.

3. Irving L. Janis, "Groupthink," *Psychology Today*, 5 (November 1971): 43.

4. Ibid.

5. Herbert A. Thelen, *Dynamics of Groups at Work* (Chicago: University of Chicago Press, Phoenix Books, 1962), p. vi.

6. Janis, p. 44.

7. D. W. Taylor and W. L. Faust, "Twenty Questions: Efficiency in Problem Solving as a Function of Size of Group," *Journal of Experimental Psychology*, 44 (1952): 360–368.

8. J. Tuckman and I. Lorge, "Individual Ability as a Determinant of Group Superiority," *Human Relations*, 15 (1962): 51.

9. H. E. Yuker, "Group Atmosphere and Memory," *Journal of Abnormal and Social Psychology*, 51 (1955): 22.

10. I. Lorge, D. Fox, J. Davitz, and M. Brenner, "A Survey of Studies Contrasting the Quality of Group Performance and Individual Performance, 1920–1957," *Psychological Bulletin*, 55 (1958): 369.

11. Kathleen J. Turner, "Social Facilitation, Conformity, and the Consciousness-Raising Small Group in the Contemporary Women's Movement," unpublished paper, Purdue University, Department of Communication (1975): p. 3.

12. Irving L. Janis and B. T. King, "The Influence of Role-Playing on Opinion Change," *Journal of Abnormal and Social Psychology*, 49 (1954): 211–218.

13. Ewart E. Smith, "Effects of Threat Induced by Ambiguous Role Expectations on Defensiveness and Productivity in Small Groups," University of Colorado, Group Process Laboratory, 1956 (Tech. Report No. 1, Contract No. 1147 (03), Office of Naval Research).

14. Harold P. Zelko, "When You Are 'In Conference,'" in Richard C. Huseman, Cal M. Logue, and Dwight L. Freshley, *Readings in Interpersonal and Organizational Communication* (Boston: Holbrook Press, 1973), p. 429.

CHAPTER 10
THE ANATOMY
OF A GROUP

Preview

An understanding of group dynamics is a prerequisite for the effective use of conferences.

All groups have a basic anatomy composed of:

• Structure
• Norms
• Leadership

Structure is developed through:

• Division of labor
• Assignment of roles
• Power relationships
• Communication networks

Norms are the patterns of behavior to which members conform.
Cohesiveness is the attractiveness of the group to its members.
Leadership consists of any act that fulfills a group need.

During a recent instructional project one of the authors had an opportunity to observe for an extended period a group of ten U.S. Navy personnel. The participants all wore civilian clothes, and no member knew any of the others prior to the seminar that brought them together for two weeks at Newport, Rhode Island.

The group was a composite of the various types of people who make up the naval establishment. Five of the members were reservists fulfilling their annual active duty requirement, while the other five were career Navy people who had been released from their regular jobs for two weeks of special training. Six of the group members were commissioned officers and four were enlisted personnel; their military ranks ranged from junior enlisted (a third-class petty officer) to senior commissioned officer (a captain, which is comparable to a colonel in the Army or Air Force). Eight of the participants were men and two were women. Their ages ranged from the early 20s to the mid-40s. The group's task was to study the question of compulsory military training and prepare itself to debate the issue with other groups in the seminar.

As the group began to assemble for its first session, members tended to get into conversations with those sitting next to them. Surveying the scene as he entered the room, one particularly handsome young man quickly found a seat next to one of the two women participants and was soon engaged in active conversation with her. Two or three of the members sat silently as they glanced through some of the materials that had been issued to them when they checked in.

When several minutes had elapsed, one of the older men, after looking around the table, raised his voice somewhat and observed that since it appeared that everyone had now found his way to the room perhaps it would be a good idea to get started. Several people nodded in agreement, and the man who had called the meeting to order made a statement concerning his understanding of the group's purpose. Several questions were asked and a number of group members added their observations to the discussion of purpose.

Almost from the beginning of the discussion a pattern of interaction began to emerge. Most of the talking was done by two of the older men in the group; when the younger members did speak, it was usually to ask a question or to voice agreement. The younger participants always addressed the two older men as "sir."

Just as the first session was about to end, one of the women suggested that all the members of the group should introduce themselves and say something about their backgrounds. Again there was a general nodding of assent, and the man who had originally begun the discussion once more took the initiative and led off the introductions. As it turned out, he was a senior enlisted man (a chief petty officer) in the Naval Reserve who, in civilian life, was a supervisor for the post office. The other older man, who had shared in dominating the first period, was also a reservist—a captain in the Dental Corps and a dentist in civilian life. The senior active duty member of the group was a youthful-appearing commander who flew jet planes off an aircraft carrier. He had been one of the more active and enthusiastic members of the group during the first session, but had also been noticeably deferential in his relationship to the two older men. The young man and woman who had paired off into a conversational group at the beginning of the hour were both active duty personnel; he, however, was enlisted (a third-class photographer's mate), while she was an ensign who had recently graduated from Officers' Candidate School.

Between the first session and the second one, less than twenty-four hours later, the group underwent some major changes. The jet pilot showed up early for the meeting, sat at the head of the table, and distributed an agenda he had prepared to each of the other members as they arrived. He continued to be buoyant and friendly, but he no longer addressed either of the two older members as "sir"; when others addressed him in this manner, he asked that they call him by his first name. The postal employee (reserve enlisted man) who had dominated the first meeting had changed his location so that he was now sitting next to another chief petty officer; although he conversed a little with his new acquaintance, he said practically nothing to the group as a whole. He was no longer addressed as "sir" by any member of the group. The handsome photographer's mate had found a new seat next to the second female member of the group, also an enlisted person, while his original spot by the new ensign had another occupant—a young reserve lieutenant just off active duty and now in law school.

In subsequent meetings of the group the relationships established during the second session tended to be maintained. There were, however, some exceptions. The captain/dentist, though continuing as a respected member of the group (he was the only participant who continued to be called "sir" or was addressed by his formal title by some of the other group members), became less and less prominent in group activities as other members began to observe that he was a particularly inept debater. At the same time, the law student took on an increasingly active role in the group as he aided others in their library research and gave instruction in debating techniques (he was a former college debater). In addition, as the group continued to meet, the atmosphere became more and more informal, with members joking and calling each other by first names. By the end of a week the group was even spending considerable time 'together outside of working hours.

In attempting to analyze the behavior of this group, one may be inclined to conclude that the members acted the way that they did because of their individual personalities. In part, of course, this is correct. On the other hand, however, if we could see the same people interacting in other groups to which they belong, we would undoubtedly observe a quite different set of behaviors. In dealing with his own staff, for example, the post office supervisor would probably be unwilling to relinquish leadership to someone else who attempted to take it over. Similarly, if the two older men in the group had been senior career officers, as the young commander unquestionably thought prior to the group's self-introductions, he would more likely have continued throughout the two weeks of the seminar to exhibit the same subservient behavior he showed during the first meeting. The nature of the particular group, in other words, has a lot to do with how its members act.

Just as with individual human beings, groups have life cycles that are uniquely their own. They come into being, mature, develop distinctive characteristics, and eventually cease to exist. Understandably, if one is to utilize groups to their fullest advantage or participate in them effectively, it is necessary to have some insight into the factors that are most influential in determining the nature of a group's life cycle. Whenever a group is formalized in an organization, it takes on all the attributes of an organized subsystem, as described in Chapter 2. A definite *structure* is superimposed or emerges. This structure becomes a communication network, with people occupying consistent *roles* and following *normative rules* that are developed within the group. Some basic elements of *hierarchy* will evolve to differentiate between leaders and followers. Finally, the group will develop some kind of *identity* or "groupness" that stems from its attractiveness or *cohesiveness* for its members.

GROUP STRUCTURE

Although the structure of any given group will vary widely depending on its membership, its anticipated permanence, its degree of formality, and the clarity with which its task is defined, every group develops within it a series of roles and relationships that can be called a group personality.

Groups develop structure because humans seem to have an innate need for predictability and stability. When we are thrust into a new group situation we immediately begin collecting information sizing up the other members of the group. We want to know what occupation people have, where they live, who they know, and what they like and dislike. Even brief and transitory relationships, such as sitting next to someone during an airplane trip, often result in the exchange of surprisingly large amounts of information of this type. The information we share, in turn, has a significant effect both on how we behave toward others and how we expect them to behave toward us. It aids us, to put it another way, in attaining the stability and predictability that we all need. Ambiguity makes us uncomfortable.

DIVISION OF LABOR One way in which structure develops is through some sort of division of labor. In some primitive societies, for example, family groups tend toward a simple, but rigid, division on the basis of sex, into hunters and gatherers. Similarly, in contemporary American society most families fall into traditional patterns of specialization in order to keep the group functioning. Typically, although such sex-related roles are increasingly being challenged and changed, husbands have worked at paid jobs outside the home while wives have concerned themselves with homemaking and child care. What is true of this division of labor in family units is equally, if less conspicuously, true (as we shall see a little later) of other kinds of groups as well. Some group members exercise leadership, others follow; some are concerned with the tasks, others do what they can to maintain relationships within the group.

ROLES   The predominant patterns of behavior, or roles, that we display in any given group setting are determined not only by our own individual personalities but also, in large measure, by the expectations others impose upon us. Four of the most important factors influencing these expectations are culture, formal agreements, precedent, and personal preference.

Culture   Nothing so determines our expectations of others as the way we have been conditioned by our culture. In the words of anthropologist Edward Hall, our systems of culture "became so identified with the process of nature itself that alternative ways of behavior are thought of as unnatural —if not impossible. . . . There is never any doubt in anybody's mind that, as long as he does what is expected, he knows what to expect from others."[1] Among the factors in American culture on which our expectations of others are most strongly based are sex, age, and occupation.

SEX. Even though women's rights groups have succeeded in changing some attitudes during recent years, a person's sex remains one of the most influential determinants of behavioral expectations. Our "knowledge," for example, that boy babies should be dressed in blue while girl babies wear pink is only the beginning. The clothes we wear, our hair styles, the recreational activities we engage in, our vocational interests, what we say and how we say it—all are related to sex. Speech, according to Hall, is one of the most prominent examples of this relationship. "Speech and sex," he writes, "are linked in obvious ways. Let the reader, if he doubts this, start talking like a member of the opposite sex for a while and see how long people let him get away with it."[2]

The extent of our effort to preserve culturally determined sex roles is illustrated by the campaign against the Equal Rights Amendment, which, as of this writing, has been stymied ever since its original introduction in 1923 almost exclusively because of the fear that it would facilitate the violation of traditional behaviors. If women are given equal rights in some areas, opponents argue, then they will also, for example, be subject to the draft and have to fight during wartime. The role of combatant, of course, is clearly unfeminine by traditional American cultural standards.

The violent reactions of many to the longer hair styles for men that became popular during the mid-1960s is a further illustration of the seriousness with which we take our sexual roles. Long hair, by American standards, was appropriate to women, not to men. For a man to wear his hair long was a violation of his sexual role—the breaking of a taboo—and to some people a just reason for severe retribution. It was not uncommon during the 1960s for long-haired youth to be ridiculed and sometimes beaten if they were unlucky enough to venture into the wrong neighborhood.

While one would not normally expect a discussion group participant to be beaten up for violating the conventions of sex, it would be unrealistic not to recognize that even today among educated and well-meaning people the relationship between sex and expected behavior is strong.

AGE. Age is also a leading determinant of behavioral expectations in American society. When our children cry we tell that that it is time they grew up and stopped acting like babies. If an elderly woman wears a short skirt we disapprove because she is not "acting her age." Although we may vehemently deny that we ourselves are "older," we know—just as well as we know that the sun rises in the east—that when the time does come we shall suddenly become "wiser," more conservative, more responsible, and of course, unable to learn any new tricks.

OCCUPATION. As with sex and age stereotypes, our images of certain vocations are constantly being reinforced. A currently popular film, for example, highlights the concern of one character—a stereotypically assertive, self-confident business tycoon (all he listens to on his car radio is the market report)—that another central character—masculine appearing, but a *hair dresser*—is a "fag."

Among other vocations that appear to be particularly vulnerable to stereotyping are military officers, librarians, college professors, salesmen, and of course, ministers ("Oops, better watch our language, here comes the preacher"). In the case of clergymen, the stereotype even extends to their children, who, as everyone knows, are always "the worst kids in town."

As we have attempted to illustrate in this discussion, when we know someone's sex, age, or occupation we think we know an awful lot about what they are really like and how they ought to conduct themselves. These expectations, in turn, translate themselves into a variety of pressures that are used to ensure that others will indeed conform to our expectations—that they will play the roles we have assigned to them.

Formal agreements Laws, constitutions, and other regulations all may, in special circumstances, contribute to the anticipated behavioral pattern of a given individual. Any job description will specify some aspects of a person's role. Thus the President of the United States has certain duties and rights that are defined by law. Most organizations, in fact, have written documents of one sort or another that specify what is expected of various employees or members under a variety of circumstances. These may extend to such matters—in the case of a country club or military organization, for example—as what attire must be worn in certain places at certain times. Even a document like *Robert's Rules of Order* has something to say about appropriate behaviors under certain conditions.

Precedent How things have been done in the past is often a major determinant of how things will continue to be done in the future. Anyone who has ever taken over a job—particularly from someone who was well liked by his constituency—has probably run into the comment, "You're not anything at all like our last . . . (manager, teacher, minister, foreman, etc.)." The remark is usually not intended as a compliment. There is, consequently, a real tendency to adopt a pattern of behavior consistent with that of those who have held the same position in the past.

Personal preferences Members often have a choice in the kind of role they occupy in a group. For example, one of the most popular tests of interpersonal relations is the fundamental interpersonal orientation-behavior (FIRO-B), developed by William C. Schutz.[3] It measures people on their apparent needs for control, affection, and inclusion. No value judgments are placed on whether a person scores high or low on any of these dimensions; people just differ. Yet these personality differences may affect a person's selection of a particular role in a group. For example, a person who has a high control need may try to exert leadership and participate actively, whereas a person who has a low need to exert control may be satisfied with less participation and may be quite happy to let others dictate what happens in the group. Members with a high inclusion need often focus on building good human relations.

Similarly, studies by Fleishman[4] and Blake and Mouton[5] stress that people differ in their orientation toward work. Some people are oriented toward the task; others are oriented toward a consideration for people. Consequently these different types will choose different roles in the conference, with the former taking task roles and the latter taking maintenance roles.

The potency of culturally determined expectations, formal agreements, precedents, and personal preferences in determining roles will obviously vary from time to time and from occasion to occasion. In spite of this variability, however, people do tend to develop expectations about how other people should act. In the face of such expectations, it is only natural that members of the group will develop the predominant patterns of behavior known as roles. Roles, as a consequence, become an important part of any group's structure.

POWER Closely associated with role theory, but distinguishable in its own right, is the concept of power. Within the context of small-group theory, power is defined as the ability to exercise influence over other members of the group. As such, power is also closely related to management and leadership.

Power is commonly described as falling into two categories—positional and earned. *Positional power*, as the name implies, is related to the title or formal position one holds. Thus if the son of a company's founder becomes chairman of the board of directors, he will be in a position to exercise considerable influence over the members of that body, regardless of what other qualifications he may or may not possess. *Earned power*, in contrast, comes about as a result of what an individual can do to help the group achieve its goals. If a participant has some special information or skill relevant to the group's task, it is more than likely that he or she will also be able to exert some influence on group decisions. Although positional and earned power may operate separately, they may also, quite obviously, be combined. The jet pilot/commander in our opening illustration demonstrated how a single individual could draw from both sources. As the most senior, regular Navy (as opposed to reservist) officer in the group, he was automatically the recipient of considerable positional power once the other members discovered who he was. In addition, however, by providing an agenda for the group's guidance at a time when it was essentially directionless, he was also able to develop a source of earned power. Under the circumstances it was almost inevitable that he would become the recognized leader of the group.

A more refined analysis of power has been proposed by John French and Bertram Raven in their essay, "The Bases of Social Power." According to these two group theorists, there are five types of power: reward, coercive, legitimate, referent, and expert.[6]

Reward power, not surprisingly, is based on one's ability to reward another member of the group. Conversely, *coercive power* depends on the ability to punish. These two sources of power are obviously closely related—in fact, they may sometimes be impossible to distinguish except in the psychological reactions of the other members of the group. Praise, for example, may be viewed as a reward by the group member to whom it is directed; at the same time, however, it is not clear whether or not the other group members will view the lack of praise for themselves as a punishment. Even though the situation may be ambiguous, it is important to understand that the effect on the group is quite different depending on whether a particular act is interpreted as reward, punishment, or neither. Actions perceived by the recipient as a reward will increase his attraction toward the power holder and, as a consequence, bind him more firmly to the group. With behavior perceived as coercive, the effect is exactly the opposite.

A real danger in the exercise of coercive power is that, rather than motivating the recipient to conform to the influence attempt, it may drive him from the group entirely as he seeks to avoid the threatened punishment. In such cases the person would be outside the range of any further attempt to influence him and would be lost as a potential group resource. For those in a position to exercise coercive power, the best advice would probably be that offered by columnist Ann Landers to disillusioned wives contemplating divorce: "Would you be better off with him or without him?" In any event, both reward and coercive power depend for their effectiveness on a combination of the magnitude of the reward or punishment and the probability, should the influence attempt be rejected, that the reward or punishment will be forthcoming. In other words, both the stakes and the odds must be right for reward or coercive power to exist.

Legitimate power is based on factors quite different from those involved in reward and punishment. It depends, rather, on one's belief that because of some special circumstance another person has the *right* to exert influence on you and that you, in turn, have an obligation to accept that influence. In American society legitimate power is probably most often associated with something like an election; its presence may be indicated by a remark such as "I personally voted against him, but let's face it, he is the President." The implication that being President confers the right to exercise influence is clear. In business organizations legitimate power seems to increase as one moves up the ladder of management. In other cultures a factor such as age might be an important source of legitimate power. A participant in a recent communications seminar sponsored by the Agency for International Development offers a good example. He was an executive in a government agency from a Middle Eastern country, a man in his late 30s with his own family. Yet when he received the opportunity to come to the United States he first had to ask his father's permission. If his father had said no, he would not have come.

That influence which is made possible because we identify closely with the person who is attempting to influence us is called *referent power*. Because we like a person and want to become more closely associated with him, we are inclined to do what he wants us to.

The final category of power delineated by French and Raven—*expert power*—is very similar to the idea of earned power discussed earlier. Ability to influence, in this situation, is related to a group member's knowledge or skill in some area relevant to the group's task. Expert power tends to be both transitory and limited in scope in that influence will normally occur only in the areas of expertise and only so long as the group requires that expertise. Expert power thus stands in contrast to referent power, where influence tends to be both general and continuing.

Whatever their source, there is no question that influence attempts occur frequently in groups. The successes or failures of these attempts constitute important differences between group members, just as their individual roles do, and as such they make a major contribution to group structure.

COMMUNI-CATION NETWORKS   Just as every group and organization develops role and power structures, it also develops a series of communication relationships. These communication networks—defined as "who talks to whom about what"—are affected by a number of forces.

1. *Large formal organizations usually regulate communications in a way carefully calculated to ensure that those who need to know will at least have access to the message,* even if they do not in all cases assimilate it. Military organizations provide a prime example of this kind of formal structuring of communication. Within the military, official communications

practically never proceed directly from the originator to the intended source. Instead, they are filtered up the chain of command, through each administrative layer, until they reach the top of the unit in which the message originated. From there the message moves to the top of the command in which the intended receiver is located, and then down again through each administrative layer until eventually it arrives at the desk of the intended receiver. Such formal systems, though they do increase the probability that all potentially interested parties will have an opportunity to become informed, are cumbersome to the point that occasional (perhaps frequent) breakdowns of communication are almost inevitable. Thus, in a case one hopes is not typical, it has been reported that a minor Washington bureaucrat received instructions from his superior to write a letter requesting an opinion as to how a certain procedure was to be performed. In due course the letter was written and introduced into the normal routing system of the agency. Some three weeks later, after being referred from one department to the next, the letter ended up on the desk of the original sender, who then wrote the answer.

2. *To help overcome the kinds of problems inherent in complex, tightly structured communication systems, a series of informal networks tends to evolve within most organizations.* Thus a large part of the organization's communication needs are met by the talk in the cafeteria or over drinks after work, at the golf course, or during the spur-of-the-moment telephone call to a friend in another department of the company.

3. *Formal communication arrangements, although they are seldom so rigid or complex as those associated with large organizations, may also be utilized in small discussion groups.* It is not uncommon, for example, that a group will agree to limit discussion to a certain topic or to discuss topics in a certain sequence, as is likely to be the case when an agenda is adopted by the group. It is also standard procedure in some kinds of groups, such as "brainstorming" sessions in which the goal is to stimulate maximum creativity, to prohibit any kind of negative comment.

4. *The need to regulate the communication of even small groups has been demonstrated by a number of studies.* In these experiments the access of group members to each other is controlled either by the use of telephones or by placing participants "in separate, but adjoining stalls so that it is possible to control the potential channels of communication by opening or closing the slots between the stalls."[7] Using these methods of control, group members have typically been arranged in the three networks diagramed in Figure 10.1.

Because the wheel and circle configurations require that a message be mediated by one or two others in order to reach all members of the group, one may be led to conclude that the all-channel network would be most conducive to task accomplishment. Such, however, is not necessarily the case. Frequently, as the researchers discovered, tasks were facilitated by the controls that are built into the wheel and circle networks. The all-

Figure 10.1. Communication networks.

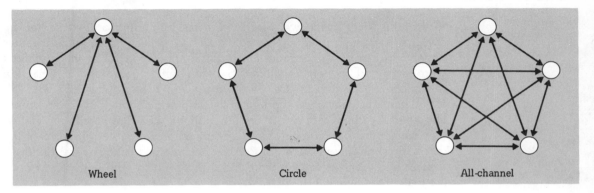

Wheel   Circle   All-channel

channel network, in contrast, seemed to provide "almost too many opportunities" for communication. A principal problem in this configuration was for group members to develop their own restrictions—to decide that they would not use all available channels of communication all the time.[8] In other words, the contingency approach leads us away from saying that there is one best type of network. The ultimate choice may depend on the type of people, the nature of the task, and the time available.

In addition to the kinds of restrictions imposed during experiments, *communication in small groups is also regulated by such factors as spatial arrangements and power structure*. Most people understand intuitively, for example, that sitting in a circle is more conducive to free-flowing discussion than a seating arrangement in which participants are further separated. Along the same lines, it is also usually true that people will interact more frequently with those seated across from them than with those sitting on either side.

Group members with high power tend to speak more frequently than those with lower status, and when they do speak their remarks are often addressed to the group as a whole. They also are inclined to spend their time giving information, advice, and criticism. In contrast, lower-powered group members usually direct their comments specifically to those with higher status. They speak less frequently, and when they do it is most often to ask for information or advice, or to express support for the ideas of those with greater power.

From the preceding discussion it should be evident that communication in groups is a complex, multifaceted phenomenon that, along with role and power relationships, has the capacity to affect profoundly the character of any discussion group. Structure, however, is not the only significant aspect of a group's personality; equally important are the dimensions we shall cover in the remainder of this chapter—group norms, cohesiveness, and leadership.

GROUP NORMS

Within the Navy group we described at the beginning of the chapter, individual behavior patterns, or roles as we called them, varied rather widely. In a number of important respects, however, all of the members were expected to behave alike. To begin with, regardless of what the reservists did in civilian life, they were all now on active duty with the Navy, and the Navy has certain rules and regulations. Every morning, for example, there appeared on the bulletin board a document called the Plan of the Day, which listed, among other things, the uniform of the day. Group members were not free to choose among the several uniforms available to them; everyone wore the same uniform—the one specified on the Plan of the Day.

The Navy also has rather specific expectations about other areas of behavior that civilians might be inclined to consider as being in the category of personal preference. One of the members—the law student—was stopped on the sidewalk one day by an admiral assigned to the base and chastised for having hair so long that it covered his ears; it was described as a disgrace to the Navy. Similarly, in the officers' dining hall those with the rank of lieutenant and below were required to eat in one area, while those with the rank of lieutenant commander and above dined in somewhat more elegant surroundings. Officers who seated themselves in the wrong area were immediately informed that they must move.

When seminar members arrived, additional expectations were imposed on them in their own group meetings. These, in contrast to the more general behavioral expectations just mentioned, were not formal regulations. They were, however, no less stringent. All members of the group, it was mutually understood, were to spend some of their free time each day doing library research on the debate topic; this was to be shared with the other group members in the morning. In fact, a little ritual developed in which the members would sit around the table each morning and distribute to the others the good pieces of evidence they had discovered the night before. In addition, once the competitive debates with teams from other groups began, all of those who were not debating that day got in the habit of attending in order to lend moral support to their teammates. On one occasion when the photographer's mate did not join the cheering section, several of the other members brought it to his attention at the next meeting of the group. After that no one missed any of the debates.

What we have been describing with regard to our Navy group is known as the development of group norms—the common beliefs, attitudes, and patterns of behavior to which all group members are expected to conform. Four aspects of norms should be emphasized. First, a norm is an idea, not to be confused with actual behavior. Many problems occur because members actually deviate from the norm. Second, it must have common acceptance. Third, it is an expectation of what members *should* do. And fourth, it is a form of social control; deviation generally results in some form of punishment by the group.[9] As is true of role structure, some norms are dictated by the general culture and, as such, impose themselves on the organizations and groups that exist within that cultural framework. Other standards of group conduct are related to subcultures, such as those associated with race, religion, or occupation. As a rule, for example, businessmen accept more outspoken and blunt behavior than schoolteachers do, and the same is true of military people in comparison to civilians; the wealthy tend to oppose government welfare programs more often than poor people do; Muslims will accept the legitimacy of violence more readily than Quakers will. An often unstated norm is that the majority is expected to prevail. Frequently small groups try to reach agreement by consensus. If this becomes impossible, the group nearly always resorts to a formal vote.

In addition to standards related to culture and subcultures, groups also develop special norms of their own. Sometimes norms can emerge very quickly in the life of a group, before majority opinion has had the opportunity to be expressed and to solidify. If in the early life of a group a member is outspoken and aggressive in his support of a particular idea, other group members will frequently acquiesce rather than risk a confrontation. Such was the case with a discussion group described by one of our students. The group, which was entirely female and intended as a forum for the exploration of issues particularly relevant to women, was dominated from the outset by a few militant feminists. Although the majority of the members tended to be much more moderate in their outlook, they found themselves either adjusting their comments so as to appear more extreme or remaining silent when they disagreed.

Sometimes organizational position may cause different norms to be applied to different group members. As many of our examples demonstrate, a group is often composed of people of unequal status, as with a superior and his subordinates. They bring these roles and their expectations of each other with them to the group. For example, Paul Wernimont[10] summarizes what supervisors and subordinates in one organization expect of each other. The superiors want subordinates who are hardworking, loyal, thorough, honest, and interested in their work; and they want subordinates who are cooperative but can take initiative and act independently when necessary. Above all, they want to be kept informed. Subordinates, on the other hand, want their superiors to give overall directions or goals but leave them with a great deal of freedom in how the work is done. They want the supervisor to have an interest in them, treat them with fairness, and provide support in dealing with the rest of the organization. When these people interact in groups, there are some common expectations that apply to everyone, but there are also some recognizable differences as to how they are to behave in terms of difference in position.

Whatever the forces that contribute to the formation of norms, however, every group does develop standards that its members are expected to observe, as Cartwright and Zander point out:

For some groups it is recognized by all that they may legitimately exert pressures for uniformity of behavior and attitudes among their members. Thus churches, political parties, professional societies, character building agencies, and others are expected to influence the membership to behave in accordance with certain norms. Other more informal groups also exert an influence over their members, but often without anyone's consciously intending to do so and without the awareness of the members that it is happening. Neighbors, bridge clubs, fishing companions, and luncheon associates; those, in short, who see each other often even though they have not created any formalized social structure, may also exert, through informal group standards, an important influence over each member's behavior.[11]

The pressures that are brought to bear on group members will vary, depending on a number of considerations: (1) the importance of the norm to the group, (2) the cohesiveness of the group, and (3) the place of the individual in the group. Most significant in determining degree of pressure, of course, is the importance of the norm to the group. Thus in a political party, where the group's very existence may depend on its ability to elect at least some of its candidates to office, failure to back the party candidate will usually result in great pressure to conform.

The degree of pressure brought on a group member also reflects the cohesiveness of the group. *Cohesiveness*, which we shall discuss in more detail later, has to do with the sense of unity felt by group members. When groups are loosely knit there is usually little effort to make a person conform, but in highly cohesive groups the pressures are often great. This is why there is so much consternation in many family groups when a child decides, for example, to marry into a different religion, join a commune, or adopt a life style different from that of the other members of the family.

In addition to the importance of the norm and the cohesiveness of the group, conformity pressures also reflect the place of the individual in the group. Peripheral members will receive less pressure to conform than a more central member. In spite of this, however, it is the peripheral members of a group who will often overconform to its behavioral standards. This is true when the peripheral member wants a more central position in the group. Thus immigrants to a country not uncommonly become superpatriots, and new converts to a religion are often more zealous in their beliefs than those born into it.

Those central to a group, such as designated leaders, will be unable to maintain their positions for long if they do not rigorously conform to the group's expectations. In fact, it is this requirement to conform that may deter some members from seeking a more central position in a group, even though that position may carry with it considerable advantages with respect to prestige, income, and personal privilege. It was reported following World War II, for example, that enlisted men sometimes turned down commissions because they knew that in their present positions they could "get away with more." Officers, in contrast, were expected to set a good example.

In the process of conforming to norms, however, leaders also place themselves in a position where they will be better able than any other group member to change the group's norms. To use an analogy, a leader gains capital by conforming to norms and then draws on his savings when he attempts to alter those norms. Thus efforts to change group standards will be successful only when they are initiated by a member with considerable power. In addition, it is helpful in such attempts if the suggestion for change is accompanied by immediate expressions of support from several other members. This creates what in persuasion theory is known as a "bandwagon" effect—the tendency of people to agree to what they think "everyone" is doing.

Except in the situations we have described, nonconformity with group norms usually will not result in a change of the standards; instead, it will result in an effort on the part of the group to bring the deviating member back into compliance. As a consequence the norm violator will initially receive a great deal of attention from other group members as they attempt to persuade or coerce him to change his errant ways. This is the reason why people who crave attention so often resort to the technique of norm violation (or the *threat* of norm violation) in order to satisfy their needs. This technique, however, has limited usefulness in that continued deviation from group norms will eventually result in the deviant's being ostracized from the group.

COHESIVENESS

Some groups are obviously sick: Attendance at meetings is poor, members are reluctant to pay their dues, and nobody seems to want to participate in the group's activities. Other groups are just as obviously healthy: Members are active and enthusiastic about belonging to the group. This phenomenon of member attraction to the group is known as *cohesiveness* and, in general, depends on two sets of conditions: (1) the needs of the individual for affiliation, recognition, and security, and (2) the nature of the group itself, such as its goals, programs, and prestige.[12]

Individual needs, of course, are so broad and varied that they defy categorization. It is, however, clear that as the needs of individuals change so, too, will their need for group membership. One of the authors recalls vividly, for example, his reluctance to affiliate with a cooperative health care clinic because of its relatively high cost until he sustained a back injury in an automobile accident. At that point he couldn't complete the membership forms fast enough. Similarly, a job becomes more important during economic "hard times"; church membership becomes more highly valued during periods of personal crisis; and a car pool is appreciated more when the family bus is laid up for repairs or an energy shortage exists.

A group may attract individuals to it both because it is the *object* of the individual's need and because it is a *means* for satisfying needs that lie outside the group. Further, when the group itself is the main point of interest, it may be either because of the people who belong or because of what the organization does. Thus one couple originally joined a gourmet dining club because they were close friends of several people who already belonged. Later, when the composition of the group had changed and the couple were no longer attracted to the other members, they continued to belong because they had become connoisseurs of the exotic foods and fine wines that the dinners regularly produced.

A group may also be attractive to an individual because it is a means by which to achieve some desired goal. A person, in this case, may join the military services to gain security or the benefits of the GI Bill once his enlistment is over, or a salesman may join a country club in order to make business contacts. In the process of making those contacts, however, the salesman may also learn to enjoy golf. In that event the country club will have become the object of his need to play golf as well as the instrument for achieving his need for business contacts.

As one would expect, the reason for a person's attraction to a group has a great influence on his behavior in the group. Psychologist Kurt Back demonstrated this point in an experiment that created groups on the basis of three different kinds of cohesiveness: personal attraction of groups of members for each other, importance of the task, and prestige of the group. On the basis of this study, Back discovered that when members were attracted to a group primarily because they liked the other members, the group's discussions were long, relaxed, and pleasant. In contrast, when the importance of the group task was the reason for cohesiveness, discussions tended to be shorter and directed only toward subjects that were relevant to the task's accomplishment. Finally, when the prestige of the group was the basis for member attraction, discussions were conducted cautiously, with the participants careful not to say anything that would detract from their own status.[13]

Whatever the source of cohesiveness, there is evidence that groups that have it tend to be more productive than groups that do not. There are, nevertheless, some potential problems related to high levels of cohesiveness. In some instances members may enjoy each other's company so much that they find it difficult to concentrate on the group task. There is also the danger that when group members are highly attracted to one another they will be reluctant to make comments that might disrupt warm interpersonal relationships. This tendency, in turn, could lead to the "groupthink" phenomenon discussed in Chapter 9.

LEADERSHIP

No other aspect of groups has been studied so frequently or so intensively as leadership. In spite of this concern, however, "leadership is still a hazy, ill-defined notion with as many approaches to its study as there are definitions."[14] The problem undoubtedly lies in the complexity of the group phenomenon itself, for as Hollander has put it, "under diverse headings and in distinctive ways, many lines of activity are pursued which speak to the question of how one person's action is affected by others."[15]

Perhaps the earliest of these "many lines of inquiry" was the theory that leaders possessed special characteristics or traits not held by others. Although this approach to the subject—known as the trait theory of leadership—remains a popular belief, it has been largely discredited by social scientists. The problem, simply, in spite of massive amounts of research, is that no one has been able to identify any physical or psychological trait that is universally characteristic of leaders. Studies that have attempted to correlate intelligence with leadership, for example, have discovered that although some leaders have been more intelligent than their followers, a significant number have also been less intelligent and many have been of about the same intelligence as other members of their groups. Similar findings have resulted from studies concerning such diverse characteristics as age, height, weight, socioeconomic background, and degree of emotional control. Summarizing the results of these studies of leadership traits, Jenkins concluded that there are "wide variations in the characteristics of individuals who become leaders in similar situations, and even greater divergence in leadership behavior in different situations."[16]

As the trait theory of leadership became discredited, social scientists began searching for alternative approaches to the subject. Emerging from this search was the idea that the key to leadership lay not within the individual but within the social situations in which people interacted. Articulating this position, Albert Murphy wrote:

> Leadership study calls for a situational approach; this is fundamentally sociological. Leadership does not reside in a person. It is a function of the whole situation. . . . The situation is fundamental and in all cases makes the leader. This is obvious in everyday life and in history. The Hitlers and the Mussolinis are made by situations and they can be understood only in terms of those situations. Their characteristics are indicative of the times in which they lived and the situations of which they are a part. Groups do not act because they have leaders but they secure leaders to help them to act.[17]

The approach to leadership outlined by Murphy has been variously referred to as situational, functional, or group centered. Whatever it is called, however, the theory is

> based on a single major premise: that leadership is the act of fulfilling the various functions relevant to group needs. Thus any group member may occupy the leadership position at a given time. For example, one member may dispel confusion by providing a summary early in the group discussion, while another may soothe the wounded feelings of a fellow member, thereby preventing an interpersonal relations crisis.[18]

Functional leadership theory clearly denies that there is any necessary relationship between leadership acts and the formal or designated leader of a group. Individuals may be given the title of leader for a virtually end-less variety of reasons. We recall, for example, observing a discussion class in which the students were divided into five-person groups and given a period of several weeks to investigate a significant social problem. Although they were not required to do so, most groups eventually elected one of their members to be the leader. Two of these groups, each with its own elected leader, reached an early crisis when, because of normal attrition, they found themselves with only three members each. The instructor decided to combine them into a single group. The new group now faced the problem of deciding which of the two old leaders would retain his position. However, when several days of polite conversation, issue avoidance, and behind-the-scenes infighting failed to resolve the issue, the group finally solved the problem by electing neither of the two former group leaders. Instead, it designated as leader a member who, until that time, had distinguished himself only by virtue of being conspicuously less intelligent, less mature, and less responsible than any other member of the group. Everyone was satisfied; the new "leader" remained as powerless in the group as he had always been, while the old leaders, feeling no repudiation by the election of such an obvious inferior, continued to perform the same kinds of leadership functions they had performed in the past.

The situation just described, though obviously atypical, is by no means unique in its disassociation of leadership behaviors from the formal leadership role. The same result may occur when formal leaders are designated by an outside authority insensitive to the requirements of the particular situation, or by the group itself when it acts prematurely or with poor judgment. Moreover, it should be understood that when this does happen it is frequently impossible to ignore the designated leader to the same degree that the classroom group did.

Designated leadership may often carry with it a number of the sources of influence delineated during our earlier discussion of power. For this reason it is clearly desirable that the individual designated as leader be someone willing and able to perform a variety of functions relevant to the fulfillment of group needs. Even the most competent of designated leaders, however, is incapable of demonstrating all of the behaviors that could be useful to the group. The most productive groups, consequently, will be those in which the designated leader actively encourages other members to seek and execute those functions.

THE CHAPTER IN PERSPECTIVE

In Chapter 9 group conferences were described as having some liabilities as well as some advantages. There is no special magic in having a group discussion or setting up a conference. They can succeed or fail, depending on how they are managed. We feel that an understanding of group dynamics is a prerequisite for anyone hoping to use groups efficiently or to participate in them effectively. The intention in this chapter was to examine the anatomy all groups have in common. Structure is necessary for coordinated activity; and if it is not superimposed by the organization, it will emerge in the group in the form of labor being divided, roles being assigned, power being distributed, and a definite communication network becoming entrenched. As the group interacts, the desire for orderliness and predictability will cause members to adopt expectations or norms to guide the behavior of individual members. The kind of interaction the members have will determine whether or not they feel very cohesive as a unit. Finally, leadership is one of the most crucial variables in the success of the group, but the same leadership style may not fit every situation equally. We hope this discussion has provided the necessary background for making group conferences work—the subject of the next two chapters.

REFERENCES

1. Edward T. Hall, *The Silent Language* (New York: Fawcett, 1959), p. 75.

2. Ibid., p. 50.

3. William C. Schutz, *The Interpersonal Underworld* (Palo Alto, Calif.: Science and Behavior Books, 1966).

4. E. A. Fleishman, *Manual for Leadership Opinion Questionnaire* (Chicago: Science Research Associates, 1969).

5. R. R. Blake and Jane S. Mouton, *The Managerial Grid* (Houston: Gulf Publishing Company, 1969).

6. John R. P. French, Jr., and Bertram Raven, "The Bases of Social Power," in Dorwin Cartwright and Alvin Zander, eds., *Group Dynamics: Research and Theory*, 2d ed. (New York: Harper & Row, 1960), pp. 613–621.

7. Barry E. Collins and Harold Guetzkow, *A Social Psychology of Group Process for Decision-Making* (New York: Wiley, 1964), p. 63.

8. Ibid., pp. 64–65.

9. Abraham Zaleznik and David Moment, *The Dynamics of Interpersonal Behavior* (New York: Wiley, 1964), p. 103.

10. Paul Wernimont, "What Supervisors and Subordinates Expect of Each Other," *Personnel Journal* (March 1971): 208.

11. Dorwin Cartwright and Alvin Zander, "Group Pressures and Group Standards: Introduction," in Cartwright and Zander, p. 166.

12. Some of the concepts in this section are from Cartwright and Zander, pp. 69–78.

13. Kurt Back, "Influence Through Social Communication," *Journal of Abnormal and Social Psychology*, 46 (1951): 9–23.

14. Larry D. Browning, "The Nature and Effect of Non-Functional Group Leadership," unpublished M.A. thesis, University of Oklahoma, Department of Speech, 1966, p. 3.

15. E. P. Hollander, *Leaders, Groups and Influence* (New York: Oxford University Press, 1964), p. vii.

16. William Jenkins, "A Review of Leadership Studies with Particular Reference to Military Problems," *Psychological Bulletin*, 44 (January 1947): 75.

17. Albert J. Murphy, "A Study of the Leadership Process," *American Sociological Review*, 6 (October 1941): 674.

18. Browning, pp. 18–19.

CHAPTER 11
PLANNING A CONFERENCE

> ### Preview
>
> **Preliminary planning by the manager is the key to productive group conferences. Factors to plan for are:**
>
> - **Group size**
> - **Purpose of conference**
> - **Agenda**
> - **Physical arrangements**
> - **Notifying the participants**

The first two chapters on group conferences have dealt with the strengths and weaknesses of group action and the sociology of groups from a practical perspective. Intensifying this utilitarian approach, the next two chapters will discuss how to make conferences productive. This chapter will focus on how to plan a group conference, and the next one will deal with the conference in progress.

KEEP THE SIZE WORKABLE

After spending his entire day in committee meetings, an exasperated school administrator vented his frustration in the following poem:

Committees of twenty
Deliberate plenty.

Committees of ten
Act now and then.

But most jobs are done
By committees of one.

Although we are unwilling to go along with the implication that groups are generally ineffective, we do like the poet's focus on group size. It has been our experience that if managers make one mistake in the handling of human resources, it is in their failure to understand the relationship between the size of a group and the nature of the task assigned to it. In general, the tendency is either to create committees that are too large or, in cases in which the administrator has no control over the size of the group, to select the wrong format.

The impulse to create big committees is understandable. To begin with, as Collins and Guetzkow point out,

when a large variety of information must be brought to bear and unusual solution alternatives must be produced, it . . . would seem that increasing the size of the group would improve the quality of productivity. These considerations might well prompt an industrial firm to bring its foremen together and have them suggest alternative proposals for a new plant which the architects then would work over before completing their final drawings.[1]

In addition, a manager is often led to create large committees by the diplomatic consideration of including anyone who might be offended if left off, or the political consideration of appointing those who might be useful in implementing the group's recommendations.

In spite of what may appear to be good reasons for increasing a committee's size, however, one must remember that a group does not have to become very large before problems of efficiency and morale begin to arise. Some insight into these problems can be gained by simply observing the way increases in group size affect the potential number of relationships among members. If a group is composed of two people, for example, there is only one possible relationship (A–B). If, however, the group's membership is increased to three, the number of potential relationships jumps to six. In this case, not only does the group have to cope with a series of individual relationships (A–B, B–C, C–A), but it also faces the likelihood that subgroups will develop and require assimilation into the group structure. Thus in a three-person group there is also potential for the relationships AB–C, BC–A, and CA–B. If group size is increased to 4, the number of potential relationships grows to 25; 5-person groups yield 90 relationships; an increase to 6 results in 301, and in 7-person groups there are 966 potential interpersonal relationships. As the group grows in size, therefore, it becomes more likely that it will be fragmented. Figure 11.1 pictures how some people become isolated, pairs develop, and some small subgroups emerge. Under such circumstances it is not surprising that Collins and Guetzkow have concluded that "the superiority of the group [over individual endeavor] may be washed out in organizational confusion if the task requires a high degree of patterning of the internal relations."[2]

Added to the difficulties of developing internal structure is the fact that larger groups simply do not allow individual group members sufficient opportunity to express themselves. If, for example, a 20-person group schedules 2-hour meetings, the average time available for each person's comments is only 6 minutes. Not only does this situation lead to low morale, it also largely negates one of the chief benefits of discussion—the opportunity to test ideas through rigorous intellectual interaction.

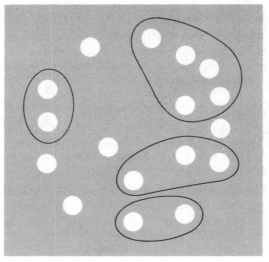

Figure 11.1. Divisions within groups.

WORKING WITH LARGE GROUPS

In view of our criticism, the manager faced with the task of conducting a conference for a large group might well wonder if there is any good solution to his problem. Fortunately, a number of formats have been found useful in dealing with groups that are too large to be constituted as a single committee.

The show-type discussion

One technique, labeled by Howell and Smith the show-type discussion,[3] places the majority of conferees in the role of auditor as they listen to a discussion carried on by a group of experts. Illustrative of this approach was a recent television program on the issue of malpractice lawsuits against medical doctors. The show's producer could conceivably have approached the problem of informing the viewing audience about this topic in a number of different ways. Even though it was a locally produced program and financial resources were undoubtedly limited, it would have been possible to video tape a series of interviews with a variety of people who had had experiences with the problem, to have conducted a debate between two opposing viewpoints, or perhaps to have had a recognized expert deliver a lecture. The producer, however, chose none of these approaches in this case. Instead, he organized a panel composed of a doctor who headed a medical organization, a lawyer who specialized in malpractice cases, an insurance executive whose company wrote malpractice insurance, and a newsman, who acted as moderator. The result was a spirited and sometimes contentious interaction. The purpose of the discussion in this case was clearly not to help the participants—either to derive a solution or to become more familiar with or sensitive to the problem—but to inform in as interesting a way as possible those who were watching the program. This, of course, is the purpose of a show-type discussion.

Because of its potential for lively interaction, our favorite format for show-type discussions is the panel; but other approaches may also be effective. Depending on the topic and the available personnel, the conference manager may wish to arrange a debate or a symposium discussion —a technique in which several experts give individual short speeches on various aspects of the subject being considered.

The principal liability of show-type discussions is that they force the majority of the group into the passive role of listener. In this respect, although structural difficulties are avoided, they have the same objectionable quality as the too-large committee. In general, group members will be more satisfied and the results of the conference will be superior if all participants are given frequent opportunities to interact with others.

The buzz session A technique that makes this possible is called the buzz session method. In this approach, first reported by Donald Phillips in 1948,[4] participants are divided into small groups of four to six members and then given a limited time (perhaps from five to fifteen minutes) in which to come up with as many ideas relevant to the conference topic as they can.

One of the authors found the buzz session extremely popular during a conference that he was asked to organize for a group of about 50 college advisers to foreign students. In this particular case, buzz sessions were utilized twice within a single afternoon session. First the conferees were formed into 10 groups of 5 persons each and given 10 minutes to list the special problems they faced in dealing with foreign students. During this activity the various groups merely congregated in different areas of the main meeting room. Nothing elaborate, such as individual conference rooms, is required to make this technique usable. At the end of ten minutes the participants reassembled and a representative of each group was given one minute in which to summarize the results of his group's discussion. The reports were followed by an hour-long panel discussion by a group of four counseling experts, who were able to react to quite a number of the points that had arisen as a result of the buzz sessions. After the panel discussion the buzz groups assembled once more, this time to analyze the panelists' ideas and to present solutions of their own to the various problems that had been articulated.

The foreign student advisers conference illustrates the stimulating results that can come from combining information-producing show-type discussions with interaction-producing buzz sessions. Although in this particular conference it was unnecessary for the group to arrive at any formal decisions or policies, this, too, can be readily accomplished simply by adding conventional parliamentary sessions to the other activities. In other words, some knowledge of group dynamics and discussion formats, combined with a little imagination and energy, can produce a variety of approaches to the communication needs of larger groups.

Nominal grouping

Nominal grouping is a relatively recent technique that is gaining in popularity. It consists of four distinct phases: listing, recording, voting, and discussing.

During the listing phase the leader gives an orientation to the procedures and presents a general overview of a problem. Typical problem areas might be the development of new products, the identification of primary communication problems, or the identification of the strengths and weaknesses of a proposed program. The leader asks each member to make a list of the needs, problems, or ideas relevant to the task. No group interaction is permitted during the listing phase because it is desirable to get each individual's perceptions without any group influence.

The recording phase involves making a master list of all the major ideas identified by the group. In order to do this, each member reads one item at a time until all nonduplicating items from all lists are recorded. Generally, it is desirable to make the list on a chalkboard or flipchart so that all members can readily see the entire list. No interaction is permitted during this phase either.

Next the members are asked to rank (privately) the items on the master list. Sometimes it is useful to have them rank only the top five or ten items that they feel are important. The group leader then computes the overall rankings and presents the results to the group.

All of the preceding steps have been means of determining what the group feels is important about the problem area, and the results thus set an agenda for full exploration and discussion. One of the principal advantages of the nominal group is that diverse viewpoints and varying perceptions surface easily and can be discussed.

Two good examples of the uses of nominal grouping are provided by Knippen and Van Voorhis,[5] who used this method in a brewery and in a savings and loan association. In the brewery, two groups of supervisors and one group of upper-level managers indicated their problems and their training needs; then they indicated the problems and training needs of the other group—that is, supervisors identified managers' needs and problems and managers identified supervisors' needs and problems. In this way it was possible not only to determine the problems and needs of each group but also to contrast the perceptions of the reciprocal groups. Consequently it could be very beneficial to explore in the discussion how and why supervisors and managers differed in their perceptions of one another's problems and training needs. In other words, the discussion phase of the nominal groups became a very useful channel for upward and downward communication.

In the savings and loan association, Knippin and Van Voorhis used a heterogeneous group that cut across levels of management and key staff personnel. (Again, the problem area was to identify the organization's chief problems and needs.) Many diverse ideas were accumulated, and the discussion indicated that some of them were apparently completely new.

Once more, the nominal group provided a greater insight into the organization than any of its members had had before.

Nominal grouping, therefore, seems to be an effective technique for generating group discussion about a variety of problems in organizations. Done thoroughly, it will often take as much as two hours to go through all four stages, but the results are often worth the time and effort.

WORKING WITH SMALL GROUPS
Although thus far we have placed major emphasis on the manager's need to recognize the differences between large and small groups when planning conferences, we have not (as you have undoubtedly noticed) been very specific about the exact numbers that constitute one or the other. Such a determination is tenuous because the number of people who can operate effectively in a committee meeting will vary depending on the skills of the participants and the nature of the task the group is undertaking. Obviously, people who are good at discussion and have worked together in the past can tolerate a larger group than those who are inexperienced and unfamiliar with each other. Similarly, there may be occasions when the nature of the task is such that input from a variety of sources is virtually mandatory. Considerations of this type may suggest to the manager the expediency of appointing a committee somewhat larger than would otherwise be desirable.

Nevertheless, there are limits that must be observed in the use of small-group discussion. As mentioned earlier, for example, if the ratio between group size and meeting time is such that it will not allow all participants ample time to express and react to ideas, there is simply no use in attempting to utilize the committee format. All other factors being equal, however, a small-group discussion should probably have somewhere between 3 and 8 participants for optimum effectiveness; 5 members would be ideal. Zelko describes the best conference arrangement as being 10–12 participants seated face to face around an oblong or oval table.[6] Further, an investigation by one of the authors suggests, even within the limited range of 3- to 8-member groups, that larger groups are significantly less efficient than smaller ones. In this case, groups with from 6 to 8 participants "found it necessary, because of the need to coordinate the activities of more members, to place greater emphasis on procedure than smaller groups."[7] In addition, "just as attention [to the task] in larger groups was more easily disrupted than in smaller groups, once a disruption did occur a longer period of time was required in large groups to restore group attention."[8] Both for the sake of member satisfaction and for the purpose of efficiency, therefore, five to ten would generally appear to be the ideal number of participants for small-group discussion. However, if the group is meeting for some reason other than discussion, the number may be increased.

CLARIFY THE GROUP'S PURPOSE

Whatever the purpose of a discussion group might be, it is important that both its general and specific objectives be understood and accepted by its members. It could be disastrous, for example, if some of the participants in a sensitivity group insisted on behaving as though the group's primary mission were to solve a problem. Equally unfortunate are occasions when the members of problem-solving groups become fixated at some preliminary stage of group development. In addition to accepting the general objectives of the group, it is also necessary that members come to a clear understanding of the group's specific purposes. A group, for example, whose purpose is to formulate a policy would very likely wish to proceed differently than if its task were simply to produce an analysis of the problem.

A useful approach to clarifying the mission of a committee is for the person responsible for convening the group to make his expectations as explicit as possible. Preparing a task for the committee, of course, has the added advantage of forcing the convener to clarify for himself what he expects the group to accomplish. An example of effective goal setting is provided by a committee on which one of the authors was recently requested to serve. The memorandum convening the group is reproduced on the next page.

In addition to drafting a memo, the assistant provost who originated the WBAA committee also appeared at the beginning of the group's first meeting to rearticulate his expectations and answer questions.

Normally, as in the situation just described, problem-solving groups are presented with the issue they are to address. Occasionally, however, a study group or discussion class requires that the group itself develop a topic for discussion. In such instances it is important that the topic selection be approached as carefully as the solution stage that will follow. Topics should be timely, significant, and controversial in order to stimulate the interest of the group and justify the expenditure of time that any worthwhile group discussion will inevitably require. Also, in order to encourage participants to take an initial stance as an inquirer rather than as an advocate, the topic should be phrased as a question. This will also promote a many-sided approach to the topic rather than the pro-con orientation that results when the subject is phrased in propositional form, as in formal debating. For example, one of the most common uses of the small group in business today is as a task force. A task force is a small group whose members represent many different areas in the organization. They are given a general problem area to investigate, and the group is assigned the tasks of defining and analyzing specific problems and then working toward solutions. One such group was assigned the task of investigating the whole internal communication system of a public utility; another was given

MEMORANDUM

TO: D. M. Berg   J. S. Miles
      F. K. Burrin   B. S. Rollins
      D. P. Bunte   K. L. Rydar
      R. O. Forsythe   W. F. Seibert
      L. L. Knodle   D. R. Smith

FROM: D. R. Brown
DATE: February 18, 1975
RE: Radio Station WBAA

I should like to ask you to serve on an *ad hoc* committee, the purpose of which will be to examine in detail selected questions concerning the functioning of Radio Station WBAA. These questions are:

1. What functions should WBAA perform for the University and the community? Wherever possible, relate these functions to the mission of other university administrative units.
2. Beyond those presently available, what personnel and physical resources are needed to serve better those functions? Wherever possible, assign cost estimates.
3. What management structure would foster serving and improving those functions? Consider both the strengths and weaknesses of (a) the present independent management and (b) an integrated management involving WBAA and the Telecommunication Center.

I should appreciate receiving a report of your deliberations by May 15th. I have asked D. R. Smith to chair the committee and he will take responsibility for calling the first meeting.

DRB/ber
cc: F. Haas

---

the task of formulating a suggestion system. Such groups are usually terminated when their mission is completed.

Finally, a better discussion is likely to result if the issue under consideration is one of policy rather than fact or value. Questions of fact (Is the United States militarily stronger than Russia?) can be answered as true or false, provided that the necessary evidence is available, while questions of value (Is abortion justified?) tend to hinge on differences of opinion that "end in the ultimate argument of 'I believe it is' versus 'I believe it isn't.' "[9] Questions of policy tend to be broader than those of fact or value and are concerned with solutions to problems. Thus a group might consider questions such as "What can the company do to reduce employee theft?" or "Should the university establish quotas for the hiring of women and minority group members?"

Although people in most organizations have tended to view group conferences almost exclusively as vehicles for decision making, groups have been found successful in filling each of the communication functions described in Chapter 3: informative, persuasive, integrative, and command/ regulative. The following discussion demonstrates how different conferences can be identified by relating them to the needs from which they have arisen.

THE INFORMATIVE FUNCTION

Information (enlightenment) groups aim at satisfying the individual task needs of their members. Rather than seeking sensitivity to others or insight into group process as their primary goals, information groups are intended to help members understand some phenomenon outside the process of the immediate group. Most organized educational activities, for example, rely heavily on information groups for their success. Thus book study clubs use groups as a means of helping their members become knowledgeable about certain literary works, and bird-watching societies meet to share information among members. The Monday morning staff meeting is basically an information group in which members regularly report to each other their plans for the week. Similarly, many managers like regional meetings because they learn what other managers are doing.

For example, Spataro and Greenbaum describe the informative meetings of a company that holds

> three supervisory staff meetings a year on Saturday mornings for the express purpose of bringing all managerial and technical staff together to exchange comments in an informal atmosphere, and learn more about the company in respect to finances and plans for the future. During these meetings, it is most usual for top management and middle management to speak with the group of 30 supervisors and technical personnel on a one to many basis.[10]

THE PERSUASIVE FUNCTION

Groups may be designed to persuade in two different ways. First, some conferences are held in order to persuade the members to adopt a certain plan. For example, when a member of the organization wants to bring in a consultant to conduct an attitude survey or help with a technical problem, he may need to get the approval of others. One strategy available to him is to call a meeting "to explore" the ramifications of hiring the consultant. However, the authors have observed a number of such meetings in which the underlying strategy is to persuade others to agree to the plan.

Groups have also been used for a slightly different kind of persuasive function based on a participation hypothesis. A group of research studies showed that group discussions were more instrumental in changing people's minds than lectures.[11] This seemed to be borne out by some observations of managers. For example, one of the authors was involved in some safety meetings held by a large steel company. Periodically, employees of the company were selected to serve on safety committees. In their meetings they discussed safety problems and made recommendations to management. The greatest value of the meetings as far as management was concerned was that the group members began to enforce the safety regulation rather than expecting management to always be the corrective agent. Thus the participation itself seemed to serve a persuasive function.

THE INTEGRATIVE FUNCTION

In one sense all groups may have an integrative function if one believes that participation itself makes one identify with the group or the organization. However, we want to examine several types that are designed primarily for integrative purposes.

1. *Sensitivity groups,* as we construe them, evolved as a means of helping individuals deal with personal problems of affiliation and self-integration. These groups attempt to aid their members in developing and internalizing awareness of and sensitivity to the feelings and needs of others. In this sense the goals and methods of sensitivity groups are similar to those of group therapy, with one important difference: Whereas group therapy is designed to make "sick" people well, sensitivity groups are intended to make people who are already well even healthier. As is true of group therapy, it is absolutely mandatory that sensitivity groups be led by someone thoroughly trained in psychological counseling and group methods.

2. The goal of *training* (T) *groups* is to develop insight into the processes of the immediate group and to conceptualize or intellectualize them. Thus they serve both informative and integrative functions. As Thelen states it, T-groups provide

a situation in which group processes can be observed and studied. The objectives are to train members to recognize when these group processes are appropriate to the group task, what the consequences of different sorts of processes are, how members contribute to determine the nature of the processes, how leaders effect these processes, how a group whose processes are inappropriate may be helped to improve.[12]

As such, the objectives of T-groups relate very closely to what we have identified as group social-emotional needs, that is, to cope with shared anxieties within the group and to deal with the establishment of group structure. To accomplish their goals, T-groups always require the services of an experienced "trainer." While they are most often made up of people from several different organizations, some managements have used "in-house" groups as instruments for their own organizational development.

3. The *buzz group,* described earlier in the chapter, also serves an integrative function because the chief reason for using it is to make people feel involved, to let them participate. Often no new information comes from such a group, but it does serve to make the participants feel that they are an active part of the group.

4. A final example will illustrate still a different kind of integration. A manager of over 133 employees conducted a survey in which he discovered that he had good rapport with his professionals but not with his technicians or chemical staff. Consequently he set up a series of meetings to

better integrate them into the department. He meets every two weeks with a group consisting of one technician from each of six divisions and one clerical worker. One-fourth of the group is changed each quarter. So far the procedure seems to have helped the employees identify more with the department and the supervisor.

THE COMMAND REGULATIVE FUNCTION

We have become so accustomed to thinking of conferences in terms of problem solving that we often forget that they can also be used to regulate behavior. It is not infrequent that conferences are held to explain policies or announce new regulations. These, of course, happen sporadically, but they do serve a vital communicative function, as is demonstrated in the following example.

A manager of a fabricating department that produced parts and components to subcontracted shops was told by his management to end the practice of receiving Christmas gifts from customers. He chose to notify all customers that gifts would no longer be acceptable, and then a printed announcement was distributed to the employees. There was a tremendous negative reaction. Finally the manager called a meeting to explain the rationale for the new rule and to analyze the negative reactions. He was pleasantly surprised, however, to discover during the meeting that some employees actually favored the new rule, and they helped convince the others to obey it.

A COMBINATION OF FUNCTIONS

As has already been indicated, many conferences serve multiple functions or may have their function vary from time to time. The following description is of a work group that covers a broad range of topics. The importance of this meeting is that it is always an open channel to serve any function its members choose to initiate. Sometimes it is informative; at other times it may be persuasive; and it nearly always serves an integrative function.

One such meeting is described very well by Spataro and Greenbaum:

Each group is scheduled to meet once a month, during normal business hours, for a period of one hour. The meeting was generally held in the conference room so as to insure privacy and prevent interruptions from phones and other personnel.

Topics for discussion at the monthly meeting come from all members of the workgroup and the chairperson. To encourage the submission of topics and problems, each worksection has several 3 × 5 index card boxes labeled prominently "Problems and Topics for Workgroup Meetings." In the office these are placed on the desk, and in the warehouse such boxes are mounted on the steel columns with a prominent paint-job to attract attention. These boxes serve as a reminder that a means for discussing matters that have not been resolved does exist and provide a mechanism for minimizing the loss of subjects that require discussion. Early in the program it was found necessary to emphasize that problem resolution should not wait for meetings, but rather that the meetings should be a kind of court of last resort for those problems and topics that had not been adequately treated.

To guide the seventeen workgroup leaders in the conduct of meetings, a meeting manual was developed and placed in the work-kit of the chairperson of each meeting. The manual stresses that the chairperson should remember the objectives and act accordingly by talking as little as possible in order to obtain maximum employee participation, that the supervisor consider subordinates as council and board of advisors, but that the group decision must have the chair's approval as the chairperson takes responsibility for group decisions.

Both before and after the meeting, the chairperson is assisted by staff personnel who prepare both hardware and software to facilitate the success of this communication activity. The hardware consists of blackboard, easel, and overhead projector. By far the most used equipment is that of the overhead projector which facilitates the review of the minutes of the previous workgroup meeting and the follow-up responsibilities noted at that time. In the software area, the staff furnishes a typed summary of the previous meeting that can be displayed on the overhead projector, a list of topics awaiting discussion as reported in previous meetings, a standard minute-taking form that facilitates the recording of minutes by a member of the worksection, and an outline of the meeting manual which very briefly highlights the important stages for the conduct of the meeting, and meeting follow-up.[13]

PREPARE AN AGENDA

When the purpose or mission of the problem-solving group has been clarified, the next planning step is to develop some sort of approach to the issue being dealt with. This may take the form of a "time-action plan," such as that adopted by the WBAA committee mentioned earlier. The plan, which is reproduced here, although brief, was sufficient for a group like this one, in which each member has some special area of expertise related to the topic.

Although for some groups and some problems a general time-action plan may be all that is required, on other occasions a more complete agenda may be called for. Sometimes, in order to expedite discussion, the manager or a designated member will do well to bring a specific proposal, spelled out in considerable detail, for the group to consider as a potential plan for solving the problem that constitutes the purpose of their meeting. Groups without specific proposals have a tendency to scratch around for a long time and accomplish little. Whenever anyone brings a specific proposal for the group's consideration, it is essential that the facilitator or group leader set the kind of climate that allows the group to examine the proposal freely and critically, considering its advantages and disadvantages, and to amend the proposal with impunity or, for that matter, to reject it entirely and call for another plan of action.

An agenda may obviously take a variety of forms and should be adapted to the specific problem being considered. A generally useful approach, however, is that embodied in the standard problem-solving discussion pattern. Even though some stages of the pattern may not be applicable to

Purdue University
Time-Action Plan

Project WBAA Ad Hoc Committee

Administrator D. R. Smith   Date Prepared 3/7/75

Action	Target Date
I. Review history and past projects of WBAA.	3/14/75
II. Identify functions WBAA might perform for the University and community as related to the missions of the University.	3/28/75
III. In light of the functions identified in II (above) assign cost estimates and predict necessary personnel and physical resources required to provide this function.	4/11/75
IV. Provide alternatives to the present management structure in light of the functions identified.	4/25/75
V. Prepare final written report for Dr. Brown highlighting the committee's findings.	5/9/75
VI. Forward the report to Dr. Brown.	

every problem-solving venture, most of them are easily adapted to special situations.

I. What Is the Problem?
  A. (Definition) What does the discussion question mean?
    1. What is meant by the wording of the question?
    2. What terms implied by the question should be defined?
  B. (Analysis) What is the nature of the problem?
    1. What are the facts of the present situation?
    2. How serious is the problem?
II. What Should Be the Solution?
  A. (Criteria) What standards must be met by any proposed solution?
  B. (Alternatives) What are the possible alternatives?
  C. (Solution) What seems to be the best solution?
  D. (Evaluation) How can the solution be evaluated after it is put into effect?

Regardless of how detailed a plan is developed prior to the actual discussion, it must be viewed only as a guideline. In all cases, if the full value of group deliberation is to be realized, the participants must be given the flexibility to determine, as the discussion progresses, how their time can best be allocated. Exceptions to this general rule should occur only on occasions when a deadline for the group's final report must be met. In cases when a deadline does not allow sufficient time for the natural development of the discussion, the responsible manager would be well advised to utilize some other decision-making apparatus.

MAKE THE NECESSARY PHYSICAL ARRANGEMENTS

When people think of small-group communication they sometimes get so caught up in thinking about group behavior that they often forget the importance of adequate physical arrangements. It is saying the obvious that all groups need a meeting room; yet from time to time a manager in charge of a group neglects to reserve a room for the meeting and the conference starts on a sour note as someone scurries about looking for a suitable conference site. The room, once reserved, also needs to be arranged properly. To be sure, members of a group can rearrange tables and carry chairs from one point to another; but a well-managed conference has the chairs and tables and other furniture in the room prearranged according to plan.

The person in charge of a conference may also want to make pencils and writing pads available to each participant. Sometimes coffee can be provided—at a minimum, drinking water. Another characteristic of a well-managed conference is the availability of essential equipment. Overhead projectors, slide projectors, chalkboards, and any other equipment that is likely to be useful in the conduct of the meeting should be brought to the room prior to the convening of the meeting. A helter-skelter search for equipment at the last minute, or after the meeting has started, usually delays, disrupts the group's progress, and generally makes a bad impression. Professionals commonly expect the manager of a conference to be a professional.

NOTIFY THE PARTICIPANTS

Unless there is a standing conference appointment or an emergency, participants should always be duly notified in advance that they are expected to participate. Even if they have been told orally, it is a wise practice to send a written reminder a day or two prior to the meeting. As much as possible, the notification should state the purpose and the agenda. Well-planned conferences are seldom enshrouded in mystery.

THE CHAPTER IN PERSPECTIVE

The success or failure of many conferences depends directly on their advance planning. The first aspect of successful planning involves group size. Large groups tend to be ineffective and dissatisfying to their members unless special formats are used. The show-type discussion, the buzz session, and nominal groupings have been suggested as ways of increasing member input and satisfaction. But for the sake of participant satisfaction and for the purpose of efficiency, five to ten would appear to be the best number of people in small-group discussions.

Once the manager has concerned himself properly with group size, he should clarify the group's purpose—both in his own mind and to the participants. Although most professional groups are concerned with decision making, groups have successfully filled each of the communication functions described early in the book: informative, persuasive, integrative, and command/regulative.

In addition, the manager should prepare an agenda for the meeting, make all necessary physical arrangements, and be sure to notify the participants.

With the preliminary planning completed, the organizational communicator is ready to conduct the conference. This is the subject of the next chapter, "The Conference in Progress."

REFERENCES

1. Barry E. Collins and Harold Guetzkow, *A Social Psychology of Group Process for Decision-Making* (New York: Wiley, 1964), p. 23.

2. Ibid.

3. William S. Howell and Donald K. Smith, *Discussion* (New York: Macmillan, 1956), p. 9.

4. J. Donald Phillips, "Report on Discussion 66," *Adult Education Journal*, 7 (1948): 181–182.

5. Jay T. Knippen and K. R. Van Voorhis, "Nominal Grouping: Technique for Increasing the Effectiveness of Organizational Communication and Problem Solving Efforts," paper presented to the Academy of Management, Seattle, 1974.

6. Harold P. Zelko, "When You Are 'In Conference,'" in Richard C. Huseman et al., *Readings in Interpersonal and Organizational Communication* (Boston: Holbrook Press, 1973), p. 423.

7. David M. Berg, "A Descriptive Analysis of the Distribution and Duration of Themes Discussed by Task-Oriented, Small Groups," *Speech Monographs*, 34 (June 1967): 174.

8. Ibid., p. 175.

9. Herbert A. Thelen, *Dynamics of Groups at Work* (Chicago: University of Chicago Press, Phoenix Books, 1954), p. 130.

10. Lucian Spataro and H. Greenbaum, "Workgroup Meetings: Dimensions of Effectiveness," paper presented to the Academy of Management, New Orleans, 1975, p. 9.

11. Ernest G. Bormann, *Discussion and Group Methods: Theory and Practice* (New York: Harper & Row, 1969), p. 44.

12. Thelen, p. 129.

13. Spataro and Greenbaum, pp. 13–14.

CHAPTER 12
THE CONFERENCE IN PROGRESS

Preview

Productive conferences are a result of good leadership and skillful member participation. Leader and participant share the responsibility for successful group behavior.

Responsibilities common to all:

- Human relations
- Critical thinking
- Effective communication

Responsibilities of the leader:

- Set overall tone of conference in terms of group purpose
- Guide the conference
- Stimulate the participants
- Control the group process
- Clarify the discussion
- Conclude the conference

Responsibilities of participants:

- Prepare thoroughly
- Be on time
- Participate cooperatively
- Share leadership
- Be a process observer
- Keep purpose in mind

Before we begin to *prescribe* what one ought to do, perhaps the most logical beginning point is to *describe* what actually takes place in most groups. Of course every conference will have its unique features, but there tend to be some characteristics common to most groups.

Robert Bales, after a series of carefully conceived laboratory studies, was able to identify 12 different categories of interaction in groups.[1] (See Figure 12.1.)

BASIC PATTERNS OF GROUP INTERACTION

Of the 12 behaviors on the Bales diagram, 6 (the first 3 and the last 3) relate to the *social-emotional climate* of the group, and 6 (those in the middle) relate to the group's *task accomplishment*. Thus, showing solidarity, tension release, and agreement are all things group members can do to build good human relations within the group. As Bales discovered, the

Figure 12.1. Bales' interaction categories.

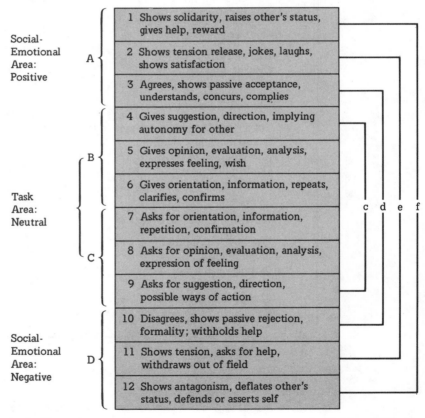

a. Problems of communication
b. Problems of evaluation
c. Problems of control
d. Problems of decision
e. Problems of tension reduction
f. Problems of reintegration

A. Positive reactions
B. Attempted answers
C. Questions
D. Negative reactions

TABLE 1   BALES INTERACTION CATEGORIES[7]

Social-emotional (positive)	1. Shows solidarity, raises other's status, gives help
	2. Shows tension release, jokes, laughs, shows satisfaction
	3. Agrees, shows passive acceptance, understands, complies
Task (giving)	4. Gives suggestion, direction, implying autonomy for other
	5. Gives opinion, evaluation, analysis; expresses feeling, wish
	6. Gives orientation, information; repeats, clarifies, confirms
Task (seeking)	7. Asks for orientation, information, repetition, confirmation
	8. Asks for opinion, evaluation, analysis, expression of feeling
	9. Asks for suggestion, direction, possible ways of action
Social-emotional (negative)	10. Disagrees, shows passive rejection, formality; withholds help
	11. Shows tension, asks for help, withdraws out of field
	12. Shows antagonism, deflates others' status, defends or asserts self

group members who were "most commonly rated 'best liked' typically have higher than average rates of showing tension release (mainly smiling and laughing) and showing agreement."[2]

Showing disagreement, tension, and antagonism, as one would expect, is behavior that tends to be destructive of the group's social-emotional climate. The fact that disagreement may be harmful to good human relations, while at the same time frequently necessary to critical thinking, demonstrates the not always compatible relationship between these two major skill areas. As suggested earlier, an adept communicator can often minimize the painful effects of disagreement but will probably not be able to eliminate them entirely. This may account for Bales' discovery that "giving suggestions, necessary as it may be for accomplishment of the task, is more likely to arouse negative reactions than is giving information or opinions."[3] One can assume that at least some of the time a suggestion will run counter to the ideas and opinions of other group members and will therefore constitute an implied disagreement. Moreover, conflict is not necessarily dysfunctional. In Bales' research a pattern seemed to emerge in some of the healthiest groups that permitted as much as one-third of the interactions to be negative without impairing the group's productivity. In fact, some completely positive groups turned out to be quite unhealthy because they were not really investigating, analyzing, and probing.

The fact that giving suggestions may stimulate negative reactions from other members has interesting implications for the person who is designated group leader or aspires to that position. Again, as Bales observes, "this tends to put the task specialist in a vulnerable position. The group commonly develops a certain amount of negative feeling toward him. Not only is he likely to lose the status of being best liked, but he may lose his position as task leader."[4] This may account for the fact that many successful discussion group leaders tend to avoid substantive contributions. Instead, they concentrate on such matters as balancing participation among the various members, providing positive feedback, summarizing group progress, and coordinating group activities. In the final analysis, then, we can say that effective participation in a group will necessitate coping with a diversity of behaviors.

There is still another pattern that needs to be described: the interaction cycle. Since some interactions help accomplish the *task* while others affect the *social-emotional climate* in the group, these two types of interactions are actually complementary; taken together, they produce a kind of cycle in the group's performance. Whenever groups begin to work on a task, they almost invariably create some social-emotional tension or human relations problem. If the problem grows in importance, it has to be solved before the group can begin to work effectively on the task again. After the group returns to the task, however, new social-emotional tensions may be created. Because of this cyclical nature of group interaction, those who participate in conferences must understand that all task groups will require some time (and, on occasion, a good deal of time) to develop the kind of roles, power relationships, and norms with which their members can be comfortable. Socializing at the beginning of a meeting is not necessarily a waste of time.

With this background in the diversity and cyclical nature of group interaction, we now turn to the skills that make participation effective.

SKILLS THAT MAKE CONFERENCES EFFECTIVE

As long-time observers and teachers of discussion, we are still surprised by what sometimes happens to people when they enter a group setting. We recall, for example, a classroom exercise in which a seemingly intelligent and cooperative young man, once he was elected group leader, turned into an insensitive, overbearing bore. Apparently personal attributes that are effective in one context can become totally ineffective in another. It is possible, in the words of Herbert Thelen,

for a group whose members are mostly educated, well adjusted, and knowledgeable to get nowhere: consider many school faculty meetings. It is possible for administrators marvellously trained to be unable somehow to run successful staff meetings. It is possible for members of a community council, highly successful as leaders in their own organizations, to be unable to work together. It is possible for people trained in research and loaded with information about what happens in groups to be unable to contribute effectively to groups of which they are a part. It is even possible for a group, highly successful in planning policy for its organization's executive secretary, to fail miserably when its co-operation with other groups is required.[5]

Although the success of any small group will ultimately depend on a large number of variables, it is still true that certain skills and behaviors are more conducive to fruitful discussion than others. Three general categories of skills are essential: (1) those that contribute to the establishment of good interpersonal relationships among group members; (2) those that enhance rigorous critical thinking about the topic; and (3) those that make the communication clear and understandable.

HUMAN RELATIONS SKILLS

There are those, unfortunately, who feel that any time spent in establishing good human relationships within a group is wasted. Even more regrettable is the fact that this kind of no-nonsense, "let's get on with the job" attitude seems especially prevalent among people who have themselves attained positions of status within their organizations. Regardless of who holds them, however, attitudes that deprecate the significance of human relations skills reflect an ignorance of group processes. As discussed earlier, social-emotional problems are inherent in any group situation and must be accomodated if the group is to realize its full potential.

It is not unusual to find people who are confused by what is meant by good human relations. Some seem to assume (perhaps this is the basis for many of the negative reactions) that it refers to an artificially polite, all-smiles, sweetness-and-light atmosphere. This is an obvious misconception. As we use the term, good human relations simply refers to the establishment of psychological conditions that will best facilitate task accomplishment. Two basic categories of attitudes and skills that tend to produce good human relations have been identified by Howell and Smith in their book, *Discussion*.[6]

1) Participants must learn to welcome opinions that are different from their own. Underlying this position is an attitude that goes well beyond merely tolerating another person's right to "believe what he wants." What is called for, rather, is the kind of disposition reflected in the maxim, "Every person is my superior in that he can teach me something I do not now know." Approaching others from this perspective implies that not only does one listen willingly to what they have to say, but an active effort is made to encourage others to contribute their ideas, to draw them out, and to express appreciation for their contributions. Appreciation does not necessarily imply agreement, however. It is entirely possible to disagree vigorously with the position taken by another group member while, at the same time, showing appreciation for the person's willingness to contribute. When approached in this manner, disagreement can occur without conflict or interpersonal hostility.

2) Every participant should from time to time assume the other person's point of view. He should try to put himself in the other's shoes and ask how he would feel if he were in that position. Establishing such a frame of reference is an excellent starting point from which to seek understanding of another person's perpsective, but good motives in and of themselves are insufficient. One must do more than merely empathize with others; one must also query them as to their meanings and feelings. In other words, it is necessary both to give and to seek *feedback*. Before leaping to, and perhaps expressing, a value judgment about something another participant has said, one must do everything within reason to ensure that he understands the other person's intended meaning. By restating in one's own words an interpretation of what the other has said, and then asking for his reaction to that interpretation, one may be able to avoid

both misunderstandings and the conflicts that so frequently accompany them. In other words, participants should listen actively, empathically and critically.

CRITICAL-THINKING SKILLS

As important as human relations skills are to a group, however, they will not in themselves guarantee the accomplishment of the group's task. Thus groups must be careful to avoid the rather common tendency to become so enraptured by good feelings for one another that they forget to concentrate sufficiently on the task at hand. Effective task accomplishment requires a second set of attitudes and skills—those related to *critical thinking*, or *reasoning*. "The distinctive feature of this type of thinking," according to philosophy professor Max Black, "is the use of *reasons*: Something known or believed to be true is repeatedly used in order to arrive at other supposed truths."[7] From Black's description it is evident that effective reasoning has two components.

1. *It requires accurate information*. What is believed to be true may not always in fact be true. Thus a person must be ready to question his own assumptions as well as those of others. An example of what can happen when assumptions are not validated was provided by a committee recently created to suggest ways in which a university's student newspaper could be improved. Many of the problems of this particular paper seemed to result from a contract with the university that governed the use and cost of space and facilities. The contract, which was negotiated in 1969 during the "days of campus unrest," was felt by many committee members to be punitive—a method of punishing the student paper for its radical stance. Believing that the university would not alter the terms of the 1969 contract, the committee spent much time and energy exploring such alternative solutions as buying or renting a building off campus. Later, when someone took the trouble to investigate the current attitude of university officials, it was dicovered that the original assumption was untrue: The university would agree to a contract with terms more favorable to the newspaper.

Part IV of this book offers some guides to research, but it should be pointed out here that critical thinking cannot take place in the absence of correct information. Moreover, it is not a safe assumption that the collective membership of a group, no matter how carefully they are selected, will have among them all the information needed to make a wise decision. To put it another way, at some time in the group's deliberations members are almost surely going to have to go out and dig for further information. Fortunately, in this search for relevant data discussion groups have the advantage of being able to divide up the labor.

2. *Once information has been sought out and validated, one must draw accurate conclusions from that information*. Since problem-solving groups cannot afford the luxury of jumping to conclusions, each member has an obligation to help evaluate the inferences from which conclusions are drawn. The principal problem in dealing with inferences is not that people

make them but that they fail to distinguish them from observations. The difference, as William Haney has pointed out, is vital: Conclusions based on observation, provided that the observations are well made, may "approach certainty," but conclusions based on inference "involve only a degree of probability."[8] Inferences, in other words, no matter how well reasoned, still involve an element of guessing. The following testimony from a defendent in a reckless driving trial should help illustrate the potential hazards of acting on invalid inferences:

I had just come out of the drugstore on Saturday morning when I noticed a car being driven by that looked like my wife's Volkswagen. I had never seen the young man behind the wheel before so I thought that the car had probably been stolen—especially since we've been having so much trouble with car theft around here lately. Anyway, I jumped in my car which was parked right in front of me at the curb and started chasing the guy to see what the hell he thought he was doing in my wife's car. I caught up with him after a couple of blocks at a red light and got out of my car to go over and talk to him, but just then the light changed and he took off. I caught him again and was trying to pass him and force him to the side of the road when I was stopped by the police.

In this case the man on trial had made some accurate observations about the situation: The car, as it turned out, was his wife's, and it was being driven by a man who was a stranger to him. Unfortunately for him, the defendant also made a critical inference that resulted in an incorrect conclusion. The car had not been stolen. Instead, it had been picked up, at his wife's request, by an employee of a local garage and was being taken in for repairs. The man driving it had become frightened and had tried to get away when he realized he was being chased by another car.

The lesson here should be apparent: People who deal with inferences must not only be alert to distinguish them from conclusions based on observation but must also learn to calculate the *degree* to which the inference is probably true and the *consequences* of acting on their conclusion if the inference should turn out to be wrong. Finally, the person working with inferences must realize that, because inferences are based only on probabilities, it is always possible to infer more than one conclusion from the same evidence. The critically thinking discussion group, therefore, will settle on a conclusion only after actively seeking alternative interpretations of the evidence with which it is working. Even then conclusions should be viewed as only tentative and subject to revision if new information or interpretations become available.

COMMUNI-CATION SKILLS

Although it is vital to the success of a problem-solving group that its members develop effective human relations and critical-thinking skills, these in themselves are insufficent for productive discussion. Group members must also manifest a sufficient number of communication skills that will help the group attain its ends.

Members must be able to express themselves accurately, fluently, and persuasively. As Collins and Guetzkow point out, "it is not enough that the information be present; it must also be presented persuasively and legitimately documented before the other group members are likely to accept it."[9] The ability to communicate clearly and persuasively has never been an easily achieved skill, but it may be even more difficult for those of us living in the second half of the twentieth century. Many experts on the subject seem to agree that our language is in an advanced state of decay, and our own observations support that conclusion. Even among those with a college education vocabularies often appear to have degenerated to the point where conversations consist mainly of fillers ("like, you know") and exclamations ("heavy," "far out," "like wow"). As *Time* magazine has observed, "with frightening perversity—the evidence mounts daily—words now seem to cut off and isolate, to cause more misunderstanding than they prevent."[10]

Unfortunately, we have no ready solution to the problem of inadequate expression. Perhaps a starting point is to recognize that language is important, that words do shape the way we think about things, and that the acquisition of communication skills is worth the effort it requires. At any rate, we should make no mistake about it: Without the ability to communicate effectively our success, both as discussion group participants and as human beings, will be severely limited.

WHEN YOU ARE THE LEADER

Leaders have the primary responsibility for what happens in a conference, and under most circumstances they influence heavily the structure, norms, and productiveness of the group. The best leader in most circumstances will be the one who is able to blend his dedication to the task with consideration and compassion for people in covering both the *content* and the *process* of the conference. The following suggestions should help make a leader successful:

1. *Introduce the conference in such a way as to set a tone conducive to the accomplishment of the task.* At a weekly staff meeting where people know one another and work together, the leader may go directly into the agenda. For a training group or task force where members come together for the first time, he may choose to see that all members are introduced or else give the participants some time to interact socially. As in the interview, the leader should begin the conference by explaining the purpose, indicating how the group is to participate, and identifying some specific end products that should be attained.

2. *Guide the conference.* Guidance refers primarily to the leader's influence over the content of the meeting. He guides it initially by the fact that he sets the agenda. But he can also guide it by means of internal sum-

maries, probing questions, and good transitions from one point to the next, and by curtailing digressions that take up time and lead the group far afield.

3. *Stimulate the participants.* "Stimulating means the constant attempt . . . to keep his group interested, motivated, and desirous of participating."[11] Basically, stimulation comes from (1) setting an atmosphere in which all can participate comfortably, (2) asking thought-provoking questions, (3) keeping the group mindful that the conference is relevant to their jobs, and (4) keeping the group moving so that there is a sense of progress toward some goal. Of all the problems groups have, none is more frustrating or more disheartening to participants than to feel that nothing is being accomplished. When this happens, the group would be better off recessing or adjourning, as the following example indicates. A church committee had been meeting for three hours one Sunday afternoon. Tempers were flaring, the discussion had degenerated, and the participants agreed that they were at an impasse. Finally someone suggested that they simply adjourn until the following Sunday. They all agreed, and a number of participants dreaded going to the next meeting. Much to their surprise, however, the discussion proceeded remarkably well and the problems were resolved. Nothing magical had happened, but the intervening time had given the participants a new perspective on what was happening in the group.

4. *Control the group process.* Most conference leaders have some choice as to how much control they will exercise and what forms it will take. Despite our common bias toward "democratic" leadership of discussion groups, there is no one pattern that is going to fit all groups or all conferences. In fact, there are different degrees of "democracy." Figure 12.2 presents a realistic range of possible behaviors available to leaders who have organizational authority.[12] The leader may choose the degree of control he wants to exercise on the basis of four contingencies: (1) his own

Figure 12.2. Continuum of leadership behavior.

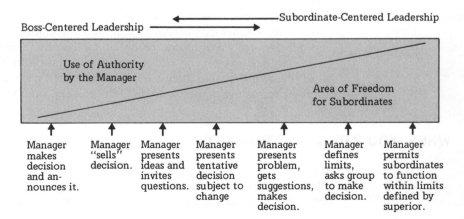

preferences for leadership style, (2) the nature of his participants, (3) the constraints of time and task, and (4) other important situational variables.

Of course these options are not open in any discussion group where leadership has to emerge rather than being superimposed by the organizational context. Nevertheless, common forms of control involve regulating the time spent on a topic, regulating the amount of participation by individuals (i.e., either discouraging those who try to monopolize the discussion or encouraging the silent members to participate), determining how decisions are to be reached, and keeping the discussion orderly and organized.

5. *Clarify the discussion.* Whenever a participant introduces an irrelevant point, the leader will do well to ask the individual to relate his contribution to the group's train of thought. This practice will either get the person to see that his thought is irrelevant at the time or get him to clarify his contribution by relating it in some vital way to the group's thinking. The leader should also be concerned with meaning. When ideas seem unclear he will try to get people to explain themselves or, perhaps, to define key terms that are being used.

An occasional drawing together or summary of what has already been said on a subject will help clarify the group's discussion. The effective group leader will usually make such internal summaries at appropriate moments; however, if he fails to do so it is highly proper for a participant to do it. Finally, outcomes often need clarification. At the end of a conference all members of the group should have a reasonably clear understanding of what information was presented, what was decided upon, or what plan of action was adopted. Thus as the group ends its deliberations the leader may want to state what he thinks the group's decision or attitude seems to be and then let members respond, either by agreeing or by correcting his statement. Participants, especially when they are uncertain about the outcome of the group's deliberations, will do well at the close of the meeting to inquire about decisions and outcomes. Such a final query will usually send each group member away feeling assured that he understands the outcome of the deliberations.

6. *Conclude the conference.* Participants generally defer to the leader, and it is generally a group norm that he be the one to bring things to a close. In so doing, however, he should make sure he describes the progress toward the group goal, explains what is to happen next, and expresses some appreciation to the participants for their time and energy.

WHEN YOU ARE A PARTICIPANT

Many of the behaviors desirable for effective participation have been implied in our previous discussions of human relations, critical thinking, and communication skills. Nevertheless, it is useful to identify some very special aspects of the participant's role, since most of us attend many more conferences than we lead.

1. *Assume some responsibility for the ultimate success or failure of the conference.* Of course the leader has the initial responsibility, but he cannot do it all himself. If he could, there would be no need for the conference.

2. *Prepare thoroughly.* Preparation can take many forms. It involves doing necessary research. In addition, you may want to review some of the minutes of previous meetings to refresh your memory about what has occurred. Come to the meeting prepared to state your point of view as well as possible. This may involve preparing a short presentation, bringing charts or graphs, or writing out questions that should be considered.

The following example told us by a manager indicates the value of thorough preparation:

A company's vice president of engineering was called on the carpet for not meeting schedules and was given one week to review the problem and offer some solutions. He directed his staff to determine the causes of not meeting the schedules, suggest some solutions, and prepare a realistic schedule. We were to meet with him to discuss these before he had a follow-up meeting with the general manager and vice president of programs. At this staff meeting one subordinate provided him exactly what he wanted: a brief summary of the problem, a solution to the problem, and a realistic schedule. Two others walked into the meeting with ten pounds of data each and a lot of excuses. They spent the remainder of the night preparing what he wanted for his 8 A.M. meeting the next day.

3. *Be on time.* In fact, it is often desirable that participants show up a few minutes early either to orient their thinking toward the conference or to socialize with the other participants. One's participation is restricted if one comes in late and does not know what the group has covered. Usually, repetition and a waste of time are the result.

4. *Participate cooperatively.* First, participants should be considerate of what the leader is trying to accomplish. In addition, they should try to express ideas clearly and remember that communication is a joint process that involves listening. Participants need to recognize the rights of others to different points of view and to recognize that groups must sometimes go through a period of real dissension before they can arrive at the best solution. Finally, perhaps the most important aspect of cooperative participation is simply to make sure you do not become a roadblock to the group's progress.

5. *Share leadership.* Leaders are not superhuman; they need all the help they can get from the participants. And running a successful conference can be a big challenge that creates a lot of tension. Moreover, the participant will nearly always be aware of things that the leader misses. For example, issues are left out, some good questions are not raised, some procedures are not followed, or some people in the group who should participate don't. If he is aware of such problems, the participant can perform

a vital leadership function by pointing them out and by helping the group use all its resources.

6. *Be a process observer and keep the ultimate purpose in mind.* Participants should use their knowledge about group processes to gauge the progress of the group in terms of what it needs to accomplish and act accordingly.

THE CHAPTER IN PERSPECTIVE

Productive conferences are a result of good leadership and skillful member participation. Three types of skills are particularly important in a general sense: (1) human relations skills, (2) critical-thinking skills, and (3) communication skills. Conference leaders should begin by setting the overall tone of the meeting and introduce the task in a manner conducive to its accomplishment. As the conference progresses, the leader has the further responsibility of stimulating the participants, using probing questions and drawing silent members into the discussion. It is also vital that he or she control the group process and clarify the discussion, using internal summaries from time to time; the leader should also state what seems to be the final outcome, allowing members to check the statement with their perceptions of the outcome. The leader should end the conference by explaining what is to happen next.

Participants should prepare thoroughly for the meeting, doing necessary research, reviewing minutes of prior meetings, and formulating ideas concerning the subject for discussion. When the conference begins, they should participate cooperatively, always remembering that communication is a two-way process involving listening as well as speaking. Participants need to recognize the rights of others and try, to the best of their ability, to practice the skills mentioned earlier: human relations, critical thinking, and communication.

REFERENCES

1. Robert F. Bales, "How People Interact in Groups," in Alfred G. Smith, *Communication and Culture* (New York: Holt, Rinehart & Winston, 1966), p. 95.

2. Ibid., p. 101.

3. Ibid., p. 102.

4. Ibid.

5. Herbert A. Thelen, *Dynamics of Groups at Work* (Chicago: University of Chicago Press, Phoenix Books, 1954), p. 129.

6. William S. Howell and Donald K. Smith, *Discussion* (New York: Macmillan, 1956), pp. 22–25.

7. Max Black, *Critical Thinking* (Englewood Cliffs, N.J.: Prentice-Hall, 1952), p. 4.

8. William V. Haney, *Communication and Organizational Behavior* (Homewood, Ill.: Irwin, 1973), p. 223.

9. Barry E. Collins and Harold Guetzkow, *A Social Psychology of Group Process for Decision Making* (New York: Wiley, 1964), p. 30.

10. "The Limitations of Language," *Time*, March 8, 1971, p. 36.

11. Harold P. Zelko, "When You Are 'in Conference,'" in Richard C. Huseman, Cal M. Logue, and Dwight L. Freshley, *Readings in Interpersonal and Organizational Communication* (Boston: Holbrook Press, 1973), p. 425.

12. R. Tannenbaum, I. Weschler, and F. Massarik, *Leadership and Organization* (New York: McGraw-Hill, 1961), p. 69.

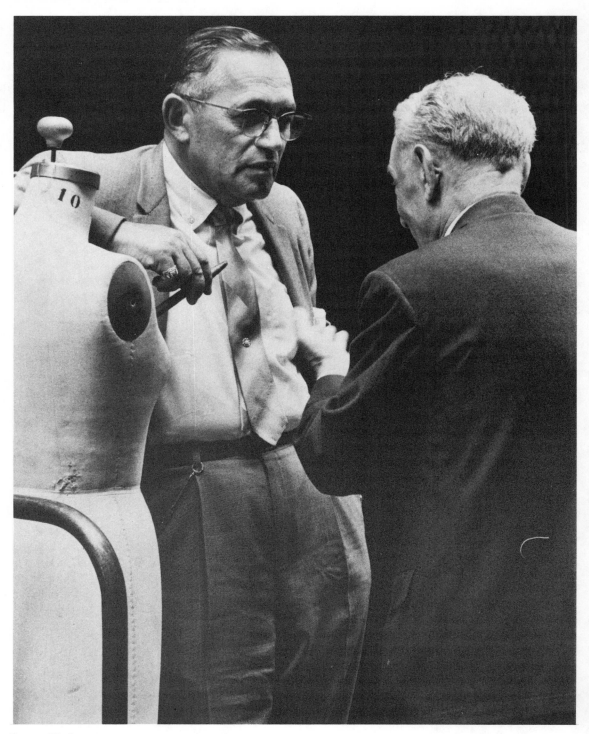

Rogers, Monkmeyer

PART IV
PERSONAL PRESENTATIONS

Although we may spend more time communicating in dyads and small groups than in giving speeches, one cannot overlook the vital role of personal presentations in business and professional settings. As long ago as 1948, S. C. Allyn, president of National Cash Register, acknowledged that "business leadership expresses itself primarily through speech."[1] Somewhat later, the economist Peter Drucker, writing in *Fortune* magazine, pointed out: "Colleges teach the one thing that is perhaps most valuable for the future employee to know. But very few students bother to learn it. This one basic skill is the ability to organize and express ideas in writing and speaking."[2] By 1967 Mark Knapp found that many companies were so concerned about the personal presentation that they intended to offer their employees training in public speaking.[3]

A company official presents data to a stockholders' meeting. The sales manager needs to present sales policies and inspire the sales force. A vice president may want to brief the board of directors on a new product the company plans to manufacture. A company representative may strive for good will as he addresses a public gathering. A research director is called on to present findings at a meeting of a professional society. A salesperson will want to demonstrate equipment at trade shows. These and many other settings call for effective personal presentations.

Our purpose in this part of the book, thus, is to explicate the vital skills and strategies of personal presentations as they apply to different types of messages. The topics covered will be the anatomy of discourse, preparation and presentation, and types of personal address. The reader will readily note that the types of presentations discussed conform markedly to the organizational communication functions set forth in

Chapter 2. The first type of personal address discussed relates to the informative and instructive functions of communication; the second pertains to the demonstrative and integrative functions; and the third involves persuasion.

After reading this part of the book, the reader should be able to

1. analyze an audience and a speaking occasion for the purpose of message adaptation.
2. discuss the anatomy of discourse.
3. demonstrate effective research techniques.
4. prepare and present a message to an audience in an effective manner.
5. discuss important concepts of informative, integrative, and persuasive presentations.
6. prepare and present meaningful informative, integrative, and persuasive presentations.

REFERENCES

1. S. C. Allyn, "Speech and Leadership in Business," *Quarterly Journal of Speech* (April 1948): 36.

2. Peter Drucker, "How to Be an Employee," *Fortune* (May 1952): 126.

3. Mark Knapp, *An Investigation and Analysis of Public Speaking in America's Largest Business and Industrial Organizations*, unpublished Ph.D. dissertation, Pennsylvania State University, 1967.

CHAPTER 13

THE ANATOMY
OF DISCOURSE

Preview

Personal presentations are used extensively in most organizations.

A speech should be adapted to the environment and to the audience.

The basic anatomy of a presentation consists of:

- An introduction that focuses attention
- An orientation to the subject
- A development of main ideas
- A conclusion that makes an impact

Long ago the Greek philosopher Plato compared human discourse to a living organism. "Every discourse, like a living creature," Plato wrote in the *Phaedrus*, "should be so put together that it has a body of its own and lacks neither head nor feet, a middle or extremities, all composed in such a way that they suit both each other and the whole." Taking this metaphor as a point of departure for this chapter, we will examine the three basic parts of personal presentations: introduction, body, and conclusion. Just as the living organism must adapt to its environment to survive, the speech must be adapted to situational constraints. Thus we will discuss basic principles regarding the anatomy of discourse in relation to audience and setting.

ADAPTING TO THE ENVIRONMENT

The archer never shoots an arrow in a random direction but aims it carefully at a specific target. His form and technique in delivering the arrow acquire meaning only as they assist him in gaining accuracy in hitting the bull's-eye. So it is with speakers, messages, and audiences. Inexperienced speakers often make a basic mistake when they are called upon to address an audience. Their inclination is to begin at once to prepare their message without regard for the listeners to whom the message is to be given. The experienced speaker, by contrast, thinks about the receivers of his message before he plans any part of his presentation. *Messages are created for the purpose of generating meaning in the minds of people.* Unless this thought is kept paramount, it is altogether possible to prepare and present a tightly developed presentation that may please the speaker but miss the audience almost fully.

1. *Members of an audience, large or small, attend meetings and speech occasions with expectations*—sometimes called an a *priori* set. At times their expectations are clearly defined, while at others they are less clear. In some instances they may be seeking specific kinds of information; they may want to impress their colleagues in some way, or they may want to spend time away from an odious task. At other moments they may be motivated by sheer curiosity, or they may attend because they are required to be there. Nevertheless, as pointed out in Chapter 3, each person has a motive in relation to the occasion, the message, and the personal relationship. The person who is attending because it is compulsory may, for example, be trying to prove to himself that the meeting is a waste of time, and will therefore approach it with negative expectations. Regardless of the motives of those in attendance at a professional event, it is vital that the speaker realize that his listeners will have motives regarding the event. Then he can conjecture about these motives on the basis of available evidence and prepare his message accordingly. William V. Haney has written:

> If one is to communicate with others, serve as a subordinate, manage others, and the like, he must have *some kind of theory*—valid or not, conscious or not—about human motivations and relationships. Otherwise he will be unable to function at all. If we are to control or to influence behavior—our own at any rate—we must be capable of predicting reasonably accurately the responses of others—and of ourselves.[1]

If a listener expects to obtain vital information but receives none, he will leave dissatisfied. If he expects to hear a careful analysis of advantages and disadvantages of a plan of action but hears only general comments, he will judge the speaker as inadequate. If he is in search of new ideas but hears only rehash of the old, he will think the meeting worthless. If someone desires clarification of concepts but encounters only an opaque and skimpy explanation, he is likely to leave in disgust.

2. *People bring points of view to a speech occasion.* In the first place, we should recognize that every member of the audience will hold attitudes about a great variety of things, be they social, political, economic, educational, or spiritual. These attitudes, which shape the individual's value priorities, are his personal guides to thought and behavior. He may vote Republican because he feels that Republican policies are best for business. He may feel that personal success should be measured primarily by economic means. He may feel that colleges and universities have gotten much too lax in their standards. These attitudes constitute the filters through which a person receives information or responds to persuasive appeal.

Just as important, members of the listening audience tend to bring points of view about the speaker and his subject to the communication event. Listeners may, for example, have a high degree of trust and confidence in the speaker's knowledge and ability. If so, his task is easy. All he needs to do is make a clear presentation. But if an audience is unsure about the speaker's grasp of his materials, he must carefully demonstrate the depth and scope of his knowledge about the subject. He should relate himself to the subject during his introduction and in that way let the audience know the extent of his experience. We often call this "setting forth one's credentials." Concomitantly, listeners hold points of view toward the subject. On the one hand, if listeners have very few preformed views about the subject, or if they are relatively neutral toward it, the speaker can concentrate on presenting as much material as possible. On the other hand, if listeners hold a strong and unified point of view about the subject, the speaker must be prepared to relate to and deal with that point of view. The biggest problem occurs when people bring strong and diverse points of view to the meeting. Then the speaker has the demanding task of not only dealing with multiple points of view but also trying to unify the group in some way.

3. *Members of an audience have distractions.* The busy schedules and complex activities resulting from our modern, multidirectional way of life make sustained attention difficult. Hundreds of factors are vying for our attention at any given moment. One person may be concerned about the report he needs to complete the next day. Another is worried about some difficulty he is having with a teenage daughter. A third is worried about what the boss really meant when he said the company might have to cut back on personnel. Such distractions give rise to private dialog and planning in the mind of the listener. While a speaker is presenting a message to him, the receiver may permit his mind to dart off and plan how he is going to proceed further with his research study or finish writing his report, or how he can arrange to attend a convention and keep his family happy at the same time.

Physical factors may also distract. One person may be hungry because he had to skip lunch. Another may have a bad cold that he seemingly can't shake. Someone else has a headache from the strain and tension of his office activity. In each of these cases the body is vying for the mind's attention. Not all the physical distractions come from within; some come from the environment. The room may be too hot or too cold. Noises of various kinds may make hearing difficult in certain parts of the room. The room may be too crowded and the seats uncomfortable. The speaker may be able to control, or at least alleviate, some of the external distractions and should do so whenever possible. If the room is too hot, he may be able to turn down the thermostat. And he may be able to shut out a lot of noise by closing a window. All the same, the speaker must compete with most of the listeners' distractions through interest value in his presentation. One can say that it is the speaker's task to distract the listeners from their distractions and focus their attention on the subject at hand. Attention-holding materials are thus vital to effective speaker-to-group communication.

4. *Members of an audience have varying listening skills.* Some may be good listeners and may be readily able to follow difficult and abstract materials; yet many are likely to be poor listeners. Effective listening is a difficult task. While reading, we may momentarily lose our concentration and fail to comprehend the material of the last two pages; but we can easily skim over those pages again. As listeners, we cannot afford that luxury; we must get it the first time. If our motivation to listen is high, we find it easy to sustain attention. But whenever we have to exert effort to concentrate on what is being said, if we are like most people, we can sustain adequate attention for no more than 15 minutes; from that point on, our attention tends to diminish rapidly. Poor communication commonly results from a presentation that lasts 45 minutes or more. A skillful oral communicator will therefore present a large body of material in short segments. For example, he may present a 15-minute segment of a report and then use another communication channel, perhaps slides or other visuals. Often merely allowing for a short question-and-answer period periodically throughout a long presentation helps sustain attention.

It is equally important for a speaker to present difficult and abstract materials in a concrete and graphic manner, for listeners are notoriously poor at retaining information, unless the information is related to something with which they have great familiarity—the fundamental principle of all mnemonic devices. Retention is also assisted if the material is presented to listeners through more than one sense receptor. Robert S. Craig of the U.S. Public Health Service reported at a national osteopathic child health conference in Atlanta a few years ago that "when knowledge was imparted to a person by telling alone, the recall three hours later was 70 percent, and three days later, only 10 percent." He further reported that when showing alone was used, "the knowledge recall three hours later was 72 percent, and three days later, about 35 percent." However, he reported studies showing that when both telling and showing were the teaching tools the recall three hours later was 85 percent and three days later 65 percent.[2] The lesson to be learned here is obvious: People gain far more information from concrete and multisensory presentations than from abstract and single-sensory messages. Presentations utilizing more than one sense assist people in overcoming their listening problems.

Realizing (1) that members of an audience have a *priori* expectations about the communication event, (2) that they will probably bring points of view about the speaker and his subject to the meeting, (3) that they are subject to distractions, and (4) that they have questionable listening skills, it becomes imperative that a skillful communicator assess these vital characteristics of the people he expects to address. He will try to make the subject meaningful in terms of listeners' expectations; he will strive to make his ideas clear and easy to follow; and he will endeavor to make his materials credible to the people receiving his message. The speech principles in this chapter should be approached from this perspective. The construction of the speech and the materials chosen for presentation should occur in relation to the audience addressed and the subject to be discussed. The anatomy of discourse, like all organisms, must adapt to its environment. Only a careful analysis of the listening audience can produce the proper adaptation.

BEGINNING THE PRESENTATION

One obviously must establish some initial contact with the audience, whether one does this through some formal greeting such as "Ladies and Gentlemen," "Members of the Board," or "Mr. Chairman and Fellow Delegates," whether one moves directly into the materials one wishes to present, or whether one observes the time-honored tripartite division of a speech—introduction, body, conclusion—and begins with an attention-getting, interest-arousing introduction. The beginning of a personal presentation should always be adapted to the purpose and subject of the address, the occasion of the speech, and the audience's predisposition to the speaker. If one is briefing a superior, be it for the purpose of information or decision, it is most unlikely that beginning with a human interest story is wise strategy. On the other hand, if one is addressing a public gathering, starting with human interest materials is usually advisable. For example, when addressing a group of company employees who have little interest in the speaker's subject, it is vital that one begin by gaining their attention and making them want to listen. Moreover, if the listeners are hostile to the speaker or harbor strong negative feelings about the subject, he must spend time gaining good will and rendering his hearers favorably disposed to what he has to say. Thus it is apparent that the answer to the question of how one should begin a presentation is not a simple one. Hence, we will identify general principles for speech introductions that can be readily adapted and modified to fit most speaking occasions.

The most basic function of the introduction is to *provide an entry into the main body of speech materials*. It usually does this by disclosing the theme of the presentation, and sometimes it limits the scope of the address and perhaps states the purpose. As indicated earlier, on some occasions the speaker may proceed very directly. Let's say he is an Army major briefing a colonel about the current status of ROTC on college campuses. He may begin quite simply:

Sir. My purpose today is to brief you regarding the status of ROTC on our nation's college campuses. I will proceed in three phases: First, I will report on enrollment trends of the last five years. Second, I will relate studies regarding the quality of training provided by ROTC as preparation for military careers. And third, I will point out what seem to be the leading problems confronting our ROTC programs today.

Ira G. Corn, Jr., chief executive officer of Michigan General, addressing the National Institute in Dallas, began his talk on tax reform in the following direct manner:

> In this particular talk I shall suggest a specific program to restore a favorable investment climate. Some aspects of this program are a challenge, so I ask you to consider it all as a package. This program involves, among other things, a higher personal income tax, a lower capital gains tax, a new approach to investment credit based upon taxes before application of investment credit, continuation of tax-free bonds, a return of interest from a fully deductible expense and a continuing use of special tax preferences. Now the logic to support this program.[3]

An executive might begin a briefing of a board of directors in a similar manner, initiating the statement with "Gentlemen" or "Members of the Board."

Other communication situations may call for a more extensive introduction focusing on interest factors or background material. In order to call attention to some of the options available, we shall examine a few introductions and analyze the tactics each speaker uses to establish interest in his speech and generate concern for his subject.

1. The first one is by Mark Hatfield, Republican senator from Oregon, speaking on "Noise."

> There is a bumper sticker now circulating which says: "Eliminate Pollution Before Pollution Eliminates You." Immediately we will think of studies which threaten a lack of water by 1980 and conjure up the words of California scientists stating that within 50 years their state will be uninhabitable for any form of life. Or we hold our breath for a moment remembering that 142 million tons of smoke and noxious fumes are dumped into the atmosphere each year. Momentarily we feel brief panic and then for one reason or another, we forget the threatening words of the bumper sticker and go about our daily duties in a comfortable shield of self-deception and false security. Unfortunately such an attitude has now brought us to a situation in which the rapidly deteriorating quality of our environment is the most hazardous challenge to not only our health and well-being but to our very lives and those of our children and grandchildren.
>
> Environmental pollution may not pose the immediate destruction that nuclear war does, but I might remind you that the effects are the same and just as lasting. And I might remind you that destruction at the hands of our environment is as immediate as your and my lifetime. And finally, I might remind you that lack of inhabitable land, lack of food, lack of good water to drink and good air to breathe are the very conditions under which men become desperate and resort to any and all means to preserve their survival. It is with these thoughts in mind that I state my firm conviction that pollution—all forms of pollution: air, water, and noise pollution, overpopulation, land and soil pollution—is the most challenging and the most crucial problem facing the man of the twentieth century. And it is with these thoughts in mind that I firmly believe that if we do not meet this problem with all the creativity and ingenuity of our age, then within a very short time nothing else will matter, for there will be nothing else to worry about.[4]

Senator Hatfield's introduction illustrates several rhetorical concepts. In the first place, it opens with the catchy bumper sticker slogan, "Eliminate

Pollution Before Pollution Eliminates You." This is the type of epigram that captures people's imaginations. Immediately Senator Hatfield has a degree of interest in his speech. He follows this with several threatening statements about the lack of water by 1980, an uninhabitable California within 50 years, and the 142 million tons of smoke and noxious fumes that are dumped into our atmosphere annually. These statements are designed to point up the *vital nature of his subject*. However, since these statements have little immediate effect on us beyond a degree of mental discomfort, Hatfield says, we tend to go about our business and wrap ourselves in a comfortable shield of false security. Hence, in the second paragraph he tries to impress upon his listeners the fact that pollution has the potential to destroy the elements on which life itself depends—it can do this with the potency of nuclear destruction. Hatfield now has pointed up the importance of his subject and has generated a *need to listen*. Then the senator leads into a statement of his subject. Thus Hatfield has used an attention-getting quotation, built a need to listen by impressing the audience with the importance of his subject, and smoothly divulged his topic.

2. The second introduction is by Frederic W. West, Jr., president of Bethlehem Steel, speaking at Town Hall in Los Angeles on the fight against inflation.

Stewart Cort, who retired as chairman of my company at the end of July, addressed Town Hall three years ago, almost to the day. You might recall that he borrowed his theme from Thomas Jefferson, quoting Jefferson's appeal to the people to "unite in common efforts for the common good."

It was good advice in 1801; it was good advice in 1971; it's good advice today. And thinking about my own talk, I decided to follow Mr. Cort's lead and look to one of our Founding Fathers for inspiration. It makes even more sense today, with the Bicentennial drawing closer.

So I've borrowed my theme from George Washington. Not *President* Washington, but *General* Washington, before he became president; in fact, before the patriots declared independence in my old home town of Philadelphia.

The words I have in mind are from one of Washington's messages to the Continental Congress. The General was near the end of his rope. His army was ill-equipped, unpaid and mutinous. They'd taken one beating after another. Things looked grim, and Washington asked, "Does anybody care?"

I'm sure you remember that question if you saw the play or movie versions of "1776." They wrote a song about it, "Does Anybody Care?"

Nearly two hundred years have gone by. Our problems are different than they were in 1776, but they're just as serious. And Washington's question still applies: Does anybody care? Does anybody care about some of the things that are going on? I mean things that are pushing our economy in exactly the wrong direction.

For example, does anybody care about inflation—the kind of double digit inflation that's been causing so much trouble?[5]

West's introduction is very different from Hatfield's. He feels no need to point up the importance of his subject, assuming that inflation is a topic vital to everyone in 1974. Instead, he begins by referring to a prior speech quoting Thomas Jefferson. This reference allows him to make a smooth transition to a quotation that he wants to use as the theme of his presentation—General Washington's question, "Does anybody care?" We can learn several things from West's approach. In the first place, *short, pointed quotations* are good interest-arousing materials in the introduction of a speech. The quotation, however, must be short, succinct, and provocative. Beginning a speech with a long quotation is usually deadly.

The second thing we can learn from Frederic West is that we may begin by referring to a historical event. West refers to a speech delivered in the same meeting hall three years earlier. This reference allows him to introduce Jefferson's quotation and get the flow of his presentation started. References to historical events are commonly used at the outset of a speech.

In addition to the use of short quotations and historical reference, there are two other tactics Frederic West uses in his introduction that are worth noting. Observe how effectively he refers to a recent event when he says, "I'm sure you remember that question if you saw the play or movie version of '1776.' They wrote a song about it, 'Does Anybody Care?'" Any such *references to recent happenings* usually add a touch of interest to a speech. Finally, we should appreciate the possibility of using a short quotation such as Washington's "Does anybody care?" as a theme for a speech. Speech themes phrased as succinct quotations tend to be memorable for the listener.

3. The third introduction we want to look at is one given by Dr. Simon Ramo, vice chairman of the board and chairman of the executive committee of TRW. Dr. Ramo spoke on "The Coming Social-Industrial Complex" at the University of Houston in 1971.

When I was a student more than a third of a century ago there would occasionally be a guest lecturer on campus to impart wisdom on some important subject and connect my brain with the real world on the outside. I confess that I can recall neither any specific individual nor a single lecture subject. This was probably because something else was very much on my mind—this much I certainly remember. It was how in the world, and when, would I get a job after graduating? There was a depression on then and no one was hiring graduates in engineering and science or business or anything else.

Also, an anti-technology wave was rolling over us. I recollect being an intramural debater in my senior year with one subject being "Resolved: The Engineers Caused the Depression." Another engineering student and I got all the way to the finals, defeating debaters from various liberal arts, physical education, and home economics schools and the like, but losing out to two fast talkers from the law school. They said the world suffered from too much technology, that thoughtless application of it, neglecting the human factor, was ruining the society. The depression was only one manifestation. Their climax was that engineers designed automatic factories that threw people out of work. In fearless, confident rebuttal, we argued that lawyers, who arranged contracts that commit to create automation systems, were just as socially responsible or irresponsible as engineers who perform on those contract obligations, assuming even that automation systems were bad for the society. But we lost the debate. Perhaps we weren't such good debaters. Engineers then as now were all well known to be inarticulate. Besides, what if we had won the debate—we still didn't have jobs on graduation.

Perhaps you see some parallels with today's situation. After a third of a century we finally have worked the society back to anti-technology and a scarcity of new jobs for graduates. But there are some great differences between then and now.[7]

Dr. Ramo opens his speech with a *personal experience*. Relevant personal experiences are invariably good speech materials and seem to be especially useful in introductions. For one thing, personal experience relates the speaker to the subject, thus enhancing his personal credibility. In addition, personal experience comes in the form of a story, and stories tend to be interesting. Thus beginning a speech with an illustration, personal or otherwise, provides a strong human interest dimension. Dr. Ramo uses his personal experience as a *parallel case*—or *analogy*—with the contemporary situation that he wishes to address. He hopes this analogy will help his listeners see the wisdom of his remarks.

4. The fourth introduction is brief but instructive. It comes from a speech by John A. Howard, president of Rockford College, on the need for traditional liberal arts.

Two caterpillars were crawling across a lawn one day when a handsome butterfly flew overhead. One caterpillar was heard to remark to the other, "Some folks may think that's the way to live, but you couldn't get me up in one of those flimsy things for a million dollars."

This morning I want to share with you some thoughts about liberal arts education, which appears to be carrying on very much like the grumpy caterpillar just quoted. The potential is there, but the creature, seemingly ignorant of its potential, is somewhat obtuse in its thinking and earthbound in its performance.[8]

Dr. Howard begins his speech with a *situation:* two caterpillars crawling across a lawn with a butterfly flying overhead. This may not make for high drama, but it does arouse curiosity and create an air of expectancy. The quotation that follows has sufficent irony and humor so that it evokes a slight chuckle and makes one wonder what direction the speaker is going to go after that story. A situational beginning borrows from the repertoire of the novelist. O. Henry, for example, begins his story "Tommy's Burglar" with this sentence: "At ten o'clock P.M. Felicia, the maid, left by the basement door with the policeman to get a raspberry phosphate around the corner."[9] The time of day, the domestic position of Felicia, the basement door, the identification of her companion as a policeman, the mission, and the destination all strongly suggest that vital action is to follow and thereby gain one's attention.

In a second short paragraph Dr. Howard does an excellent job of setting up the subject of his speech by relating it to the grumpy, earthbound caterpillar. This introduction illustrates how swiftly a speaker can generate at least a degree of interest in the minds of listeners with a short, well-designed introduction.

5. The final introduction we want to cite is taken from a speech given by one of the best public speakers of our time. President John F. Kennedy, who was well known for his pungent wit and humor, began his speech in Miami at the opening of an AFL-CIO convention as follows:

> I'm delighted to be here with you and with Secretary of Labor Arthur Goldberg. I was up in New York stressing physical fitness, and in line with that Arthur went over with a group to Switzerland to climb some of the mountains there. They all got up about 5 and he was in bed—got up to join them later—and when they all came back at 4 o'clock in the afternoon, he didn't come back with them. They sent out search parties and there was no sign of him that afternoon or night. Next day the Red Cross went out and they went around calling "Goldberg—Goldberg—it's the Red Cross." And this voice came down the mountain, "I gave at the office."[10]

Humor is one of the most common devices used to begin a speech. If used effectively, as we think it is used here, it arouses listener interest and gains good will for the speaker. Yet we offer a word of caution. Not all speeches need to begin with humor. Too many speakers have the idea that one cannot begin a speech without telling a few of the latest jokes. Not everyone can relate humorous anecdotes effectively, and worse yet, far too often "the latest jokes" aren't funny—or have already been heard. Humor, to be effective, needs to be appropriate to the audience and occasion and, just as important, to be pertinent to the subject.

The length of the introduction should of course depend on the needs of the moment: Some speech topics require longer introductions than others; some occasions require the speaker to make appropriate references to the event or to other dignitaries present; some audiences need more warming up than others. Seldom are introductions too long—especially student introductions. Time spent in presenting a well-prepared, carefully polished introduction to one's speech is usually time well spent. It not only gains attention but also begins the speech on an impressive note.

REVEALING THE SUBJECT

As a rule it is best to divulge one's subject specifically and directly in business and professional speeches. In some instances of persuasion, as books on the subject often advise, it may be best to proceed inductively and present issues and data prior to telling the audience what one's stance is regarding the subject; at the same time, we know of very few instances in business and professional settings when the added clarity and comprehension that tend to result from a direct statement of theme early in the speech are not desirable. The introduction should lead directly into a statement of the theme, like the following introduction used by attorney James M. Thomas, speaking to the Savannah Optimist Club on politics and politicians:

Obviously, I am here to talk about politics and politicians. What I seek is a re-examination of the quality and purpose of political leadership in America and the standards by which the citizenry may judge them. In essence I shall be speaking of what Tacitus would call "statecraft."[11]

Fabian Linden, director of consumer research for the Conference Board, opens his speech on consumer spending with a brief introduction setting up his topic and then discloses his subject:

In looking to 1980, it is fashionable for public speakers these days to proclaim that the changes in the Seventies will be far greater than in any comparable past period. My message this morning is also that the changes in the Seventies will be far greater than in any comparable past period. And what's more, I believe it. For convenience, the subjects I plan to review can be grouped under three headings—demographic changes, social changes, economic changes— though, evidently, there will be some overlapping.[12]

In addition to noting how Linden discloses his subject, a second dimension of his statement warrants attention. After he has made it clear that the changes in consumer spending in the 1970s will be far greater than in any comparable period, he partitions his subject into three topics or compartments: demographic changes, social changes, and economic changes. This forecast of the body of the speech greatly assists the listener in gaining a perspective on the address and helps him follow and remember it.

Quite often a speaker not only will state his theme at the outset of his address but will proceed to limit and define what it is he intends to cover. Grayson Kirk, formerly president of Columbia University, limits the scope of his topic.

Tonight I have been asked to talk with you about the responsibilities of the educated man. This, in itself, is no small canvas on which to sketch a few fragmentary ideas—and to do so in that span of time between this moment and that speaker's warning signal when the first stifled yawn in this audience is observed. Therefore, to reduce the canvas to a manageable size, let me say that I propose merely to talk about some of those responsibilities that ought to emerge from, and partially to be a product of an exposure to *formal* higher education. I say, "ought to emerge" because we all know that no formal education can guarantee that the graduate will in fact have all, or any, of the qualities I propose to mention. There are different kinds of responsibilities and different levels of responsibility, and some of our friends who hold an array of degrees appear to have managed with great skill to avoid both. Also, I have used the term, "formal education," because I would like to focus our thinking upon the task of the college and university in that brief segment of a student's life which it can influence. When the student has become an alumnus, the University virtually has finished its effective effort toward his education. It may still be able to educate him about the virtues of philanthropy, but that is about the limit of what it can do in later years.[13]

Often it is useful to define a critical term used in one's topic statement. This practice should be followed whenever there is any question as to whether the audience fully comprehends the terms. One of our favorite speeches is one that was given by a student, Ernie Link, on project Head

Start. Having disclosed his subject, Link wants to be sure his hearers understand what he means by disadvantaged children.

Perhaps you are wondering what I have in mind when I speak of disadvantaged children. Exactly what is a disadvantaged child? Is he a child who lives in an urban slum area, a child who has a number of siblings and only a mother to support them? Is he a child who lives in the hills of Kentucky or Tennessee and has never seen a city, a zoo, a museum, even a train or a bus? Is he a child who lives in a rural area of New England and attends a one-room school with children from grades one through eight, a child who has never walked in a park or ridden on a bus, who has been no farther than his grandparents' house 40 miles away? Disadvantaged children could be any of these things, but the one common element is that they are the victims of social and economic misfortune. They are affected by environmental factors that limit their aspirations and achievements. William E. Amos, Chief of the Division of Youth Employment and Guidance Service of the United States Employment Service, defines the disadvantaged as "those who have heavy liabilities which lessen their chances for competing successfully with their fellow citizens in all phases of life."[14]

Link's definition is quite clever. Instead of routinely presenting a dictionary type of definition, he begins with a series of questions designed to give breadth and scope to the problem he plans to discuss. At the same time, the questions vividly depict what kinds of children are often disadvantaged. It is only at the conclusion of his definition that he gives a concise statement of what is meant by disadvantaged, drawing on a quotation from William E. Amos. Quoting Amos not only defines the term but also gives an authority base to Link's definition of *disadvantaged*.

DEVELOPING THE BODY OF THE DISCOURSE

Just as the human body is governed by nerve impulses from the brain, a speech has a central controlling idea. This central idea, often called the *theme*, is developed through a series of supporting ideas or main points. Thus the main body of the speech should develop a series of supporting ideas, relating these to each other and to the central thrust of the presentation. In the remainder of this chapter, therefore, we shall be concerned with idea development and arrangement.

IDEA DEVELOPMENT Some presentations, such as a talk on the function of a new accounting system, have explanation as the entire thrust of the address. Even though other speeches may have persuasion as their objective, explanation plays a vital supportive role. Regardless of the speaker's purpose, ideas, above all else, need to be explained.

1. *Good explanation is clear and complete.* However, it need not and should not be dull. Our favorite example of explanation comes from a

speech that is very old. It was given in 1866 by Thomas Henry Huxley, speaking on the "Method of Scientific Investigation." Here Huxley explains the process of induction to his audience.

Suppose you go into a fruiterer's shop, wanting an apple—you take one up, and, on biting, you find it is sour; you look at it, and see that it is hard and green. You take another one and that too is hard, green, and sour. The shopman offers you a third; but, before biting it, you examine it, and find that it is hard and green, and you immediately say that you will not have it, as it must be sour, like those that you have already tried.

Nothing can be more simple than that, you think; but if you will take the trouble to analyze and trace out into its logical elements what has been done by the mind, you will be greatly surprised. In the first place, you have performed the operation of induction. You found that, in two experiences, hardness and greenness in apples went together with sourness. It was so in the first case, and it was confirmed by the second. True, it is a very small basis, but still it is enough to make an induction from; you generalize the facts, and you expect to find sourness in apples where you get hardness and greenness.[15]

2. *Illustrations, both hypothetical and real-life stories, can hardly be overused in a speech.* Well chosen and well presented, they are always interesting; they clarify and intensify the speaker's meaning and increase the credibility of the idea. Huxley is well aware of this and begins his explanation with a hypothetical illustration, "Suppose you go into a fruiterer's shop, wanting an apple . . ." This illustration allows the audience to involve itself directly in what the speaker is saying and makes the thought concrete through a comparison. An everyday happening, such as biting into an apple, is the vehicle for getting the nineteenth-century lay audience to understand the scientific process of induction.

3. *Contrast is another device often used to explain, clarify, and sharpen the impact of a point.* For an example, we turn to a speech given by Jean Dohrer, a student. Speaking in behalf of a new Indian policy, Dohrer tries to make vivid certain differences between Indian and white children in order to demonstrate that current educational practices impose white thought habits upon Indian youth.

The modern white child is ruled by the clock. He must attend school before a certain time or he is deemed tardy; he eats lunch around 12 o'clock and recess (time to do anything but study) occurs only at midmorning and midafternoon. He finishes studies at around three-thirty in the afternoon and anticipates supper around five. Some time after supper is usually set aside for homework, and bedtime arrives sometime after eight o'clock. But in the Sioux language there isn't even a word for *now, tomorrow, time.* The Indian eats when he is hungry, he sleeps when he is tired and is regulated by his physiological and psychological needs rather than by society. Indian time is indefinite; it is spoken of in terms of moons rather than by seconds, minutes, and hours. Few school curricula take this cultural differentiation into account when they label the Indian students as being slow, lazy, and tardy. We may, then define Indian education as the imposition of white American educational institutions upon American Indian communities—and never the twain shall meet.[16]

Dohrer's use of direct contrast sharpens her point. Without the contrast, the impact of her point would be substantially less.

4. *Business and professional presentations often require the use of certain technical jargon.* To be sure, such jargon should be kept at a minimum and used only when absolutely necessary. But when you find it necessary to use jargon, be sure your audience understands your terminology. A good rule of thumb is to explain and define all difficult terms that you think might prove sticky to the listener. In private conversation we often pause in our discussion and ask, "What do you mean by that?" But members of an audience will seldom do that. The speaker thus should assume the initiative in asking himself what he means by his terms and providing appropriate explanations. Sometimes a dictionary definition will suffice; often rephrasing the statement will make it clear; but at other times you may need a more extended definition. Note how Martin Luther King explains what he means by a just law in a speech on "Love, Law, and Civil Disobedience."

> Well, a just law is a law that squares with a moral law. It is a law that squares with that which is right, so that any law that uplifts human personality is a just law. Whereas that law which is out of harmony with the moral is a law which does not square with the moral law of the universe. It does not square with the law of God, so for that reason it is unjust and any law that degrades the human personality is an unjust law.[17]

King uses contrast to make vivid his concept of a just law. But sometimes negation is used to good effect. Lauralee Peters, a student, uses this technique in a speech on totalitarianism.

> To begin with, totalitarianism does not mean simply any government which is not democratic in nature. To employ such a definition for the term would render it completely meaningless, for to be sure there are many forms of non-democratic rule in our present day world. Nor does the term *totalitarianism* denote any dictatorship. The dictatorships, for example, of most of South America and South East Asia, overthrown with great regularity as they are, reflect, not a totalitarian state, but a situation of intensified political struggle among the members of the power elite of the nation. What then does it mean?[18]

The devices we have discussed so far sharpen and make vivid the ideas the speaker is trying to develop. A second level of rhetorical devices, used primarily in persuasive speeches, is used to make an idea credible. Sometimes we refer to these devices as *proof* or *evidence*. Regardless of the terminology used, credibility devices serve the dual purpose of clarification and documentation. Such devices stem from a number of sources. Two of the most vital are the specific and the general. By the specific is meant the example, and by the general, statistical quantification. Usually it is strategic to use the specific and the general in concert: The example makes the idea concrete by referring to actual instances; statistics give breadth and scope to the idea. If one were to argue that the American Red

Cross is an effective social agency, one could do this by describing a specific instance of its assistance—for example, a family victimized by a flood. This example would make vivid what the impact of the Red Cross assistance can be. The idea being developed could then be given scope by citing statistics showing how many other families were similarly helped by the Red Cross.

ORDERING IDEAS

1. *The order of one's points sometimes has little significance.* On some subjects and on some occasions, it matters little which idea is presented first, which second, and which last. At the same time, instances do arise when it is strategic to order one's points in a definite sequence. Clarity may demand that a subject be unfolded one way as opposed to another. If one is to explain how the company's suggestion system works, it is useful to unfold the method the company uses in processing every suggestion received. Moreover, in a persuasive speech it may be wise to take up one point ahead of another because of the effect it may have on listener receptivity to the message. In every case, one is wise to look for the most logical and the most strategic order for arranging one's points.

2. *The subject itself often suggests the best pattern of arrangement.* Many subjects can be broken down into natural or intrinsic categories, as is the case, for example, with the topic "higher education," which can easily be divided into teaching, research, and service. In addition to such natural divisions of subjects, certain stock patterns or partitioning designs can often be used. For example:

Theory and practice	Political, economic, and social
Structure and function	Symptoms, cure, and prevention
Resemblances and differences	Top to bottom
Specific and general	East to west
Past, present, and future	Physical, mental, and spiritual

Whatever the division of the subject or the order in which the points are arranged, the important thing is to design and structure one's presentation according to some definite and strategic plan. Business and professional presentations normally require a high degree of clarity of thought, and careful arrangement is integral to this end.

3. *A vital aspect of arrangement is the transition, or the thought bridge that links one idea to another.* Good transitions are vital to the flow and continuity of the speech. Each point needs to be rounded off and related to that which follows. Too often points are left suspended as though in midair, with no way of coming down; the speaker jumps from one point to the next, never concluding a point, never tying the speech together. We turn to a speech by Dr. Karl Menninger, an eminent psychiatrist, for an illustration of terminating a point. After developing the observation that

mental illness is something that may occur—in some degree—in the lives of all of us, he contrasts mental illness with physical disease and terminates the point.

> This, of course, is not quite like the notion of some physical diseases. One can have many degrees of arthritis. But one either *has* malaria or does not have it. The same is true with many other diseases. But in the case of mental illness, it seems that any of us can—indeed all of us *do*—have some degree of it, at some times. That is my first observation. Now for a second observation.[19]

Sometimes transitions may be simple and abrupt. Menninger moved from his first point to his second with the concise statement, "That is my first observation. Now for the second observation." This transition is not terribly poetic, but it is functional in that it lets the audience know what's happening in the speech. Examples of other transitions might be: "Thus the results of the first experiment are somewhat uncertain. However, the results of the second experiment leave no room for doubt." "Our city certainly faces an impelling problem. My solution to the problem, however, is a simple one." Often an internal summary telling the auditor what has already been covered, followed by a forecast of the next point, is helpful: "Now that we have seen that capital punishment is barbarian revenge and that it sometimes executes the innocent, let's see if it acts as a deterrent to crime, as is sometimes alleged." In sum, transitions are the parts of the anatomy of a speech that tie the other parts together and help them function, not as separate entities but as integral parts of the whole.

4. An outline of a single idea of a speech may look like the following:

I. Ambition and desire are necessary ingredients of success.
   A. Howard H. Kendlen, noted psychologist and author of *Basic Psychology*, says, "Without ambition one has little power, accomplishes little and has little respect."
   B. Without ambition Bill Bradley could not have been a three-time All-American basketball player and a Rhodes scholar.
   C. Without desire John Walker could not have run a 3:49.4 mile.
   D. Sometimes exceptionally talented football players are relatively ineffective because they lack desire.
      1. They may lack desire because they are overpaid.
      2. They may lack desire because they have no goals.
   E. Eddie Stanky, a highly successful baseball player, was once described as a slow runner, a bad fielder, and a poor hitter.
   F. The same principle holds true in salesmanship.
      1. Jimmy Jones is an example of a salesman in our company who never had a really big day in selling but never had a bad day either—he hustled all the time.
         a. He may not have as much natural selling ability as a lot of our salesmen.
         b. But because of intense effort his sales totals are always good.

    2. Fred Green aspired to improve his sales total each year.
        a. He became the number one salesman of the company.
        b. He is now vice president of the company.
G. It is thus not hard to see what roles ambition and desire play in salesmanship. They are necessary ingredients for success.

ENDING THE PRESENTATION

Speeches should be brought to a strategic close instead of just stopping. To illustrate vital characteristics of effective conclusions, we turn to a speech on the need for international cooperation by J. K. Jamieson, chairman of the board of Exxon.

An international approach has the best opportunity to meet the stringent criteria for solution to this problem: First, funds must flow to consuming countries in rough proportion to their oil-related trade deficits. Second, a substantial proportion of the producer country surpluses must be converted from short to long-term claims. Finally, the transfer of funds must be accomplished without adding undue instability in foreign exchange markets.

So we have to deal with supplies and prices, both current and for the long-term. We have to develop resources. We have an enormous world balance-of-payments problem. All this constitutes a long and difficult agenda. It will not be resolved quickly. But it must be resolved at some point—and resolved cooperatively—if nations are to achieve lasting harmony and stability in their economic relations with each other.

I remember something that Prime Minister Mackenzie King said toward the end of the Second World War when I was still living in Canada. He was speaking on peace, security and prosperity, and he made quite clear the importance that he attached to interdependence.

"We maintain," he said, "That prosperity, like security, cannot be the possession of any nation in isolation. We believe that lasting prosperity will come only through international cooperation. In particular, we are convinced that Canada's prosperity and the well-being of our people, in all regions, and among all classes are bound up with the restoration and expansion of peacetime world trade."

That statement was made nearly 30 years ago. It would be entirely consistent with its spirit to extend these views beyond trade to the international sharing of resources, to monetary cooperation and to cooperative solutions for the many serious problems which now afflict the world economy. In these enlarged terms, Prime Minister King's words still ring true.[20]

Jamieson begins his conclusion with an explicit *restatement of his central theme*: "An international approach has the best opportunity to meet the stringent criteria for solution to this problem." Second, he *summarizes* his points clearly and concisely. He then reiterates a few key thoughts: "So we have to deal with supplies and prices, both current and for the long-term. We have to develop resources. We have an enormous world balance-of-payments problem." He next points to the difficulty involved in solving the problem and the *urgent need* for doing so. Finally, he begins his end-

ing note, using a quotation from Prime Minister Mackenzie King as his vehicle. Since he was delivering the address in Toronto, the rationale for his choice of quotations is obvious. Short, pertinent quotations in a conclusion tend to be effective; but again we add a warning: Avoid long quotations. After quoting King, Jamieson effectively relates the quotation to his subject and ends with a *strong final sentence:* "In these enlarged terms, Prime Minister King's words still ring true."

From Jamieson's conclusion we can learn a number of factors that go into an effective ending of a speech: (1) a restatement of the theme, (2) a summary of the key ideas, (3) a final interest factor to give lasting impact to the speech—in this case a quotation, (4) a brief application of the quotation, and (5) a strong and definite final sentence.

We have noted that Jamieson tried to give a degree of urgency to his message as part of his conclusion. This strategy is often of vital importance in a persuasive speech. To further illustrate the concept we turn to a conclusion from a speech by Malcolm C. Todd, president of the American Medical Association, speaking against national health insurance.

> Let me serve notice that anything that *de*-personalizes the care of man's dearest possession—his health—is a cruelty to our minorities. For the assertion of personality is now one of their greatest strivings.
>
> Human emphasis is not only kindness—it is common sense. *De*-personalized planning has gone into Britain's National Health Service . . . and into our own Indian Health Service. Now the British system is plunging toward disaster . . . and the Indian service is a tragic disappointment.
>
> There is an old Indian lyric that says, "My sky is full of the dreadful sound of the wings of failure."
>
> Let us spare our minorities . . . and all our countrymen . . . from a health-care system that is full of that sound.
>
> Let us have programs that work *for* them by working *with* them . . . so that the wings they hear will be their own.[21]

Here we have a crispness of style that brings the address to a climactic close. Moreover, the short quotation is especially well chosen, since it is taken from a minority group in our society—the group for which Todd argues that national health insurance would prove tragic. In addition, his final sentence has lasting impact: ". . . so that the wings they hear will be their own. "Regardless of one's attitude toward national health insurance, one feels a good deal of urgency surrounding the problem of depersonalized health care at the close of this speech.

A most effective concluding technique, whenever it is appropriate, is to refer back to material used in the introduction. Again we turn for an example to the speech by Ernie Link on Head Start. Link begins this speech by relating the plight of Tommy, a little boy who lived across the street from him in a small western Kansas town. "Sometimes I would walk by [Tommy's house] and see a red toy tractor lying on one of the patches of grass. It had only one wheel." He goes on to describe the condition of the house and the size of Tommy's family. He points out how Tommy was his age and how he remembers Tommy's first day of school in the first grade.

"In the first grade almost everyone talked a lot, but Tommy didn't talk much the first day. Nor did he talk much the second day either. Sometimes our teacher would ask Tommy questions, but he would never answer them. He only shook his head and looked down at the top of his small, wooden desk. Tommy was different; he didn't speak well, and he couldn't express his thoughts to others." In the body of the speech Link discusses the four main problems of the disadvantaged child: language insufficiency, lack of curiosity, difficulty with authority, and physical problems. After discussing how Head Start can assist the disadvantaged child in all four areas, he leads into his conclusion, referring back to Tommy's red toy tractor.

In my mind's eye I can still see Tommy's red toy tractor with one wheel missing lying on a patch of dry, brown crabgrass. I can still see Tommy looking down silently at the top of his small wooden desk when asked a question by his teacher. I can still see the agony Tommy suffered from being unable to compete with the other children in his class. Head Start would have been invaluable to him. It would have helped his language development; it would have improved his ability to speak; it would have given him many of the kinds of experiences that most of the other children had had at home and at nursery school.

Bringing the auditor back to Tommy and his red toy tractor seems to tie the speech together and give it unity of emotion. Link ends the speech with a passage from which he has taken the title of his address: "Come Take My Hand."

Initially describing Project Head Start, Mrs. Lyndon B. Johnson called it an effort to reach out to the younger children "lost in a grey world of poverty and neglect." She said, "Some don't know even a hundred words. Some don't know how to sit in a chair because they don't have as much as a chair. Some have never seen a book or held a flower. . . . There is no more important task in our communities, than for such children to hear a voice say, "Come take my hand."[22]

Conclusions for informative reports or simple explanations quite obviously need not be as elaborate as endings for addresses that seek to influence attitudes or to stimulate and inspire. Quite often a simple summary or rounding off of the information is sufficient.

But the best advice concerning speech conclusions may come from an oft-quoted poem:

The coffee's cold, the sherbet wanes,
    The speech drones on and on . . .
Oh Speaker, heed the ancient rule:
    Be brief. Be gay. Be gone!

To be sure, a speech should not be cut off abruptly but should be brought to a strategic close. At the same time, some speakers seem unable to end their discourse. Theodore Roosevelt was notorious for this. He might say, "And now in conclusion . . . ," and then speak for another twenty minutes. Occasionally a speaker takes the advice concerning summarizing his thoughts so literally that he in effect gives his speech a second time. He should remember that his "train" of thought should reach a terminal.

THE CHAPTER IN PERSPECTIVE

A personal presentation involves one speaker addressing a group of people, large or small. And members of this listening group bring expectations about the event to the meeting. They may, for example, expect to receive vital information, to hear a succinct discussion of pros and cons concerning a course of action, or to be inspired by a tribute to a fellow worker. In addition, they bring attitudes concerning all kinds of matters— social, political, economic, educational, spiritual—as well as points of view about the speaker and his subject. Their busy schedules and complex lives make them subject to mental distractions, and listening is sometimes difficult for them. Hence, a skillful communicator will carefully assess the vital characteristics of the listening group and adapt his preparation and presentation to them.

Personal presentations may be introduced in a variety of ways, but the goal should always be to enlist the listener's interest, relate the subject to him in terms of need and importance, and make a meaningful disclosure of the subject. The main body should stem from a carefully thought out central theme and should develop a series of supporting ideas, which should be related to each other and to the central thrust. Points of the presentation should be carefully explained and ordered according to a definite pattern of arrangement. Finally, the conclusion should focus strongly on the central theme, perhaps summarize the main points of the body, and generally round out the thought of the presentation. The conclusion is a final attempt to give impact to the message.

A good speaker will view a personal presentation as a communication event—not merely an opportunity to throw out some thoughts or bits of information. Since oral presentations usually allow little time for direct interaction between the participants in the communication event—or the audience is so large that size entirely prohibits interaction—the speaker should demonstrate special concern that his audience will receive and understand the message he is presenting to them. Perhaps more illustrations and explanations are necessary than in a dialogical situation that allows the other party to ask questions and exchange ideas as the interaction occurs.

REFERENCES

1. William V. Haney, *Communication and Organizational Behavior*, 3d ed. (Homewood, Ill.: Irwin, 1973), pp. 150–151.

2. Conwell Carlson, "Best Memory by Eye and the Ear," *The Kansas City Times*, April 19, 1967, p. 13A.

3. *Vital Speeches of the Day* (July 15, 1974): 584.

4. Ibid. (December 15, 1969): 130.

5. Ibid. (October 1, 1974): 766.

6. Ibid. (December 15, 1966): 152–153.

7. Ibid. (November 15, 1971): 80.

8. Ibid. (November 1, 1974): 56.

9. *The Complete Works of O. Henry* (Garden City, N.Y.: Doubleday, 1953), II, 1201.

10. *Public Papers of the Presidents of the United States, John F. Kennedy* (Washington, D.C.: GPO, 1962), p. 786.

11. *Vital Speeches of the Day* (September 15, 1974): 731.

12. Ibid. (July 15, 1974): 591.

13. Ibid. (May 15, 1964): 471.

14. Ernie Link, "Come Take My Hand," in Wil A. Linkugel and David M. Berg, *A Time to Speak* (Belmont, Calif.: Wadsworth, 1970), pp. 139–140.

15. Thomas Henry Huxley, "The Method of Scientific Investigation," in Donald C. Bryant and Karl R. Wallace, *Fundamentals of Public Speaking*, 3d ed. (New York: Prentice-Hall, 1960), p. 484.

16. Jean Dohrer, "Our Forgotten Man," in Wil A. Linkugel, R. R. Allen, and Richard L. Johannesen, *Contemporary American Speeches*, 3d ed. (Belmont, Calif.: Wadsworth, 1972), p. 271.

17. Martin Luther King, "Love, Law, and Civil Disobedience," in Linkugel, Allen, and Johannesen, p. 77.

18. Lauralee Peters, "What Is Totalitarianism?" in Wil A. Linkugel, R. R. Allen, and Richard L. Johannesen, *Contemporary American Speeches*, 2nd ed. (Belmont, Calif.: Wadsworth, 1969), p. 51.

19. Karl Menninger, "Healthier Than Healthy," in Linkugel, Allen, Johannesen, 2d ed., p. 56.

20. *Vital Speeches of the Day* (November 15, 1974): 86.

21. Ibid. (August 15, 1974): 126.

22. Linkugel and Berg, pp. 156–157.

CHAPTER 14
FROM PREPARATION TO PRESENTATION

Preview

Preparing for a speech can be a rich learning experience because research adds to one's store of knowledge.

Visual aids reinforce verbal messages, and audiences generally appreciate them. Excellent visuals are a trademark of a really professional organizational communicator.

A well-developed outline helps give the audience a sense of progress. Notes can be used, depending on the speaker's style:

- Extemporaneous speech
- Manuscript speech

Even certain aspects of the delivery can be planned:

- Voice
- Body

As our chapter title indicates, the processes of preparing and presenting a speech are indissolubly linked. While he is searching for ideas and materials, and while he is designing his presentation, the speaker should always keep in mind the audience he is to address, mentally testing his ideas and materials as to their probable effectiveness. Conversely, when he is delivering the speech he must be alert for needed adjustments, adding data when extra proof or additional clarity is needed, subtracting perhaps whole points when time is running short or if he is in danger of overextending his line of reasoning. This chapter takes the reader through the process of speaking from preparation to presentation, from beginning to end: research, note taking, notes for speaking, visual aids, delivery, and finally, adapting to the unexpected.

FINDING MATERIALS

The richest source of speech materials lies within you—your knowledge, your experiences, your attitudes and beliefs. A speech is a personal statement from you to others. It therefore makes good sense to begin the preparation process by taking stock of what you already know, noting everything you can draw out of your mind and jotting down the kinds of factual information you will want to research. Ideas are born from observation and reflection. To see that which happens around us and to fit it into meaningful patterns is to create; to think long and diligently about problems is to forge solutions. Inspiration is as much mental labor as it is genius. Anyone holding a position that requires him to speak frequently should be continually alert for thoughts worthy of being communicated to others.

The second step in preparation is to consult your speech file. A speech file may be the executive's best friend. Franklin Roosevelt, one of the most effective speakers of our time, started such a file early in his career, and he used it extensively when he was President. "Whenever something catches my eye which I think will be of value in the preparation of a speech," he once said, "I ask her [his personal secretary] to put it away in the speech material file." Roosevelt's "subject file" consisted of 24 file boxes, each 4 inches deep. Sixty-three manila folders were used to file the materials under alphabetical headings such as "Accomplishments," "Unemployment," "Agriculture," and "Apt phrases." When he was preparing a speech, relevant materials were removed from the overall file and placed in a separate folder for that occasion. Later they were refiled. Roosevelt's speeches always bore the imprint of his subject file.[1]

There will be times when we can speak from our personal knowledge, perhaps supplemented by a speech file, without doing library research. But more often than not we are likely to have to draw on outside sources. Many major corporate offices maintain private libraries, and even small organizations keep documents related to their line of work. Any library is a storehouse of an almost unbelievable amount of information. If we know how to use it and are willing to search, the library will usually yield in abundance the information we are seeking. Moreover, reference librarians, being perhaps the world's most helpful people, will gladly introduce a person to the many guides to reading matter that exist in the library.

Let's suppose that we are going to give a presentation on job enrichment to an audience of young executives, and let's take an imaginary trip to a municipal or university library in search of information. Our first stop will be the card catalog. The card catalog lists all books in the library alphabetically, a commonly known fact. However, it is less well known that each book will usually have cards in three places in the catalog, one filed by author, another by title, and a third by subject matter. In addition, each card contains much useful information. It lists the date of the book and its general contents; it indicates whether the book contains a bibliography or reference list; and at the bottom of the card are listed two or three subjects under which you can look for additional books. We will begin our search by looking under the subject heading "Job." If that term yields nothing, we'll shift to a related, somewhat broader term, which, in this instance, might well be "Employment." Whether we look under "Job" or "Employment," we will want to thumb through the cards under that heading, looking for critical subheadings—in this case, "Enrichment." If we find no mention of enrichment, we will want to try "Climate" or "Conditions" as key subterms.

Completing our search for books in the card catalog, we will step into the reference room and look at appropriate indexes listing journal articles. The most basic index is the *Reader's Guide to Periodical Literature*, an up-to-date listing of practically all magazines and periodicals in America. Once more, we will not limit our search to the heading "Job Enrichment" but will try key related terms. *Poole's Index* is useful chiefly for articles published before the *Reader's Guide* was begun (1900). If we want to check foreign periodicals, we will turn to *The International Index to Periodicals*. Other indexes we may want to consult are the *Educational Index*, which lists articles appearing in almost all scholarly and educational journals; the *New York Times Index*, which lists by subject and author (if an author's name appears) all articles that have been published in the *Times*; the *Vertical File Service Catalog*, which helps us locate pamphlet materials published by a great variety of organizations; the *Monthly Catalog—United States Government Publications*, which lists all publications issued by the various departments and agencies of the government; and the *Public Affairs Information Service*, which lists not only periodical articles but books, pamphlets, and documents related to all subjects pertaining to public affairs. In addition, there are many indexes that are restricted in scope, for example, the *Agricultural Index*, the *Engineering Index*, the *Industrial Index*, and the *Speech Index*. If we want statistical information, we may want to turn to one of the following sources: *World Almanac and Book of Facts* (1868 to present); *Information Please Almanac* (1947 to present); *Survey of Current Business*; *Monthly Labor Review*; *Statistical Abstract of the United States* (1878 to present); or *Statesman's Yearbook: Statistical and Historical Annual of the States of the World* (1867 to present). For biographical information we turn to any of several "who's who's." There is the general *Who's Who* and *Current Biography*, as well as the very specific *Directory of American Scholars* or *American Men of Science*. Certain information we are seeking may be sufficiently general so that we can find it in any of the encyclopedias that every library possesses.

NOTE TAKING

Let's hope that we thought to take note cards with us on our imaginary trip to the library, because we will want to note useful information. Cards (4 × 6) are better than full pages of paper if we are going to take a lot of notes. For most purposes cards are faster to handle and sort; they can be classified better according to topic, since they can be sorted into piles. It is best to restrict each card to a single idea or example. We will want to place an appropriate heading at the top of each card so that at a later time we can readily tell what's on the card. For our speech on job enrichment we may use such labels as "Texas Instruments example," "Monsanto example," "'humanizing' work," "conceptual foundations," and so on. To avoid repetition, we may proceed by writing down a bibliographic listing once and then assigning a number to it; for each additional reference to that source, we will simply place the number in the upper right-hand corner. Beginning researchers often have the problem of either writing down far too much of what they read or else taking such sketchy notes that they have little meaning at a later time. Usually, a lot of time and space can be saved by paraphrasing ideas rather than writing down the exact words of the source. Economy is a virtue when it comes to note taking. At the same time, we want to be certain that what we write on each card is sufficently complete so that at a later time we can determine what information we noted.

Once we have completed our research, we will want to read through our notations and sort them into topical categories. Then we will want to go back to the thoughts we noted earlier out of our own knowledge and background and relate them to the notes we have taken from library research. Out of this will come the structure of our presentation. We will want to outline the development of each idea and note what factual and illustrative materials we expect to use under each heading.

For our purposes let's sketch out an outline of our speech on job enrichment as it might look at this stage of preparation. We will assume that we will have three major points concerning job enrichment: (1) its nature, (2) its conceptual foundations, and (3) its practical limits. Thus our outline might look something like this:

Job Enrichment
   I. The Nature of Job Enrichment
      A. What is it?
      B. Where has it been used?
         1. Texas Instruments
         2. Monsanto
         3. H. R. Grace
         4. General Foods
         5. Procter and Gamble
      C. How does it work?
  II. The Conceptual Foundations of Job Enrichment
      A. An attempt to "humanize" work
         1. Explain what is meant by "humanizing" work
         2. Based on F. Herzberg's theories of motivation
      B. An attempt to use intrinsic motivation to increase productivity
      C. An attempt to adapt to workers' attitudes

III. The Practical Limits of Job Enrichment
   A. Differences in workers
   B. Differences in tasks
   C. Contingency theory says it probably would not succeed in all cases.

This outline is by no means final—some of the statements are in rough form; more subpoints will probably be added later; we still need to work up an introduction and conclusion—but it does begin to give us a picture of what our presentation is going to be like. In fact, our speech is sufficiently well developed so that we will want to determine at this time what, if any, visual aids we want to use as part of the presentation.

VISUAL AIDS

We may choose from numerous visual vehicles. The simplest and most basic is the *chalkboard*. We may either draw diagrams and sketches on the board prior to the speech or write on the board as our ideas unfold. Chalkboards are a convenient and relatively effective means of picturing vital data and important terms for the listener. At the same time, it is difficult to draw intricate pictures on the board, and use of a chalkboard seldom produces as great an impact as other types of visuals that allow for color and more careful design. We therefore may want to consider *posterboard* drawings. Posterboards can be prepared in advance and can be made as professional as skill and budget allow. They do have the disadvantage of being somewhat clumsy to handle, especially if more than two or three are needed. A *flipchart*, consisting of drawings on a poster-like, large paper tablet displayed on an appropriate frame, simplifies handling problems. A *flannel board* allows us to place things on the board while we are talking about them instead of having to unveil the entire visual at once. This single focus keeps the listener from becoming so intrigued by the total chart that he loses track of the speech. The *cutaway* will be very useful if we plan to show a progression of information, and especially if we want to picture a design, for we can begin with a very basic outline and gradually progress to a complex drawing. A doctor discussing the human heart might, for example, make effective use of a cutaway. Cutaways require considerable time and artistry in their preparation. But if our organization has a design department we may want to consider a cutaway for an important speech that we expect to repeat on numerous occasions.

If the necessary equipment is available, we may consider using an *overhead projector* or an *opaque projector*. The overhead projector is used for displaying charts and graphs on a large overhead screen. These visuals are easily prepared, and the overlays can be erased and used many times.

The opaque projector allows us to display pictures or charts directly from books or periodicals without duplicating them. The opaque projector, however, has the disadvantage of requiring a slight darkening of the room. *Slides* and *filmstrips* should be considered if we plan to repeat the presentation a large number of times. These media will project a professional tone and allow for skillful color usage. Like the opaque projector, slides and filmstrips require a dimming of the light.

For some subjects, actual *objects* or three-dimensional *models* will be the best visual aids. For explaining how an automobile carburetor works, the best extraverbal aid is a real carburetor. The speaker can point to its parts and show how they function. Three-dimensional models are miniature picturizations of the real object. For example, an architect will often display a model of the edifice he has designed in any presentation concerning the building. Such models are exceptionally good visual aids because they are vivid representations.

Many times, the best type of visual aid, if the size of the audience permits, is the mimeographed handout, especially if figures are involved, as in budgetary statements. The handout can also be used effectively to outline essential information, which may eliminate the need for note taking by the listener, thus allowing him to listen more closely. We think the handout so helpful that it can hardly be overused—at least it seldom is.

Now that we are aware of our choices of visual vehicles, we must decide whether we want to use a chart, a model, a graph, or a map. *Charts* are often used to impart specific information. A speaker wishing to explain Maslow's hierarchy of human needs might use the chart shown in Figure 5.1, page 68. This chart serves a dual purpose: It provides the listener with a picture of Maslow's hierarchy and assists the speaker in presenting this part of the speech.

Single-dimensional *models* drawn on paper are a frequently used visual aid. One can hardly pick up a book on communication today without finding at least one communication model portrayed in it. Often these models consist simply of circles representing people and lines and arrows showing communication flow. (See Figure 14.1.) Some authors try to humanize the communication model and use drawings of people speaking, showing either the head and neck or, in some instances, the entire body, since the whole body gives off nonverbal message cues. Models are most useful for illustrating the flow of things—such as communication, money, or organizational authority.

Graphs are of several types and are useful for presenting trends. We are all familiar with the *line graph* showing, for example, monthly rainfall amounts. Gross or net profits are often portrayed on a monthly or annual basis with line graphs in order to indicate trends. (See Figure 14.2.)

The *bar graph* depicts quantity. A simple bar graph literally uses bars to indicate amounts. (See Figure 14.3.)

Figure 14.1. A communication model.

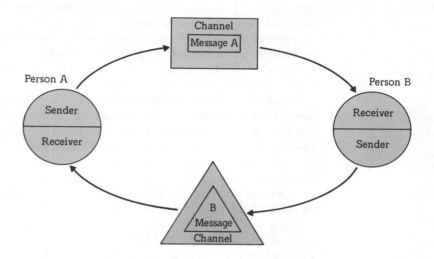

Figure 14.2. Line graph of gross income.

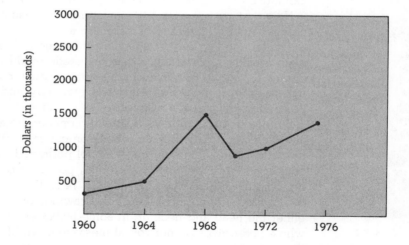

Sometimes pictures are used to indicate amounts—caricatures of humans, for example; the larger the man in the graph, the greater the amount represented.

Anything can be used to represent the bar: animals, buildings, coins, ships, and so forth.

Maps can be used in a great variety of ways. We are all familiar with road maps, maps picturing terrain, and maps showing political territories.

Figure 14.3. Comparisons of worker productivity.

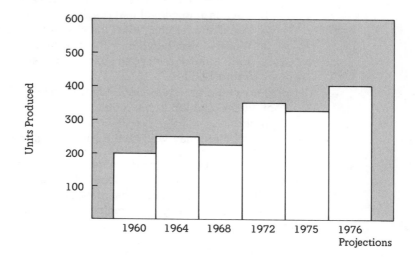

At the same time, the organizational communicator can use maps to show how sales are progressing in different states, where the company is considering opening branch offices, or where population is concentrated. Line graphs show trends, bar graphs amounts, and maps locations.

Finally, here are a few thoughts concerning the effective use of visual aids:

1) Visuals should be large enough so that each member of the audience can easily decipher them. Visuals that are hard to discern are worse than none at all.
2) Visuals should be displayed so that they can readily be seen by everyone. This usually means placing them high enough so that people sitting in front will not obstruct the view of those sitting farther back.
3) Avoid standing directly in front of a visual while you are explaining it. When writing on the chalkboard, for example, try to avoid obscuring what you are writing and avoid standing with your back to the audience.
4) Remove the visual after you are finished with it. Failure to remove a visual often allows the individual listener to keep his attention focused on it while the speaker has proceeded to other matters.

POLISHING THE OUTLINE

We are now ready to finish our speech. Let's decide to begin it by discussing the problem of worker productivity. After all, every manager is interested in maximizing output, so worker productivity should arouse his interest. The outline of our introduction might look like this:

I. Every manager is interested in productivity.
   A. One of the most vital cogs in productivity is the individual worker.
      1. Yet it is at this level that breakdowns often occur.
      2. We all are familiar with "the sleeper." (See Figure 14.4).
      3. We are also familiar with "the time waster." (See Figure 14.5.)
      4. And almost everyone knows someone who daydreams. (See Figure 14.6.)
   B. If we could enrich the individual worker's job so as to eliminate some of these problems, we could perhaps increase production significantly.
II. Job enrichment may well be the answer to this problem.

Since visual aids are good interest devices, we are using them freely early in our speech. We have decided to use a flipchart because we will have quite a few visuals and most of them will be charts and graphs.

We have expanded the first main point of the body of our speech in the following manner:

I. The Nature of Job Enrichment
   A. What is it?
      1. It is an attempt to put into work opportunity real achievement.
      2. It is oriented toward the individual worker's motivation and satisfaction.
      3. It includes many different procedures that encourage a worker to grow in his job.

Figure 14.4

Figure 14.5

Figure 14.6

B. Where has it been used?
   1. Texas Instruments
   2. Monsanto
   3. H. R. Grace
   4. General Foods
   5. Procter and Gamble

We are using a chart to show where job enrichment has been tried. (See Figure 14.7.) This chart will make impressive the point that job enrichment has been widely used by important companies.

We are going to conclude the first point concerning the nature of job enrichment with a discussion of how it works.

    C. How does it work?
        1. Job enrichment is best implemented after the organization has diagnosed its specific problems.
        2. The employee is given greater responsibility in making decisions about the job.
        3. The employee is given immediate feedback through regular appraisals.

Our second main point hasn't changed much.

  II. The Conceptual Foundations of Job Enrichment
    A. It is an attempt to humanize work.
        1. Explain what is meant by "humanizing" work.
        2. Explain F. Herzberg's theories on motivation as the basis for humanization.
    B. It is an attempt to use intrinsic motivation to increase productivity.
        1. Explain what is meant by intrinsic motivation.
        2. Explain how intrinsic motivation should increase productivity.
    C. It is an attempt to adapt to workers' attitudes.
        1. Explain that each worker brings a set of attitudes to his work.
        2. Explain how job enrichment seeks to adapt to those attitudes.

Our third point is going to offer reservations concerning job enrichment. We want our auditors to know that job enrichment is not a panacea for all worker problems.

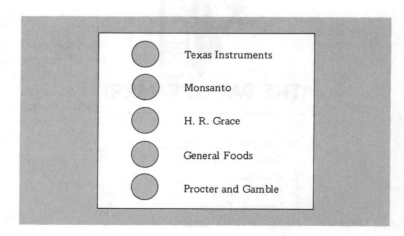

Figure 14.7.

III. The Practical Limits of Job Enrichment
   A. Differences in workers (Depict on flipchart)
      1. Motivational differences
      2. Differences in career objectives
      3. Personality differences
   B. Differences in tasks (Depict on flipchart)
      1. Technical competencies
      2. Amount of coordination required
      3. Staff versus line operations
   C. Contingency theory says job enrichment probably will not succeed in all cases.
      1. Explain contingency theory.
      2. Explain why contingency theory projects that job enrichment will not always work.

This concludes the body of our presentation. Our conclusion will restate our theme, summarize our main points, and finally seek to give impetus to our key idea.

   I. Job enrichment is an attempt to increase individual worker productivity. We have tried to explain:
   A. The nature of job enrichment
   B. Its conceptual foundations
   C. Its practical limits
   II. But it has been warmly received in the major companies where it has been tried. It might work for you.

NOTES FOR SPEAKING

An organizational communicator will give most of his speeches extemporaneously. By *extemporaneous* we mean a speech carefully prepared, thoroughly outlined, rehearsed but not memorized, and delivered from notes rather than manuscript. At the same time, virtually every executive will sooner or later deliver a speech so important that he will want to give it from a manuscript. We will therefore consider both the use of notes in extemporaneous speeches and vital characteristics of manuscript addresses.

**EXTEMPO-
RANEOUS
SPEECH**
If we decide to deliver our speech on job enrichment extemporaneously, which in all probability we will do, we will want to prepare notes that we can use as special aids in delivering our address. These notes, which serve mainly as an aid to memory, need take no special form. The form that is most helpful will be suitable—key phrases, complete sentences, or key

words. We must guard against an inclination to prepare notes much too elaborate for our needs. The authors have often encountered students who relied heavily on notes in giving a presentation and discovered later that they could have given their addresses without notes—and with much better eye contact. Notes, for many, are a crutch that allows them to look away from the audience. This tendency defeats communication. The speaker's purpose is to talk to people, not to a lectern or a set of note cards. We will thus want to limit our notes to key or "trigger" words.

Next we will have to decide whether we are going to use note cards or sheets of paper. Sheets of paper are entirely suitable if we are going to lay them on a lectern and leave them there. They have the advantage of allowing us to visualize a larger segment of the address at one time than is allowed by smaller note cards. In fact, we may be able to get all our notes on one sheet of paper. At the same time, if we plan to use the chalkboard or at any time move away from the lectern, or perhaps use no lectern at all, note cards are highly preferable to a sheet of paper. Note cards are easier to manage than sheets of paper. Usually 4 × 6 cards are the most functional; you cannot get enough on smaller cards, and larger ones tend to be awkward. It probably will be wise to limit ourselves to three cards at most and to place notations on one side only. We will want to number our cards; then, if we should happen to drop them or get them mixed up, we will be able to rearrange them easily.

We can make either content or descriptive notes. *Content notes* consist of key phrases, sentences, words, and visual aids, all of which give the exact materials to be used. *Descriptive notes* merely give reminders as to what comes next. Thus descriptive notes might simply say, "Give statistics concerning increased productivity," whereas content notes might say, "Each worker increased productivity by 10 percent." For especially difficult and unfamiliar subjects it is probably wise to make key sentence notes; the sentences will help one word one's speech more fluently on the platform.

There was a time when speakers were advised to write their notes as small as possible, on a very small card, and to hide the card in their hands while speaking. This practice seems foolish to us. In the first place, it is wise to write large enough so that you can read your notes easily while speaking. Typed notes are best. And we want to be sure we don't crowd our notes together so that it is very difficult to discern main ideas. Then, when speaking, we will do well to use them openly and freely. In fact, we should feel free to gesture with them if it is helpful. If we try to hide our cards, the audience will probably detect our attempt at deception. Although overreliance on notes impedes eye contact with the audience, a certain use of them indicates that we have prepared our address and are not talking off the cuff. Notes for our speech on job enrichment might look like this:

I. Managers Want Productivity
   A. Vital cogs . . . individual worker.
      1. Sleeper
      2. Time waster
      3. Daydreamer
II. Nature
   A. What is it?
      1. Opportunity for achievement
      2. Individual's motivation and satisfaction
      3. Procedures for worker growth
   B. Examples (refer to visual)
   C. Works?
      1. Diagnosis of problems
      2. Worker responsibility
      3. Immediate feedback
III. Conceptual Foundations
   A. Humanize
      1. Explain
      2. Herzberg's theories
   B. Intrinsic motivation
      1. Explain
      2. Effect on productivity
   C. Worker's attitudes
      1. Explain attitudes
      2. Effect of job enrichment
IV. Limits
   A. Differences in workers
   B. Differences in tasks
   C. Contingency theory
V. Conclude
   A. Restate three points
   B. End with . . . not panacea but liked where tried.

MANUSCRIPT SPEAKING Manuscript speaking has come of age in our day of radio, television, and public address amplifiers. That it is important in organizations is illustrated by the *Manpower Resources* report, which shows that in terms of "communication abilities utilized by the various organizations," speech writing is ranked fourth in importance in the "business" category. Busy industrial executives and political figures must guard against inaccuracies and avoid the possibility of being misquoted. Without doubt, extemporaneous speech is best for most purposes and for most occasions. A common weakness of manuscript speaking is poor delivery resulting from the loss of eye contact with the audience. In addition, most people do not read as well as they speak. They tend to read with too narrow a pitch range, read too fast, fail to highlight key thoughts, and stumble over words. Manuscript speaking, to be effective, should sound like extemporaneous address. Its words, phrases, and sentences should spring forth with a conversational freshness suited to the thought and occasion. Faulty language usage is a common reason why manuscripts often do not speak well. The language of a speech to be read aloud should resemble as nearly as possible the language and style of extemporaneous speech. A manuscript speech is not an essay read aloud but has its own oral style. Winston Churchill, for example, always read every sentence of his manuscript aloud several times to make sure it spoke well. Franklin Roosevelt used the same practice. A good way of developing a speech manuscript is to use a tape recorder or a dictaphone. In this way our thoughts will be expressed orally, and they can be modified and polished as we see fit, always giving an ear to how our sentences and phrases sound rather than how they look on the page or read silently. Finally, when delivering his speech the manuscript speaker must concentrate on his ideas rather than his words. He should live anew the thoughts and feelings he is expressing, sensing their vitality and importance. Practice is essential. One should practice a manuscript speech until one's eyes relate with the audience at least twice as much as with the manuscript. A communicative spirit is essential.

DELIVERY

The day has arrived. We are going to give our speech on job enrichment to a real audience. What about delivery? What thoughts concerning effective delivery should we keep in mind as we try to achieve our purpose? Since we will want to get our speech off to a flying start, we will want to walk to the lectern with definiteness of purpose, make sure our visuals are in proper order on the display stand, turn, look at the audience, and start speaking. We will want to have the first few sentences firmly in mind so that we won't stumble at the outset and can get the speech started on a strong, positive note. Next we will want to remember that effective delivery maintains a *spirit of communication*. The skillful speaker talks with his listeners; he maintains as much eye contact with as many people as he can. He will speak with them in the spirit of sharing ideas with them instead of projecting vocal sound into the air, much like a radio broadcaster, letting the sound fall where it may. We will also want to *make our ideas sound important*. Hardly anything turns off an audience more quickly than an indifferent, I-don't-care, listless, ultracasual speaker. Every word and phrase should be worthy of the listener's respect and attention. Commitment to our thought is essential. Finally, we will do well to remember that words like *energy*, *animation*, *vitality*, *movement* reflect an attention-holding style of speaking. Good speakers get themselves keyed up for a performance much like athletes or actors. They have something worth-while to say, and they want to say it well. They communicate through voice and action.

VOCAL COMMUNICATION

The human voice is central to speech communication. When used effectively, the voice is a fantastic attention holder and a great aid to meaning. The professional actor, for example, can project fine shades of meaning concerning critical words through his voice—sarcasm, joy, sorrow, optimism, despair—the audience hanging on his every word. To help us achieve a minimum vocal standard in our speech, we will remind ourselves of three questions concerning oral delivery.

1) *Can everyone hear me?* If we can't be heard, there is no point in speaking—we will just be engaging in a kind of expressive ritual in front of a group of people. We should watch for telltale signs of hearing problems. Are any listeners squirming about, turning their heads, leaning forward, or even cupping their ears? If so, we must speak up. To be heard requires adequate and sustained vocal loudness, vocal energy, and proper projection of the voice to the back of the room.

2) *Can I be understood?* Diction should be clear and precise. We should not mutilate our words by omitting or adding sounds or syllables. Careless, slipshod, indistinct mumbling not only annoys and disturbs the listener but gives the impression that the speaker is fuzzy and careless about his thinking. At the same time, when a listener concentrates on how a speaker is saying something, he may neglect what the speaker is saying.

3) *Is my voice quality pleasant?* Good speakers modulate their tones and control the intricacies of inflection, tempo, volume, and rhythm to make listening easy and enjoyable. A *monotone* is someone who hardly varies his vocal pitch. He drones along, creating the same sounds for the duration of his speech. A *monorate* is a person who says everything at the same pace, never slowing down for clarity or accelerating for emphasis. His tempo hardly varies; it is as regular as the count of the musician. Nothing is as boring as a one-note, one-rate, one-force, one-tune speaker. A voice that is rigid, stiff, and unresponsive to changes of mood and meaning is distressing to the listener; a jerky, hesitant delivery cluttered with random and meaningless "uhs" and "ers" is equally annoying. A flexible, expressive voice, on the other hand, is pleasing.

BODILY COMMUNICATION

The total person talks. All our bodily activity sends nonverbal message cues to our audience. Posture, shrugging of the shoulders, head movements, hand gestures, facial expressions, and eye glances all add to or detract from our message. Bodily action is an important part of the natural code for communicating thought; as the poet once remarked, "He speaketh not and yet there lies a conversation in his eyes." This remark indicates that a speaker cannot escape bodily action as part of the communication code. In addition, effective bodily communication can clarify, emphasize, and reinforce thought.

Facial expressions are probably the most crucial nonverbal message cues accompanying our spoken words. The speaker's face reflects his thoughts, emotions, and attitudes. And the eyes are the focal point of the face. Have you ever noticed how terribly distracting it can be to talk with someone who is wearing glasses so dark that you can't see his eyes? It is with the eye that the speaker pierces the minds of his listeners. Therefore he should look directly and constantly at them. The glance at the floor, the vague gaze over and above the audience and at the ceiling, and the mechanical sweeping of the eyes from one side of the room to the other like a water sprinkler are habits that distract and annoy listeners.

Posture tells the listener much about the speaker's attitude. Speaking with a slouch, for example, will probably indicate a degree of boredom with the message or the audience addressed. Other forms of awkward posture result from leaning heavily on the lectern, rocking back and forth from one leg to the other, and the wooden soldier pose—characterized by a stiff, uncomfortable stance like someone rigidly standing at attention. Good posture is a stance that makes a person seem alert and dynamic. It does not mean undue erectness, nor does it allow for apathetic slouching.

A speaker's hands represent one of the most expressive agents of bodily action, superbly convenient and useful for description and emphasis. The answer to the novice's inevitable question, "What shall I do with my hands?" is, "Talk with them." We can let our hands clarify ideas, describe physical objects, and point to critical thoughts on the flipchart. We will want to use our hands to help make our ideas clear. At the same time, we can use our hands and arms for emphasis. The writer can put an exclamation mark at the end of a sentence to give added emphasis to his thought; so can we as speakers—we can use an emphatic gesture. The public speaker may gesture sharply and firmly. Gestures can dramatize thought and add importance and excitement to a presentation.

BEWARE OF THE UNEXPECTED

We have now met all the vital problems from preparation to presentation. We have researched our ideas, prepared appropriate visuals, prepared speaking notes, and reviewed good delivery habits. But there is one factor that haunts every public speaker at one time or another—the unexpected. Here are a few examples. Say we have prepared our notes for our speech on job enrichment with the expectation that a lectern will be available to us in the speaking room. But what if there is none? The lack of a lectern can be especially problematic if we have planned to speak from manuscript. One of the authors of this book can recall when this happened to him. To heighten the problem, he had written many changes in the margins of the manuscript; on one page he had written three lines all the way around the perimeter of the paper. He felt quite foolish turning his manuscript in rotary fashion in full view of the audience as he read these lines. Had there been a lectern, he could easily have handled the revisions. Here are other examples. What if we expect to use a microphone but none is available? What if we're told there would be a display rack for our flipchart but it was forgotten? What if we are asked to speak from a stage so removed from our audience that people can hardly see the words on our flipchart? The same author recalls giving a high school commencement speech when he spoke from a stage with the audience seated on chairs on the basketball court in front of him. There was one small problem: The graduating class was seated directly behind him on the stage. To whom should he speak, the audience or the graduating class? In a gallant effort to communicate with both, he tried to turn repeatedly from one group to the other, with the result that he probably gave the bulk of his speech to the space between the two groups. The speech, needless to say, was a failure. The next night he gave the same speech with great success to another audience seated differently.

Another author recalls speaking in a large auditorium when a fight broke out among members of the audience seated in the balcony. Should he continue speaking and ignore the pugnacious few in the balcony, or should he pause and wait for the fight to subside? When order was restored, he continued speaking—only to have a stagehand accidentally pull the microphone cord from its socket. Some speeches are like that! Anybody who has done a fair amount of speaking has at least one such horror story to tell. What to do about it?

We will want to anticipate as many problems for our speech as we can. Much like the baseball fielder who plans what he will do if the ball is hit to him, as public speakers we should be ready to field the unexpected. We may not be able to settle a fight or conjure up a lectern. Yet, at a minimum, we should not be flustered and panicky if these things happen. A cool head and a quick mind are the answers to most unexpected problems.

Lest this discussion be ended on a downbeat, it should be pointed out that most audiences are polite and receptive, most speaking situations are without special problems, and most manuscripts have their pages in the proper order. A good speech well delivered is as exhilarating for the speaker as scoring the winning touchdown.

ANSWERING QUESTIONS

Every speaker making a personal presentation should be prepared to answer questions from the listening audience. Usually these questions will come at the end of the address in a forum period; but as suggested previously, not only may questions come at any point of the address but some speakers even encourage them at regular intervals as a kind of feedback on listener comprehension. The ability to handle questions (or objections) with poise and dexterity can be as vital as presenting the speech. Through the interaction resulting from the question-and-answer process, a speaker may make even better contact with the listening group and satisfy their needs and desires more fully than with his planned presentation. We therefore suggest the following principles as guidelines for answering questions.

1) Make sure everyone in the audience knows what the question is. In a large room or auditorium it is always good practice to repeat the question before answering it and in that way tell everyone what you are responding to. It is most frustrating to listeners if they do not know what question the speaker is trying to answer. If a moderator is presiding, he can profitably repeat the question, addressing it to the speaker. This procedure has the added benefit of giving the speaker extra time to formulate a response. In a small room with a small audience, the speaker probably does not need to repeat the question. At the same time, he may find it useful to rephrase it somewhat and make it part of the beginning of his response.

2) Do not let a single questioner dominate the forum. Sometimes a particular person has an ax to grind and will either ask far too many questions or pursue one line of thought long after others in the audience have lost interest in it. Either the moderator or the speaker himself should exercise control in such instances. Usually it is desirable to let as many people as possible ask questions. If time is running short and some people are interested in further discussion, it is wise to tell them a few minutes in advance that since you must close shortly you will entertain only one or two additional questions and they should therefore limit themselves to vital inquiries. Then, if your schedule allows, you may suggest that interested parties are invited to talk further with you privately after the meeting.

3) What if you expect questions and get none? Sometimes a forum period is planned as a vital and integral part of a personal presentation. If this is true, it is usually wise to arrange with one or two people in the audience to ensure that initial questions are raised. Often people who do not respond with questions immediately will raise them if someone else asks the first question. If on the other hand, you do not think questions are essential to the success of your presentation and no questions are raised, thank the audience and terminate the address.

4) Are there any special techniques for answering questions? If additional information is requested by a listener and you have it, simply relate the information. If clarity is the problem, further explanation may be the solution; at the same time, the use of clarity devices, especially comparison, can be most helpful. Relating the unfamiliar with the familiar greatly increases clarity and will usually dissolve existing confusion.

Some questions are best answered by another question. A counterquestion is often a good strategy in handling a query involving an objection. The counterquestion will tend to put the challenger on the defensive, and his response will often suggest the best approach to answering his original objection. This device should not be overused, however, and should be used with extreme tact lest the speaker seem contentious.

5) Finally, do not allow the questions to get too far afield from the original presentation. There is a danger that questions may digress so far that the discussion will be turned in directions that were in no way covered in the speech and perhaps are irrelevant to it. If irrelevant issues are raised, tactfully indicate that you think you would like to stick with the subjects covered in your speech. Moreover, if someone asks for information you do not possess, an admission of ignorance will often do more to raise your credibility with the audience than an uncertain, stumbling, and perhaps inaccurate response. If your answer is based on personal conjecture, tell the audience so; but if you know where the exact information can be found, tell them that.

THE CHAPTER IN PERSPECTIVE

This chapter has taken you through the process of preparing and presenting a speech. Briefly reviewed, this process involves finding the necessary speech materials—drawn from your personal experiences, from your speech file, or from careful library research, note taking, and outlining of ideas. On the assumption that the more communication channels the speaker can employ the more effective the message, it also involves the selection and preparation of extravisual aids. Research indicates that the listener can recall more than six times as much about a message when "telling" and "showing" are both employed as communication vehicles than if telling alone is employed. When delivering the message, the speaker should maintain a strong spirit of communication through direct eye contact and an attitude of sharing ideas. Vocal delivery should be clear, loud enough to be heard, and pleasant. Bodily action should be viewed as an integral part of the natural code for communicating thought. The speaker's body, especially his face, reflects his thoughts, emotions, and attitudes. Finally, beware of the unexpected. Microphones may stop functioning, audio equipment may be of the wrong kind, or a fight may break out in the audience!

REFERENCE

1. Ernest Brandenburg and Waldo W. Braden, "Franklin D. Roosevelt," in Marie Kathryn Hochmuth, ed., *A History and Criticism of American Public Address* (New York: McKay, 1955), pp. 471–473.

CHAPTER 15
INFORMATIVE PRESENTATIONS

Preview

Effective informative presentations are judged in terms of:

- Accuracy
- Completeness
- Unity
- Meaningfulness

Informative presentations are used extensively in organizations. The basic types are:

- Explanations
- Reports
- Briefings

Above all else, speech communication is situational. We address the boss in his office; we explain an annual report to our stockholders; we address the Kiwanis Club; we explain the company benefit program to our employees; we present our departmental budget requests to the executive staff. These and many other situations characterize our speech activities. Although no two situations are totally alike—people change, the organization changes, we ourselves change—we can safely identify moments when business and professional people give similar personal presentations. George Brown may, for example, brief his boss on new affirmative action guidelines in Cincinnati while Judy Jones briefs her boss on the same subject in Dallas; the speakers and listeners are different, but the type of presentation is similar. We think it profitable, therefore, to identify the main types of presentations that business and professional people are most likely to give at some time and to relate key theoretical principles concerning each type. To implement this end, we are using three categories of personal presentations: informative, integrative, and persuasive. This chapter is concerned with the informative.

MEASURES OF INFORMATIVE DISCOURSE

Informative discourse is concerned with factual statements. In order to clarify this thought, we suggest that statements can be classified in three categories: observations, inferences, and value judgments. Reality is factual, but when we perceive it through our senses it becomes observation. It is no longer the actual thing, but what we think it is in terms of what we have seen, heard, felt, sensed, or tasted. When we reason from or go beyond our observations, we are making inferences. And when we say whether our conclusions are good or bad, useful or useless, desirable or undesirable, we are making value judgments. To be sure, when we are called upon to explain or report—in other words, impart some kind of knowledge—we are expected to limit ourselves to the realm of reliable observation. If we are guessing, we should say so, and if at any time we find it useful to interpret or make vital inferences, we should tell the receiver that we are doing this. On the other hand, value judgments should always be reserved for moments of persuasion or decision briefing.

Four criteria can be established for informative discourse. Since genuine understanding by the auditor is the speaker's goal, he must present an accurate, complete, unified, and meaningful view of his subject.

1. *Informative discourse calls for highly diligent and professional preparation;* accuracy is a result of careful observation, study, and research. Sometimes small inaccuracies seem unimportant to us; after all, everybody should be allowed a small margin for error. At a minimum, however, what is at stake when a speaker is inaccurate is his own credibility. At most, inaccurate information may be used with tragic consequences. For example, a decimal point out of position may be responsible for a disastrous economic decision; an incorrect date could lead to important breakdowns in work scheduling. The old axiom that "close" counts only in horseshoes is appropriate here.

2. *The importance of completeness* may not be equally obvious. After all, one cannot include every detail. But by completeness we mean all the information essential or integral to a proper understanding of the subject. If I tell you in great detail how an engine functions but neglect to tell you how to start it, I have imparted knowledge of questionable value. To make the thought even more graphic: If an airplane pilot is assiduously taught how to take off but given no instruction in landing, he is likely to return to terra firma with considerable impact. The same thing is true in the business world when making a critical report. A presentation may omit one vital feature of a proposed sales plan, and that feature could be the critical one in judging its acceptability.

3. *Unity of information is equally important.* An informative presentation that covers a number of subjects, skips around without a clear thought progression, or has no central focus is less than successful.

Wilson and Arnold, in *Public Speaking as a Liberal Art*, offer us a useful illustration of the concepts of accuracy, completeness, and unity.

> The speaker who undertakes to explain how a tape recorder works will err seriously if he alleges that all tape recorders use vacuum tubes for sound amplification (many use transistors), he will err in a different way if he neglects to discuss the play-back systems most recorders have, and he will err in another fashion if he does not make it clear that the entire mechanical system exists to preserve sound and re-present it for later examination. . . . His listeners may not reject him as a person for his error of fact, his omission, and his disregard for the total meaning of his material; but they will not understand tape recorders unless they understood them before. Why? The speaker did not put into his discourse those things that must be there if talk is to inform or teach: accuracy, completeness, unity.[1]

4. *We would add one further criterion for informative discourse: meaningfulness.* One may impart a set of statistics, for example, with great accuracy, completeness, and unity without the listener's comprehending what they mean. In such a case the speaker has failed to find the unit of presentation that will lead the auditor to a proper understanding of the subject. The informative speaker must often translate technical language into everyday terminology, define key terms, transform the abstract into the concrete, and find the most appropriate unit of quantification—be it percentages, fractions, comparative numbers, or numerical totals. Often an abstraction can be made concrete with a single example. One could, for instance, spend considerable time explaining to a group how to prepare an income tax return, but what surer way of transforming this abstract information into concrete knowledge than by using a tax form as an example? To say that we had a lot of absenteeism last year surely is not as meaningful as saying that the company lost 480 work days because of absenteeism. A church budget committee may report that it proposes a budget of $85,000 for the next fiscal year. It could increase the meaningfulness of this figure by pointing out that this budget calls for an average contribution of $580 per member. Percentages are usually meaningful units of quantification, as are fractions. As a general rule it is useful to present statistics in more than one unit of measurement. For example, "Our debate squad won 438, or 75 percent, of its debates last year." The figure 438 fails to tell the total number of debates participated in, or what relationship the figure has to a perfect record of 100 percent.

TYPES OF INFORMATIVE DISCOURSE

We will divide informative presentations into three categories: explanations, reports, and briefings. As you approach these informative presentations, remember the criteria of accuracy, completeness, unity, and meaningfulness—measures that will guide you toward effective informative discourse.

EXPLANATIONS Explanations are frequently needed within an organization. An organizational communicator may be called upon to explain the workings and uses of new equipment that a department has acquired. At another time he may need to explain a new program or new procedures to a group of employees. New bookkeeping techniques may need explanation; a new sales program may have to be presented and explained to the sales staff; or explanations of what others have said or written may be needed for the staff to understand properly the document under consideration. The organizational communicator may also have to conduct various orientation or training sessions. He may, for example, need to orient new employees to company sick-leave policy or to orient outside representatives from the home office to company operations.

When presenting explanations, the first thing to consider is the method of unfolding knowledge to the audience. One's approach to the process can be of vital importance. If, for example, one attempts to explain a new sales program, it may be helpful to give a basic overview of the program before getting into specific aspects of it. When explaining a new piece of equipment, it may be helpful to identify key working parts of the machine before explaining the process of the machine. Then, when presenting the explanation, it is useful to check with the audience at appropriate points concerning their absorption of the materials. To ensure comprehension, it may be useful to ask one or two listeners to feed back critical thoughts about the explanation that has been presented. Occasional review of material covered before proceeding to the next point is another wise tactic. At the end of the presentation it is sensible to make some check of listener comprehension. Simply inviting them to ask questions may often be sufficient. At other times it is useful to employ once again the technique of asking specific auditors for direct feedback concerning their understanding of the subject discussed.

Explanations should never be treated lightly. They may represent some of the most productive moments of oral discourse in which the organizational communicator engages. If employees properly understand information vital to the organization's functioning, both productivity and worker morale may be strongly affected.

REPORTS Reporting is similar to explaining except that it does not involve the "how to" dimension. Whereas explanations within the organizational context quite often intend to teach an employee how to do something, reports are essentially statements of affairs or research findings. Financial reports or year-end departmental reports are statements of the condition or status of an agency. The financial reports given at every stockholders' meeting are often of primary interest to such gatherings. Annual departmental reports are commonly presented to a board of directors as well as to groups of employees. For example, the sales division of General Motors may report its activities for the preceding year. Likewise, reports of research findings to management constitute a vital organizational activity. The *Manpower Resources* report, under the heading "Rank Order of Communication Abilities Utilized by the Various Organizations," states that in the "Business" category oral reporting is rated first in importance and in the "Industry" and "Health-Related Professions" categories it is ranked second.

Visual aids are essential to most reports, especially financial reports. The speaker will either hand out mimeographed statements to the audience or use an overhead projector for picturing vital data. If the overhead projector is used, it is helpful to limit the amount of information displayed at one time. Listeners find it difficult to cope with a large set of statistics displayed simultaneously. It is much more effective to give them the information in small units. Careful and complete explanation is another important feature of such reports. Too often the listener is left to grapple with a huge amount of statistics without having the slightest idea what some of the numbers represent. The layout of the report and the meaning of the numbers should be carefully explained.

Reports of research data commonly follow a definte pattern of arrangement: (1) a precise statement of the problem or topic studied, (2) an explanation of the procedures used to gather the data, (3) identification of the universe of subjects tested or surveyed, (4) an explanation of how the data were analyzed, and (5) the conclusions drawn from the analysis. Sometimes some speculation as to the implications of the results is included. Although reports are usually put in writing, they should always be accompanied by an oral presentation. Written reports by themselves are too easy to file and forget. Full discussion of the results of research by organizational executives when they first see the report is critical to effective utilization of the data gathered.

BRIEFINGS

The term *briefing* is most commonly associated with the military. It stems in part from a "need for extreme accuracy, absolute thoroughness, and attention to detail on one hand, and brevity, speed, and almost instantaneous response on the other . . ."[2] There are four types of military briefings: information briefings, decision briefings, staff briefings, and mission briefings. Each type has as its purpose the compressed presentation of selected information. Although the term *briefing* may not always be used, the business world makes use of similar oral presentations. For example, the following incident was reported by a manager in the airline industry:

A visitor to our plant had requested briefings on the status of several aircraft models and derivatives. I arranged for my program managers to do these briefings.

After the briefings I received an excited call from one of the program managers. His interpretation of some of the comments made by our visitor added up to some important marketing information.

As a result the other program managers were called in, and their versions of the visitor's comments were pooled.

1. The *information briefing* involves the presentation of vital knowledge to a company executive. The purpose of the briefing is to keep the executive abreast of the current status of the operation or to supply him with specific requested information. It is purely informative discourse, and the desired response is comprehension. This type of briefing does not include conclusions or recommendations but limits itself exclusively to facts. The use of charts for statistical data and visuals for key ideas is often vital for maximizing the potential of the presentation. In many respects the information is just another name for the average report, except that briefings may be thought of as special reports and quite often have been directly solicited by the executive or military commander. For example, an executive has reported the following:

My supervisor confronted me with the assignment of briefing top management the next day on the subject of manufacturing controls. I asked him what approach I should use or if he had a preference. He only said, "You know what I want."

Such immediate requests are not uncommon in most organizations. In this case it was not unreasonable, either. First, the executive had given similar briefings on the same topic. Second, his long relationship with his boss had conditioned him to the kind of role relationship his boss wanted to maintain with top management; consequently the executive knew his boss' preferences about such a presentation.

2. The *decision briefing* will be discussed under persuasive discourse. Although it relies heavily on the presentation of factual data, the desired outcome is decision—the formation of an attitude or belief leading to one course of action as opposed to another.

3. The *staff briefing*, even though it may ultimately lead to a command decision, is informative in purpose. "It is known and used at every military echelon to keep the commander and his staff informed of the current situation. The anticipated response is a coordinated or unified effort."[3] In the staff briefing each staff representative may be called upon to present information pertinent to his particular activity. A staff briefing may also involve a lesser officer presenting findings of a special study that the staff has requested. Again the parallel within the business community is obvious. Organizations have frequent executive staff meetings. In this setting each executive may be called upon to brief the others on the activity of his branch of the company in order to better coordinate the organization's efforts. At other times the executive staff may request a special report from someone outside of their group.

4. In the military the *mission briefing* is designed for actual combat

operations. "Its purpose can be a combination of any or all of the following: to impart information, to give instructions, or to instill an appreciation for operational conditions that will lead to the successful execution of the mission."[4] The military handbook goes on to say, "The purpose of the mission briefing can be summarized as the final review of a forthcoming military action that is designed to insure that those taking part are certain of their objectives and the particular problems that may confront them."[5] Once again the parallel in the world of commerce is easy to see. The key concept in the mission briefing is "the successful execution of the mission." Whenever a company is ready to inaugurate a new program or launch a special effort designed to achieve added productivity, quite often the personnel expected to implement these efforts will receive a final mission briefing. The purpose of such a briefing is to impart vital information, give specific instructions, and instill an appreciation for the operation. The appreciative aspect of this briefing represents an integrative or motivational dimension. Nevertheless, the bulk of the briefing is purely informational. A chance to ask questions is often vital to a successful mission briefing. Everyone should seek clarification of an aspect of the mission not absolutely clear to him. After making a presentation, skilled mission briefers will often question listeners concerning vital details of the mission, thereby assuring comprehension. The success of the mission may depend on every participant's clearly understanding his role in the endeavor.

THE CHAPTER IN PERSPECTIVE

This chapter identifies three vital types of informative presentations: explanations, reports, and briefings. The organizational communicator is frequently called upon to explain such things as company sick-leave policy or the vital attributes of a new sales policy. Reports are statements of affairs or research findings. Financial reports, for example, are a common type of presentation made by company executives. Informative briefings are of four types: the information briefing, the decision briefing, the staff briefing, and the mission briefing. Briefings are usually given on a one-to-one or one-to-few basis; they do not involve large groups as explanations and reports commonly do.

Four criteria have been suggested for informative discourse: accuracy, completeness, unity, and meaning. All organizations thrive on vital information and the effective transmission of that information to key personnel. Informative discourse thus plays an important role in managerial communication.

REFERENCES

1. John F. Wilson and Carroll C. Arnold, *Public Speaking as a Liberal Art* (Boston: Allyn & Bacon, 1964), pp. 165–166. We are indebted to Wilson and Arnold for the criteria of accuracy, completeness, and unity.

2. *Military Speaking* (Fort Leavenworth, Kan.: U.S. Army Command and General Staff College, 1973), p. 3–1.

3. Ibid., p. 3–3.

4. Ibid., p. 3–4.

5. Ibid., p. 3–5.

CHAPTER 16
INTEGRATIVE PRESENTATIONS

Preview

An integrative presentation is basically ceremonial. It generally has a strong emotional tone and attempts to fill the organization's integrative function. Basic types are:

- Introductions
- Welcomes and farewells
- Awards
- Nominations
- Inaugurations
- Tributes
- Celebrations

They call for more eloquence than is normal for most other personal presentations. Often they are designed to impress by the speaker's use of:

- Diction
- Imagination
- Metaphor
- Structure

Integrative presentations find their meaning in the display of feeling. They are not strictly informative, since they often have little information to impart; nor are they totally persuasive, for they do not call for the acceptance of a belief or the inauguration of a policy or plan of action. Integrative addresses make evident how someone feels about something or someone and thereby inspire and uplift the spirits of those who listen. These speeches are ceremonial in nature and relate to special occasions. Keynote speeches, speeches of welcome and response, farewell and response, presentation and acceptance, nomination, commemoration, tribute, and dedication all represent moments of personal address expressing emotion. Humorous after-dinner speeches may also be included in this category. Such presentations are not integral to the work line of the average organization. Nevertheless, they do perform a valuable integrative function, as described in Chapter 2. It is at such occasions that personnel are likely to feel pride in being part of the organization or satisfaction that a fellow employee is receiving some deserved recognition. Such integration into the organization is a highly desirable goal; thus the importance of these types of presentations should not be minimized.

BASIC PRINCIPLES

Integrative speeches are essentially linguistic exercises. They involve using words and phrases, sense images and stylistic constructions that strike chords of emotion within the breast of the auditor. They are thus purely demonstrative. Any information they may contain is usually not important knowledge for future consideration; their persuasive value lies in their uplift of spirit. Therefore special attention should be given to finding expressive words and phrases. One of the most outstanding demonstrative speeches in our nation's annals is General Douglas Mac-Arthur's "Farewell to the Cadets," delivered at West Point in the twilight of his life. This address contains everything MacArthur disclaimed at its outset: "Unhappily, I possess neither that eloquence of diction, that poetry of imagination, nor that brilliance of metaphor to tell you all that they mean." For example, consider the eloquent diction, the poetic imagination, and the brilliant metaphor of the following passage from the general's speech:

> You are the leaven which binds together the entire fabric of our national system of defense. From your ranks come the great captains who hold the nation's destiny in their hands the moment the war tocsin sounds.
> The long, gray line has never failed us. Were you to do so, a million ghosts in olive drab, in brown khaki, in blue and gray, would rise from their white crosses, thundering those magic words: duty, honor, country.[1]

To be sure, many simple expressions of welcome or response to welcome, acceptances of awards, or introductions of speakers do not require the style or the poetry of imagination one finds in this passage from MacArthur. At the same time, other demonstrative moments have enough connotation so that they call for an impressive style that makes ideas sharp and clear, emotions intense and bright. Long ago Aristotle observed, with his usual wisdom, that "weighty matters shall not be treated in a slipshod way, nor trivial matters in a solemn way." Obviously, you do not want to overstate a pedestrian occasion; nor do you want to profane a moment of sublimity. The following factors, based on MacArthur's disclaimer, should help achieve a display of emotion but should be carefully adapted to each integrative speech setting.

ELOQUENCE OF DICTION Grayson Kirk, former president of Columbia University, has aptly observed that

> The uneducated man generally is lazy in his speech. When asked to describe something he says, "Oh, I guess it was kind of bluish." He is saying in reality

that he has not been observant or that he has not been trained to distinguish anything more than the primary colors. He relies upon such vague descriptive generalities as "that kind of thing" or "you know what I mean." . . .[2]

Mark Twain, with his usual wit, once said that a difference between the right word and the almost right word is the difference between lightning and a lightning bug. Since integrative speaking occasions usually call for brevity, economy of style, resulting at least in part from precise diction, is desirable.

Often simply eliminating empty expressions such as "the fact that" or "it would seem to me" will greatly tighten one's speech. Avoiding overuse of the word very will add a certain precision. One of Churchill's most admired statements was, "Never in the field of human conflict was so much owed by so many to so few." Reworded, this same statement might read: "At no previous time in the history of the world have so many people been so heavily indebted to so many other people in wartime." Not only is Churchill's statement more precise; it has greater impact because of its precision. Another of Churchill's most enduring statements was, "I have nothing to offer but blood, toil, tears, and sweat." Franklin N. Turner has wisely observed that

Sir Winston's famed blood, sweat and tears that
   sparked the English nation,
Would never have endured with
   sweat dressed up as perspiration.

**POETRY OF
IMAGINATION**

Since to a great extent an integrative speech is a linguistic exercise designed for sentimental purposes, the imagination brought to the presentation greatly determines its level of success. Sometimes being imaginative simply consists of uncovering key ideas that will trigger the desired response. When President Kennedy spoke in West Berlin in June 1963, he found the key thought for the occasion: "Two thousand years ago the proudest boast was '*civis Romanus sum.*' Today, in the world of freedom, the proudest boast is '*Ich bin ein Berliner.*' "[3] Kennedy's expression of pride in being a Berliner in the German language brought a tremendous response from the German audience—clapping, waving, crying, and cheering.

At other times, being imaginative may mean calling to mind special factors that generate a feeling of pride and satisfaction in the hearts of listeners. General MacArthur was able to develop a phenomenal sense of pride in the West Point cadets by calling to mind in his farewell address the valor of the American soldier in serving his country. In the process the general made abundant use of sense images. Imagery can make us see, hear, and feel the speaker's ideas. It always has a poetic, imaginative quality. MacArthur's use of imagery is well illustrated by the following passage:

As I listened to those songs, in memory's eye I could see those staggering columns of the First World War bending under soggy packs on many a weary march, from dripping dusk to drizzling dawn, slogging ankle-deep through the mire of shell-pocked roads, to form grimly for the attack, blue-lipped, covered with sludge and mud, chilled by the wind and rain, driving home to their objective, and, for many, to the judgment seat of God.[4]

A well-chosen example is often sufficiently imaginative to be effective. When presenting an award to an outstanding athlete or to a company worker who has gained special distinction, calling to mind a specific instance when the individual especially distinguished himself may produce the proper sentiment for the occasion.

BRILLIANCE OF METAPHOR Certain integrative speeches, especially tribute, commemoration, and dedication, can profit greatly from skillful use of figurative language: metaphors, similes, personification, and epigrams. *Metaphors* embody an implied comparison, like Sandburg's "The fog came on little cat feet" or Martin Luther King's "tranquilizing drug of gradualism" or Churchill's "iron curtain." A *simile* is a direct comparison: "as soft as drifting fog," "as gentle as a mother's love," "as dark as a cave." *Personification* consists of ascribing personal attributes to inanimate objects and abstractions. One might speak of Wall Street as "a crouching dragon" or say that "the sun smiled on us." *Epigrams* are sharp, terse, memorable statements such as Adlai Stevenson's "There are no gains without pains" or Russel Conwell's "You need common sense, not copper cents." Metaphorical language will in most cases display feeling far beyond direct address. It should not be overlooked as a means of producing effect at demonstrative moments that call for an elevated expression of thought.

STRUCTURAL IMPRESSIVE-NESS We add structural impressiveness to the three factors MacArthur identifies. It stems from special stylistic constructions of sentence and phraseology. One such construction is the *balanced sentence*, which has two parts weighing against one another to create antithesis. A good example is Kennedy's oft-quoted line, "Ask not what your country can do for you—ask what you can do for your country." And again, "Let us never negotiate out of fear. But let us never fear to negotiate." *Parallelisms* are a second means toward structural impressiveness. Parallel phrases are frequently used by skillful speakers, as Lincoln did in the peroration of his second inaugural: "With malice toward none, with charity for all, with firmness in the right . . ."; Lincoln's famous "of the people, by the people, for the people" is another example. A special construction often used is the "rule of three," which consists of using three words in a group, such as the alliterative campaign epithet of 1884, "Rum, Romanism, and Rebellion." Sometimes parallel groupings of two are used for structural impressiveness, as in "We must have faith and courage, patience and perseverance."

Aristotle warned in his *Rhetoric* that style should "neither be mean nor above the dignity of the subject but appropriate." The speaker's ability to adapt himself and his ideas to constraints of the moment lies at the center of effective speech. Daniel Webster was so conscious of stylistic propriety that his "Seventh of March, 1850" varies in ornateness from point to point within the speech. He speaks of the abominable fugitive slave law simply and directly, but he talks grandly about Americanism.

TYPES OF INTEGRATIVE DISCOURSE

We have identified eleven different types of integrative speeches that are of importance to the organizational communicator. We will now examine each type briefly and provide a general outline of pertinent topics as a handy reference.

THE SPEECH OF INTRODUCTION

From time to time a manager finds it necessary to introduce a guest speaker. He may even find himself introducing a member of the corporate headquarters who has come to talk to a training group or a plant assembly. The primary goal of such introductions is to provide the listener with key information about the speaker and, in that manner, increase the speaker's prestige and persuasive potential. A general outline for such an introduction might be the following:

1) Narrate key biographical data concerning the speaker. Be selective, however, and avoid telling every detail. The most important information is that which bears directly on the subject of his address. For example, if he is going to speak on some phase of atomic energy, be sure to focus on biographical detail concerning his vitally related experience.
2) Indicate the importance of the speaker's subject. You can be of great service to the speaker if you help him generate a genuine feeling of need and concern among the members of the audience.
3) Introduce the speaker. For most occasions, use appropriate titles if he has any.

A few words of caution: Do not steal the speaker's time by giving too long an introduction, and do not steal his speech by overextending your attempts at building up the importance of his subject. Moreover, introductions call for stylistic simplicity and directness. You are not the speaker; you are introducing him. Do not confuse the audience by speaking too grandly when introducing someone else.

THE SPEECH OF WELCOME

By a speech of welcome we have in mind more than mere recognition of someone's presence. We have in mind a formal welcoming statement by the host party. A visiting dignitary may, for example, be given a formal welcome at an annual convention. Or a representative from city hall may extend a formal welcome to an association holding a convention in his or her city. The prime examples of speeches of welcome may occur at our political nominating conventions. If the convention is held in Chicago, for example, an Illinois dignitary will deliver a stirring welcome to the visiting delegation; this was certainly the case in 1952, when Adlai Stevenson spoke so eloquently in welcoming the Democratic party that the faithful drafted him as their nominee for the Presidency.

The degree of eloquence appropriate to a speech of welcome depends on the grandeur of the occasion. In the instance of the political nominating convention, brilliance of metaphor is recommended. But in the case of welcoming an out-of-towner to an organizational business meeting, a somewhat plainer style is expected. For most speeches of welcome the following guidelines should be helpful:

1) Begin by stating what individual or group you are welcoming to your midst.
2) Indicate genuine pleasure at having the welcomed party in the city or at the meeting.
3) Speak a few words of praise about the welcomed party.
4) Inform the welcomed party of vital facts of interest about the group or city for which you are speaking.
5) Wish him pleasure and edification during his stay in your midst; if the party is a permanent addition, wish him success and indicate your desire for a meaningful relationship.

THE RESPONSE TO A SPEECH OF WELCOME

Most speeches of welcome warrant a formal response. Thus if you are officially welcomed you may want to respond as follows:

1) Express gratitude for the cordiality and warmth of the welcome.
2) Praise the group or person doing the welcoming.
3) Indicate your purpose for being there, if it is not known to the audience.

THE FAREWELL SPEECH

Farewell speeches are commonly given when a prominent person who has served the organization especially well retires or leaves the organization to join another. Quite often these speeches are part of a farewell dinner or banquet and, thus, are a blend of levity and sentiment. The style is straightforward, sometimes rising in eloquence as the speech reaches its climax. When bidding formal farewell to someone,

1) Tell him how sorry you are to see him leave.
2) Tell him you have enjoyed your association with him and how much this association has meant to you and to the organization. You may want to give at least one example that illustrates your thoughts.
3) Tell the audience where the individual is going and what he expects to do.
4) Wish him success in his future endeavors, or, in the case of retirement, wish him joy and happiness.
5) Tell him goodbye.

THE RESPONSE TO A FAREWELL SPEECH

A formal speech of farewell usually calls for a response on the part of the departing individual. In making such a response, be sure to adapt your remarks to the farewell presented by the organizational spokesman. Keep your remarks short; resist the temptation to deliver a long speech. Here are some guidelines:

1) Express appreciation for the farewell remarks of the previous speaker.
2) Tell the audience that you have enjoyed your associations with them and that you will enjoy these associations in the future. You may want to give one illustration of a particularly satisfying past association.
3) Indicate what you think the future holds for you.
4) Say goodbye.

THE PRESENTATION SPEECH

Gifts, certificates, and awards are frequently presented at annual dinners, farewell banquets, or other special occasions. For example, an award may be given to employees who have made the most significant suggestions, or a certificate may be given to the supervisor of the work unit that has the best safety record for the year. Essentially, a presentation is a special form of a speech of tribute, which we will discuss in detail later. The vital essence of a presentation is to make clear special attributes of the recipient. Presentations of awards are usually straightforward and are given in a plain style; yet at certain highly sentimental moments the tone may assume some of the loftiness of the speech of tribute. In making a presentation, consider the propriety of the following thought lines:

1) History of the award
2) Name of the donor or donors
3) Description of the award
4) Conditions for awarding (if won)
5) Virtues and accomplishments of the recipient

Present the award with congratulations.

ACCEPTANCE OF A GIFT OR AWARD

As you accept the award, adapt your remarks to the presentation speech. In all cases, keep your response simple and brief. Your response should do the following:

1) Express gratitude.
2) Praise associates or the other contestants.
3) Praise the donor.
4 Express pleasure at owning the gift or award.
5) Say thank you.

THE NOMINATION SPEECH

When you think of nomination speeches you may call to mind the long-winded orations given every four years at national political conventions. These speeches are as ritualistic as they are functional. On the other hand, when you think of nominating someone for office in your club, fraternity, or sorority you may call to mind the practice of simply calling out, "I nominate Mary Lou Gulick" or "Bob Saeger." Less prominent is the fact that meaningful nomination speeches of varying degrees of formality are often given at stockholders' meetings, board of directors' meetings, and professional association conventions. At such moments a carefully designed nomination speech may tip the balance to your candidate. Style in these instances should be adapted to the formality of the occasion. Sometimes, as at a large convention, a high degree of eloquence may be entirely appropriate; at less formal moments a very direct statement of the nominee's qualifications will serve your interests better.

Generally speaking, a well-designed nomination speech will do the following things:

1) Set forth the particular needs of the office. This involves developing criteria against which any candidate may be measured. The needs of the office should be developed in terms of organizational interests.
2) Show how your candidate meets the needs of the office. His or her special qualifications, virtues and accomplishments should be carefully related to the office.
3) Predict the degree of success of the nominee and the organization if the candidate is elected.
4) Formally nominate your candidate.

THE INAUGURAL SPEECH When we think of inaugural speeches we usually think of a newly elected American President taking office and addressing the nation. Not many of us will have a chance to give that speech! So why bother with inaugural addresses at all? Inaugural addresses can be more than political. It is the custom in many professional associations, for example, for a newly elected president to make an inaugural statement. In a work organization a new chief executive may choose to address his employees in the same manner. These rhetorical moments may be of considerable importance in setting a tone for the organization in the next few years. Although not everyone will get a chance to deliver such a speech, we think it is sufficiently important to be included here.

After a bitterly contested election a political inaugural address will invariably begin with a plea for unity. The speaker will try to get the constituency to transcend party differences and return to the orderly conduct of public and personal affairs. If such a struggle has occurred in an organization's election, the incoming officer will also want to direct people's thoughts to the greater good before talking about future action. Organizational inaugural speeches can ordinarily be organized around the following thought lines:

1) Thank people for their support.
2) Indicate the problems you think the organization faces.
3) Make a general statement of the policy you intend to pursue. You may not want to be highly specific, but set a tone or direction in which you intend to go.
4) Enumerate some general goals you hope to achieve.

THE SPEECH OF TRIBUTE   The most common speech of tribute is the eulogy commemorating the life and services of a prominent person. Upon the death of one of its members or of a high-ranking federal officer, Congress, for example, sets aside time for eulogistic services. Some of the finest literary achievements of the public platform occur at such moments. The speech of tribute, however, is given equally often in behalf of the living. Most of the time it is combined with the presentation of an award or gift. But not always. Tribute may be paid to someone who is leaving an office that he has served exceptionally well or to a person who has achieved unusual distinction. Retirement dinners are common settings for such speeches. The speech of personal praise is such a time-honored rhetorical event that it dates back at least to the ancient Greeks, for we know that Aristotle speaks prominently of this speech form.

A speech of tribute may present us with our finest opportunity for distinctive address. Poetic imagination and brilliance of metaphor may well be used in the speech of tribute, since sentiment is the criterion of this rhetorical event.

We invite you to consider the following suggestions for this integrative speech:

1) Avoid making your speech a mere biographical sketch.
2) Organize your speech around the person's leading characteristics, such as courage, imagination, or integrity. Or discuss his virtues first and his important accomplishments next. As a final point, you may want to show what effect his life had on those around him or what his accomplishments did for mankind.
3) Bring in pertinent biographical data in the development of your main points. They are a type of supporting material.
4) You may want to end your speech by pointing out to the audience what can be learned from this person's life.

THE CELEBRATION SPEECH   The fourth-of-July oration, once an American institution, has gone the way of many other hallowed oratorical traditions. The orator who called to mind the greatness of America, the uniqueness of our Constitution, and the special fiber of our people would be an anachronism today. We simply don't give patriotic speeches in the broad, expansive terms so familiar to our grandparents. Nevertheless, the celebration speech remains. We hold dedicatory services; we observe commencement ceremonies; we celebrate the anniversaries of our organizations. And whenever a new building is constructed we dedicate the edifice linguistically. At such moments the organizational communicator must be prepared to be called upon to deliver a speech of celebration. We thus invite you to consider the following thought lines for celebration speeches:

1) On anniversary occasions, what was the original importance of the event? At dedicatory moments, what was the original intent of the subject for dedication?

2) What has been its influence in the past? What were conditions like prior to obtaining the subject for dedication?

3) What is its meaning and significance today? How will the subject be used?

4) What is its probable influence on the future?

It is easy to see from the questions just listed that for both anniversary and dedicatory speeches some form of past-present-future pattern of arrangement is useful.

THE CHAPTER IN PERSPECTIVE

Integrative presentations are not integral to the work line of the average organization, but they do provide a valuable organizational function. It has been suggested that it is at these moments that personnel are likely to feel pride in being part of the organization or satisfaction that a fellow employee is receiving some deserved recognition. Such integration into the organization is a highly desirable goal.

Integrative speeches are essentially linguistic exercises in that they involve using language to inspire the auditor. Emotion and imagination are often vital qualities of such addresses. This chapter identifies eleven different types of demonstrative speeches that are of importance to the organizational communicator. Speeches of welcome, farewell, presentation, nomination, tribute, and celebration are examples of integrative speeches. All of these presentations call for the use of language for sentimental purposes.

Although these demonstrative presentations may seem peripheral to managerial communication, there is hardly a manager who is not called upon at one time or another to make such a speech. Able managers do not shun them but, rather, seek them out. They know that integration and morale are vital to the organization.

REFERENCES

1. Wil A. Linkugel, R. R. Allen, and Richard L. Johannesen, *Contemporary American Speeches*, 3d ed. (Belmont, Calif.: Wadsworth, 1972), p. 288.

2. Wil A. Linkugel, R. R. Allen, and Richard L. Johannesen, *Contemporary American Speeches*, 2d ed. (Belmont, Calif.: Wadsworth, 1969), p. 146.

3. Linkugel, Allen, and Johannesen, 3d ed., p. 294.

4. Ibid., p. 286.

CHAPTER 17
PERSUASIVE PRESENTATIONS

Preview

Persuasion is an attempt to influence a listener's attitudes, beliefs, or behavior.

A speaker has several different basic appeals from which to draw:
- His own credibility
- The acceptability of his ideas
- The emotional involvement of the audience

Persuasive speeches are used in organizations to:

- Show good will
- Sell ideas and products
- Implement decisions

The organizational communicator will often confront persuasive speaking situations. He may be called upon to make a public good-will speech, to sell a proposal to the company's board of directors, to motivate a sales force to greater action, to inspire regional representatives, to reply effectively to criticism of self or company, or to engage in decision briefings. As can be seen from the settings just mentioned, persuasion involves attitude formation, strengthening, or changing, and finds its end in belief and action.

Quite often when we think of persuasion in an organizational context we think only of salesmanship—selling door to door or urging customers to buy a specific product. Assuredly, the sales speech is a vital persuasive endeavor; however, there are many other persuasive contexts at least as important to personal and organizational success. The *Manpower Resources* report, under the heading "Rank Order of Communication Skills Utilized by the Organizations," lists persuasion as third in the "Business" category. Every time we try to influence someone's attitude in any way, we are engaged in persuasive communication. If it may be said that communication is the lifeline of an organization, responsible persuasion is the main artery. Intelligent decisions of many kinds stem from careful consideration of evidence and argument persuasively presented. Thus our purpose in this chapter is to examine briefly the concept of persuasion and then to relate this information to specific types of persuasive presentations that the organizational communicator may give at one time or another.

THE ART OF PERSUASION

Has it ever happened that two people told you the same thing and you believed one but not the other? If so, you were influenced by the ethos of the speaker. By *ethos* we mean the personal persuasiveness or credibility that seems to reside in the communicator. This concept is very old, dating back at least to the ancient Greeks, from whom we get the word itself. Aristotle believed that the speaker's ethos might be the most potent factor in persuasion. In extreme cases people may accept almost anything simply on the grounds of who says it. The converse is also true. In an organizational study William H. Read discovered that the things that make a difference are the subordinate's trust in his superior's motives and intentions, and how much influence in the organization the superior is perceived to have.[1]

Generally speaking, ethos involves three factors: expertness, trustworthiness, and good will. We must be quick to point out, however, that it is how the listener perceives the speaker's expertness, trustworthiness, and intent (good will), not necessarily what actually resides in the speaker, that makes the difference. A person may have great knowledge of a subject, but unless the audience has developed prior awareness of this fact, the speaker must speak so as to reveal a sufficient degree of expertness, or else he loses his potential for persuasion. The same is true of trustworthiness and intentionality. This makes it imperative that anyone cast in the role of communicator develop a good prior reputation as well as the skill of projecting his personal worth when speaking. The speaker's antecedent reputation we can do little about; but we can offer suggestions that will help him project, in the words of Aristotle, that he is "this or that kind of a man" through the speech itself.

DESIRABLE QUALITIES Desirable qualities of personality and character, although not necessarily revealed by the speaker's language, will shine through the presentation and create an image of the speaker in the minds of the listeners. It is difficult to say with exactness how the speaker can paint a desirable portrait of himself in the minds of others, but we feel that the following factors will add shades and tints that will brighten his image.

1. *Project an image of sincerity.* The best way to appear sincere surely is to be sincere. But it will also help for the speaker to make up his mind where he stands on controversial questions, for this will help him speak

with conviction. People quite often have greater tolerance for someone who is wrong than for someone who is insincere. One's opinion on a question should be based on a careful study of the matter. If one can develop a reputation for carefully weighing available evidence before making a decision, one's credibility will be greatly enhanced by that alone. Then additional benefit will result from speaking with greater authoritativeness due to the increased knowledge.

Moreover, one should always show good intentions toward one's audience and toward one's subject. If people feel that you are a person of good will, they often will trust you despite other shortcomings.

2. *Project an image of fairness and accuracy.* It is important to be fair when treating other people or their ideas in a speech. Scoffing at ideas or speaking of people caustically will usually stamp a person as a bigot. One may often show objectivity simply by demonstrating awareness of opposing arguments, perhaps even admitting that these arguments have a degree of merit. An aspect of fairness is accuracy. If you are uncertain of statistics or any other data, say so. You can enhance your reputation for accuracy, and also fairness, by giving exact figures, by citing sources for your data, and by quoting another person's opinion just as he phrased it. It is vital not to misquote or to quote out of context.

3. *Project a likable image.* A person displaying warmth, friendliness, good humor, tact and diplomacy, and a reasonable amount of modesty and humility will usually be personally attractive to an audience. Our manifest personality will always be constrained by what we really are; yet with a little effort we can present ourselves at our personal best. A spirit of friendliness will go a long way toward producing a favorable image.

4. *Project a dynamic quality.* *Energy*, *enthusiasm*, and *vitality* are words that frequently describe a successful speaker. The listener perceives such a speaker as a person of action, someone who gets things done. People respond more favorably to active personalities than to passive ones. They want to feel that the speaker is on top of things and that he has a good, positive attitude. Perhaps this explains why Demosthenes said that the three foremost qualities of a good orator are "action, action, action." Most great leaders, whether in the professional, political, or business worlds, usually reflect a high degree of personal dynamism. In an examination of selection procedures it was discovered that the primary characteristics recruiters look for in job candidates are enthusiasm and motivation.[2]

5. *Project your expertise.* The surest way of projecting expertise is to be exceedingly well prepared for your presentation. Then, careful documentation of assertions is critical. And, if done modestly, it is helpful to relate what experiences you have had in relation to the subject. This can often be done through personal illustrations and by specific reference to prior experience. The person who introduces you, if a formal introduction is used, will usually help the audience appreciate your expertness. This

means that it is useful for you to inform him of vital personal data, especially as they relate to your subject.

6. *Show respect for your audience.* You can do this in three ways:

a. By making listening easy. Prepare charts and graphs for vital data, and try to make your presentation interesting in all respects.

b. By showing respect for people's sensibilities. Avoid irreverence— to people, ideas, or institutions. Show your listeners the kind of courtesy in all respects that you would like to receive from them.

c. By not talking down to your audience. Any display of arrogance on your part will suggest that you are convicting the audience of ignorance. Although they may be seeking information from you, people are highly sensitive about their basic intelligence.

7. *Project a professional attitude.* As a representative of an organization you are a professional. Professionals dress appropriately, conduct themselves with discretion, and avoid extremely negativistic thought. Perhaps lack of professionalism will convict an organizational communicator faster and more fatally than any other factor.

CREDIBILITY OF IDEAS   Communicator credibility, as we have just seen, is fundamental to persuasion. A second vital source is the *credibility of the ideas* presented. In our discussion of ethos we learned that the immediate source of messages is closely related to their acceptability. Extending this thought, it is easy to see that the source of speech content is equally vital. Where does the idea come from? How well grounded is it? How typical is it? These are examples of questions people ask about message content. Strategic documentation is thus critical to persuasive speech. A speaker is unlikely to be able to make his ideas acceptable to all members of the audience; his position and that of some auditors may be too far apart to be reconciled during a single persuasive presentation. At the same time, if he skillfully uses available sources for making ideas believable, he should be a reasonably persuasive communicator.

The question of what to document and what to state as accepted fact in a personal presentation is problematic. Certain ideas are obviously acceptable to all. "Water freezes at 32 degrees Fahrenheit" will not be challenged by anyone. At the same time, the question of whether the fluoridation of water is beneficial to health has long been debated. To a great percentage of people today the statement is factual; to others it is still speculative; but to some it lacks veracity. Whenever people agree with the idea expressed, documentation is unessential. In all other instances it is crucial to offer supporting data. Thus we should proceed by trying to determine two things: (1) the most favorable grounds for argument and (2) the assumptions we can make about the knowledge and beliefs of the audience. Let's take the topic of academic freedom as an example. College professors will readily accept the idea on principle. A group of parents living at some distance from the university, however, might not accept the concept of academic freedom on the same basis. This by no means says they might not be willing to embrace the concept. Perhaps if we were to argue that it is vital for professors to be free to research, to inquire, to express ideas of all sorts if the citizens' children are to receive a quality college education, the same people might accept academic freedom as a tenable and desirable policy. Another audience, ultraconservative in orientation, might be convinced that academic freedom is essential because the lack of freedom could be used against their conservative values just as readily as for them. Thus on every subject for every listener there is probably one most favorable position for argument. The speaker should strive to find the best approach for the entire audience.

Once the position for argument has been decided, the speaker should make an assessment about the knowledge and beliefs the audience probably holds regarding the ideas he wishes to present. If the audience is large, he obviously will try to reach the greatest number of people, or at least the segment of the group that he deems especially important. If the audience is small, he may be able to make a highly accurate assessment. At any rate, he uses his analysis of the audience to determine what ideas they will accept at face value and what ideas they will want documented. Our concern here is with ideas that need documentation. We will discuss five types of support: examples, statistics, testimony, analogies, and related signs.

1. *Make ideas credible with examples.* An example is a specific case. Suppose we want to argue that teachers' salaries are so low that they find it difficult to subsist. We might point to the example of a full-time art teacher in Topeka, Kansas, with four children, whose income was so low in terms of total dependents that he was eligible for food stamps. Our example has the advantage of being specific and concrete. The Topeka art teacher is a person with a name; his wife and children have names; and they live in a specific locale. This specificity humanizes our argument. We should appreciate, however, that although some audiences will accept an argument from example, one or two examples do not warrant broad generalizations. Surely this Topeka art teacher must be the exception! At the same time, examples do establish that there may be a genuine reason for concern, provided that the examples cited are a fair sample, are typical, and are relatively numerous. Ordinarily it is wise to couple examples with quantitative data.

2. *Make ideas credible with statistics.* There are different kinds of statistics, and the kind the speaker chooses ought to be consistent with his intended impact. Whenever the desired end is to impress the listener with size or amount, the speaker may, for example, cite the total number of people employed by the construction industry, the amount of profit realized by Chrysler last year, or the total number of work days missed in the organization for the month.

On the other hand, it is sometimes more meaningful to present the average. We may need to know the average cost of producing a given product or how sales this year compare with the average for the past five years. In some cases it suits our purpose best to use percentages or ratios.

Statistics should always be presented in the most meaningful form. To say that a bond issue will cost the city $93 million has great impact; to say that it will cost the average taxpayer only $6 seems of no real consequence. When a medium-sized city sought to increase its taxes by 15 mills, the amount of increase seemed small enough; but when the city newspaper translated this rate into $100 per taxpayer per year, great concern was soon expressed. It is usually wisest to present factual data in more than one form. Often the total quantity coupled with a fraction, such as three out of four, is meaningful—or the total quantity coupled with percentages.

As supporting material, statistics have the advantage of giving scope to an idea. If we argue that teacher salaries are so low that 35 percent of our nation's high school teachers are supplementing their income by moonlighting, we have moved from the realm of isolated instance to a significant universe. It is not difficult to see that examples and statistics are best used in concert. One is concrete, the other comprehensive. The example gives a qualitative dimension to what might otherwise be quantity in the abstract.

A specific example of a speaker using quantification will be useful at this time. We turn to a speech by Charles Schalliol on air pollution. Schalliol begins with the example of the time a thick fog hit Donora, Pennsylvania, holding fumes from the big steel mills to ground level.

> Before the clouds of fog lifted from Donora, twenty had died, and 6,000, or half of the population, were bedridden. Donora was the site of America's first major air pollution disaster.
> The concern of public health officials is no longer for small towns like Donora. What happened there in 1948 is now happening in New York City, Los Angeles, and Washington. If New York is struck in the same proportions as Donora, 12,000 will die, and 4,000,000 will be driven to their beds.[3]

Schalliol gives the number of fatalities of the Donora disaster and the number who were bedridden from the incident. He quickly follows the statistic of 6000 bedridden with the restatement that 6000 constitutes half of the city's population. The potential of similar disasters, if they should occur in the future in denser population centers, is given significance by quantifying what the equivalent numbers of dead and bedridden would be in New York City.

3. *Make ideas credible with testimony.* Now that we have the specific (the example) and the general (the statistic), we can further enhance the acceptability of our idea by linking key people to it. Testimony lends additional credence to an idea but seldom proves it. In the law court the

testimony of eyewitnesses to a crime may very well demonstrate the guilt of the accused. Yet most testimony is simply opinion, expert or inexpert. The average citizen commenting on the state of the economy is lay opinion, but the testimony of a distinguished economist on the same subject is considered expert. People tend to attach considerable credibility to expert opinions; therefore a speaker should not overlook this source of believability. When using expert opinion it is wise to identify briefly the authority's credentials: the position of the authority, his special interest and background concerning the subject, and the source from which his testimony is taken.

4. *Make ideas credible with analogies.* Analogies, often called parallel cases, draw comparisons between objects, things, principles, happenings, and concepts. Cases are said to be similar when essential factors are the same. Suppose we want to argue that the consolidation of three branch offices would result in more efficient use of personnel and materials. One way of proceeding would be to point to a parallel case in another company, quite similar to ours, where three branch offices consolidated and the move enhanced efficiency and economy in all essential respects. The very existence of an analogous case strengthens the plausibility of our argument. If a company executive were to try to predict the effect of a second coffee break on worker morale and output he or she could look to other instances in which it had been tried. Analogies are as believable as they are parallel. If the cases are highly similar, especially in vital details, then they usually constitute an acceptable form of documentation.

5. *Make ideas credible through related signs.* Reasoning from sign is reasoning analogously. Signs are meaningful to us because we remember what they meant in the past. We know that a black cloud may bring rain because we remember that this has happened in the past. Economists reason extensively from sign, using vital economic indicators to predict future trends. Businesses, too, are constantly involved in the process of prediction and look to signs for indications of probability. Plausible signs, expertly used, greatly assist in making ideas credible.

Thus far we have identified the speaker's ethos and the credibility of his or her ideas as vital factors in persuasion. A third important factor is *motive appeal.* It is doubtful if any of our behavior is random, although we are often uncertain as to what lies behind some of our actions. Philosophers and psychologists have long searched for ways of charting the phenomenon of human behavior, but no one has yet found a complete answer to the question.

It is not our purpose in this book to become involved in an intensive discussion of human motivation; rather, we want to develop the idea that people have motives and that they are intrinsic factors in persuasion. All advertising, for example, is based on motive appeal. Aristotle pointed out that "our judgments when we are pleased and friendly are not the same as when we are pained and hostile." It is toward rendering the mind of the listener favorably disposed toward his subject that the persuasive speaker must direct his force and art. A. H. Maslow, whom we mentioned in Chapter 0, has come up with a helpful general theory of motivation. You may recall that Maslow lists five basic needs, ranked according to their prepotency: physiological, safety, belongingness and love, esteem, and self-actualization. The speaker will do well to ground his ideas in at least one of these motives, always remembering that motive appeals, for maximum effectiveness, should be personal. Each listener should be led to picture in his mind how the speaker's proposal will affect him directly. Suppose a member of the city's school board is speaking to an audience of taxpayers and trying to convince them that they should vote for an increased mill levy to support an expanded special education program in the city's schools. How might he proceed? In the first place, he will want to get the listener to apply the results of the levy to himself and his family. Thus it will be useful to point out some of the specific things the increased mill levy will allow. Perhaps a special program for gifted children may include his child. An expanded speech correction program may provide opportunity for better therapy for a child with articulatory problems. A new technical program may be just the ticket for one of his children who does not want to go to college. In an appeal to the single person or childless couple in the audience, he may point to the potential for expanding adult education opportunities.

The second level of appeal may be the sympathies and emotions of the audience. Many listeners, for example, may not be directly affected by an expanded speech correction program, but perhaps they can be made to empathize with the child who has a speech problem. At the same time, they may be led to see how special training for the gifted may be of value to the community and the nation. Perhaps the community has a significant percentage of unemployed; then the audience might accept the mill levy on the grounds that technical training added to the school's curriculum will increase employment. Finally, an appeal to personal pride in being a citizen of a city that provides such excellent educational opportunities as this city can with the added revenues resulting from the tax measure may be used to clinch the speaker's purpose. When carefully blended with argument and documentation, motive appeal, effectively used, may indeed influence the judgment of the listener.

In striving to produce persuasive effects, typical questions a person might want to ask himself regarding motive appeals are the following:

1) Can I relate this subject to the listeners' basic needs? Does it involve their security in any way? Will it enhance their immediate existence? What about their families? What are the economic implications?
2) Can I relate this subject to the listeners' self-esteem? To their sense of personal worth? Will it fulfill their goals in any way?
3) How will my plan help people fulfill their collective goals? Pride in the community? A better, more prosperous community?

TYPES OF PERSUASIVE DISCOURSE

Although persuasion enters into much, if not most, professional discourse, we think one can profitably identify at least five types of presentations that specifically have persuasion as their end and quite often are of great importance to the organizational communicator. The first is the good-will speech, which solicits a favorable personal attitude from the listener; this attitude may be directed toward a person or a company. The second strives to intensify commitment, and we will refer to it as an attempt to inspire and motivate. The third type of speech seeks to sell a product. The fourth is a bit more abstract in that it strives to sell an idea. And the fifth type is the decision briefing. We shall discuss each type in the remainder of this chapter.

THE GOOD-WILL SPEECH

Most speaking done by an organizational communicator is, in a general sense, for the purpose of good will, for himself and for the organization. A business executive speaks to the Kiwanis Club; an army officer addresses a high school assembly; a corporate official delivers the commencement address. These and many other speeches may be political, economic, or educational in orientation, but the speaker's overall target is to increase the good will between his organization and people he is addressing. Some major companies believe in this so much that they create speakers' bureaus and hire professionals to train anyone in the company who wants to give speeches.

At the same time, there is a genre of good-will speech that has good will as its direct and primary aim. When an IBM official talks to an audience about IBM, explaining the company's operation, new developments in instrumentation, and the company's future goals, his sole purpose is to generate good will. At such a moment he is not trying to sell a product; rather, he is selling the company to the audience. Representatives of colleges and universities annually make presentations on College Day or Career Day in our nation's high schools, talks in which they give vital information about their institutions to interested students as well as extolling the virtues of their alma mater. Educational programs are often arranged by school authorities and civic organizations. Speakers are asked to talk about their professions or business operations. If a motion picture company is located in town, it may, for example, send a representative to the school or civic club to explain some of the intricacies of film production. As part of his talk, the representative may show portions of several films in order to illustrate his points and impress his auditors with the quality of the company's productions. More than a thousand good-will speeches are often given in one year by representatives of a single large corporation. But business firms are not alone in this practice; schools, clubs, public institutions, churches—all employ the good-will speech.

A good-will speech is largely informational, telling about the organization for which support is sought. It seeks to impress the audience with the worth of the company, organization, or institution the speaker represents. At the same time, interest value is essential. Dull presentations seldom generate good will. Novel approaches are thus quite helpful, as is a liberal amount of good humor. In addition, vital facts should be presented unobtrusively. A representative who is too "pushy" for his organization will often turn off more people than he turns on. Being unobtrusive includes avoiding too strong a request for listener approval. Finally, it is helpful to show some relation between the organization or profession represented and the lives of the people listening. Sometimes people have no real awareness of how their lives are affected, either directly or indirectly, by an organization and its products. Many people, for example, may not know how far-reaching the computer is in their lives today. An IBM representative might very well wish to illustrate this phenomenon for them.

INSPIRING AND MOTIVATING Perhaps the best examples of inspirational presentations occur at sales staff meetings. The sales manager will want to encourage, motivate, and challenge the sales force to top performance. Repeated stimulation of this type is essential. If this were not true, the athletic coach might begin the season with a pep talk and then forget about it for the rest of the year. The half-time oration would lose its meaning. Similarly, sales personnel are likely to become self-satisfied or disheartened and need renewed motivation. The convention keynote address is another example of a speech given for the purpose of inspiring and motivating. The keynote speaker seeks to whip up enthusiasm for the convention and for the coming year or campaign, whatever the case may be. The pep talk will have meaning and utility as long as an organization or group of people functions collectively. Any manager of people must become expert in motivation in order to get the best from his or her personnel.

Inspirational discourse requires strong motivational appeal. Appeals to pride and principle, to economic and personal goals, to fighting spirit and self-advancement—all are useful in this type of speaking. Inspirational speeches should also be concrete and specific. Don't talk abstract principles; set forth concrete objectives and rewards. You may be able to stir the imagination of the audience by using vivid imagery; such imagery creates mental pictures that make concrete the advantages of intensified effort. Generally speaking, slogans inspire and motivate. This is why political parties are so slogan conscious. The religious community's "each one reach one" slogan is a good example of slogan power. Finally, speeches to inspire and motivate require a vital and animated delivery. No athletic coach is going to be listless as he tries to inspire his charges for the second half. *Dynamism, energy, movement, vitality*—these are the terms one commonly associates with inspiration.

THE SALES SPEECH Products or services are most often sold in a dyadic exchange of questions and answers between the salesperson and the customer. Such one-on-one selling occurs in settings ranging from department stores to executive offices. In addition, there are instances when an organizational representative has an opportunity to address a group of people concerning his product or service. As mentioned earlier, group insurance representatives are sometimes asked to explain the advantages of their companies' policies at a group meeting. Agents of educational and instructional equipment often have a chance to sell their products at professional conferences. Representatives of office machine companies may be given a chance to tell a group meeting about the merits of their contractual repair services. These and many other instances call for the traditional sales speech by one person talking to a group of people. Space does not allow us to explore the art of salesmanship in depth; besides, there are many excellent books on the subject that the interested student can read. Our intent here is to set forth in a concise manner the vital characteristics of the sales speech.

We think the pyramid in Figure 17.1 is a useful representation of the sales speech. The pyramid is used in order to portray the thought that everything funnels down into one vital act—the decision to buy.

1. *The contact phase of the sales speech is similar to the normal speech introduction.* Its purpose is to render the listeners favorably disposed toward the speaker and the message he intends to bring them. Generally speaking, contact should be made quickly and efficiently; fewer social amenities may be in order in the sales speech than in most other addresses.

2. *Salesmen are want creators;* they must get their customers to want something they don't already have. A salesman is more than a need ful-

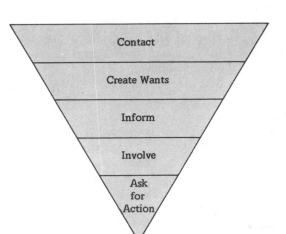

inverted pyramid

Figure 17.1. Format for sales speech.

filler. People tend to buy very few things that they really need. They buy things because they want them. And this is the salesman's task—to make people want something. To do this, he must develop internal tension in his listeners. We are told that

> People aren't moved or motivated until they feel a certain internal tension. This usually comes about when they're striving to reach a goal and realize they have to overcome some kind of obstacle, or solve some kind of problem, before the goal will be reached.[4]

This inner tension, in the case of the sales speech, should surround a desire to be able to do what the speaker's product would enable the buyer to do. This process is greatly assisted if the speaker can get his listeners to visualize the satisfaction they will receive from his product. Sometimes visualization can be achieved by using an example of another person who obtained the product and is now extremely happy with his decision. Dialog involving such a person discussing his satisfaction is often useful.

3. The third aspect of a sales speech, which relates to and is sometimes integrated with the creation of want, involves the *presentation of essential information regarding the product*. Precise language, descriptive adjectives, and apt comparisons are useful tools for this purpose. All relevant information (without boring the listener with unessential detail) should be included in the speech. A well-designed and carefully executed demonstration will help imprint ideas in the minds of the audience. It is thought by many salespeople that television stands head and shoulders above other advertising media because sponsors can demonstrate their products to the viewing audience. "Do you know why the demonstration generates the maximum persuasion power?" the authors of *Counselor Selling* ask. "You're right. It's because the prospect is able to convince himself."[5] Demonstrate how the product works; show some of its possible uses; illustrate how aspects of it function.

But what if you are selling a service instead of a product? This appears to be all the more reason for a demonstration.

> Sure, you may have to substitute something for the real product. The life insurance agent uses a graph or chart to "show" how life insurance proceeds are combined with other assets to provide income to a widow. Each asset's a different color. The prospect can "see" how much income his family would receive if he died, and from what source.
> And, it's easy for both the agent and the prospect to understand where and how new insurance would be used. If the graph is created right in front of the prospect, with his help, he participates in the demonstration.[6]

Finally, we are told that "the more tangible you make the intangible, the more likely you are to make a sale."[7]

4. The preceding statement from *Counselor Selling* leads very naturally into the next phase of the sales speech: *involvement* or, if you wish, *participation*. The best salesman is not the speaker but the product itself. Thus it is vital to bring customers in direct contact with the product. If the

product is small, pass it around and let them look at it; if it is large, invite them after the presentation to come up and handle it, work it, or use it. In this manner the listeners can visualize using the product; this, in turn, will intensify their desire for it.

5. *It is useful to ask for a specific action.* If the sale involves an order form, it may be helpful to have the members of the listening group fill one out as part of the speech; in other words, take them through the form step by step, asking them to write in the necessary information (even if they don't think they want to order—they may want to later and then they will know how to fill out the form). If the order form is written out, it is much easier for the customer to turn it in; this also increases the likelihood of his doing so.

Price objections will often arise. The speaker should be prepared at all times to discuss price in its most advantageous light. Sometimes if cost is expressed in terms of benefit units, then the price seems less imposing. Regardless of the approach the speaker wants to use, he should know in advance how he plans to respond to price objections.

The speaker giving a sales speech should not come across as a "pitch man"—someone who would hustle anything with fast talk and a smooth line. By contrast, he must come across as someone who fully *believes* in what he is selling. If he is not 100 percent sold on his product, his sales results are likely to be fractional also. Belief leads to enthusiasm and vitality, which of course are hallmarks of successful public speaking.

SELLING IDEAS
From time to time we all have ideas we would like to see adopted and implemented. Some of our ideas are proposals in response to specific problems; others are simply for the purpose of advancement of company or community interests. Our proposals may range from a simple suggestion concerning use of the lunchroom to a complete new organizational structure for a major department. Sometimes, instead of offering a proposal to company executives, we may present a proposal to outside agencies in behalf of our organization. Proposals are so common that Will Rogers once said that everybody has a plan and therefore his plan was to abolish all plans.

Products, to a great extent, sell themselves. The new-car salesman will ask the buyer to sit in the car and even to drive it—to try it out. The clothing salesperson will ask the customer to try on the garment. The music store operator will ask him to play the piano. The jeweler will place the ring on the customer's finger. But a proposal, by contrast, is an idea. You can't ask people to try it on, drive it, touch it, or, in a literal sense, look at it. An idea will not sell itself; it must be sold by the speaker. A visual dimension can sometimes be employed however. One may, for example, build a model of proposals for physical objects; one may draw a diagram or prepare a chart for systems ideas. But in the last analysis the words of the speaker will determine the sale.

Let's assume for the moment that you are presenting a proposal for solving a specific problem. How to proceed? In the first place, you will want to determine how aware your audience is going to be of the problem and, if they are aware of it, how concerned they are about it. If they are neither aware of it nor concerned about it, a graphic explanation of the problem, coupled with a demonstration of the need for concern, should constitute the initial section of your speech. Then present your proposal; explain it carefully and show how it will solve the problem you have outlined and how it will produce beneficial results. This type of presentation is often called a problem-solution speech. As a variation of the procedure just outlined, sometimes it will be vital to identify principal causes of the problem and show how your proposal will successfully treat these causes.

At other times the organizational communicator may present a proposal to a board of directors or a research funding agency. Quite often in these cases the proposal is not so much directed toward solving a problem as it is benefit oriented. The speaker is concerned with the feasibility, practicality, and benefits of his plan. He will strive to give his policy an air of promise and excitement, and to get the listener to picture the value of the results accruing from it. Proposals are often highly technical in nature, and the average listener will have difficulty comprehending them fully. The ability to translate technical language and ideas into everyday thought and expression is therefore one of the most vital attributes of the successful organizational communicator.

Policy speeches are given by the organizational communicator within the organizational structure as well as in external settings. Political ideas, economic theories, and so forth are frequently presented by the business executive to public audiences. The selling of ideas is one of the most vital rhetorical activities occurring in our society.

THE DECISION BRIEFING The decision briefing is, in many respects, similar to selling a proposal: It involves presenting and advocating a policy. However, there are some vital differences. In the first place, the decision briefing is usually given on a one-to-one basis or by one person to a small group. An army captain briefs a colonel; a lower-level manager briefs a top-level executive. The briefing topic in these instances involves a course of action. What course of action should be followed regarding a specific question or issue? At the outset of the presentation the briefer will make very clear what question he is addressing himself to. Moreover, he will identify the courses of action that merit consideration. Each of these approaches will usually be explored in terms of its strengths and weaknesses. The speaker will present last the policy he thinks is best and show why he believes it will be wiser and more effective than the other approaches. It is easy to see that the emphasis in these briefings is on evidence and crystal clear identification of issues. Most executives will not be interested in emotional appeals or human interest diversions at these moments but will want to hear issues, arguments, and evidence. In many ways academic debate is the best training ground for the decision briefer. Debate stresses the very things that are vital to a decision briefing.

The briefer should be prepared for interruptions and questions during his presentation. When questioned, he must respond specifically and succinctly to the query. If the question is unclear to him, he will do well to say so rather than trying to answer it. Sometimes he may want to state how he understands the question and then ask the executive if this is congruent with his inquiry. Valuable information can be imparted during this type of interchange if the briefer handles these situations skillfully.

THE CHAPTER IN PERSPECTIVE

Persuasion involves attitude formation, strengthening, or changing and finds its end in belief and action. Often when we think of persuasion in an organizational context we think only of salesmanship. However, there are many other persuasive contexts in organizational communication. Managers are often called upon to give good-will speeches in behalf of their organizations; they sometimes need to inspire and motivate at staff meetings; and they need to sell their ideas to higher management. From time to time, too, they will be asked to give decision briefings to their immediate superiors.

The art of persuasion involves many things, but communicator credibility, idea credibility, and motive appeal seem to be central factors. The speaker must be personally believable, must present his ideas in such a way that they seem plausible to the listener, and must relate his position to the vital needs of those he is trying to reach. Otto Lerbinger has said that "the term *persuasion* properly describes symbol manipulation designed to produce action in others. An appeal to both intellect and feeling is used to obtain some kind of psychological consent from the person who is being persuaded."[8]

REFERENCES

1. William H. Read, "Upward Communication in Industrial Hierarchies," *Human Relations*, 15 (1962): 5.

2. Calvin W. Downs, "Perceptions of the Selection Interview," *Personnel Administration* (May 1969): 12.

3. Wil A. Linkugel, R. R. Allen, and Richard L. Johannesen, *Contemporary American Speeches*, 3d ed. (Belmont, Calif.: Wadsworth, 1972), pp. 260–261.

4. "The Questioning Process," in *Counselor Selling* (Minneapolis: Wilson Learning Corp.), p. 13.

5. "The Presenting Process," in Ibid., p. 10.

6. Ibid., p. 11.

7. Ibid.

8. Otto Lerbinger, *Designs for Persuasive Communication* (Englewood Cliffs, N.J.: Prentice-Hall, 1972), p. 3.

AN EXAMPLE OF A SPEECH SELLING AN IDEA

"Nothing Happens Until Somebody Sells Something"*
Arthur H. "Red" Motley

This speech by Red Motley was given in Richmond, Virginia, to an audience of 2000 salesmen. Motley, himself a distinguished salesman—being the first man ever to receive the Oscar from the National Sales Executives as America's outstanding salesman—has conducted numerous rallies for large groups of salesmen. He was introduced on this occasion by Jack Lacy, who traveled with Motley to numerous rallies.

I was delighted to come down here tonight with Jack Lacey. Last night we were in Norfolk, tomorrow night we are going to be in Greensboro and Thursday night we are going to be in Winston-Salem.

Jack and I are here because we believe that what you and we do for a living is important. And I am delighted to come down here with Jack and talk to you men and women.

I am delighted because I believe that anybody in selling or distribution ought to be willing to plow back a little of his own time and his own money into the activities of our profession . . . the profession of selling.

I didn't come down here to make a speech tonight. I came down here to sell an idea. Like Lacy, I have been selling for 30 years, and like Jack, I like what I have been doing. Because I like what I have been doing, it appears to like me. It's an idea that I have been talking about for 20 years, and God willing, I will talk about it for 20 more.

I accept the fact that we are all human, and in spite of the fact that we are told something, we don't always remember it. And it is well to be reminded of it. And so I am going to sell you an idea—give you a little advice which I hope will improve your operation and improve the money and the commission check or the pay check at the end of the week.

The title of my talk tonight is, "Nothing happens until somebody sells something." Nothing happens until somebody sells something.

Understand what you are doing The first thing I want to sell you men and women tonight is basic and fundamental. Unless you and I—those of us engaged in selling—retail and wholesale, printed and personal—understand what we do—and understand it in terms of benefits to others than ourselves—we will never do it well—we will always be vulnerable. The first thing any man who is going to realize on the great potential or capabilities he has in selling—the first thing he must do is understand what he is doing.

Salesmen are want creators *Why* selling? Let me see if I can make that crystal clear and give you a better understanding of what you do. A lot of people talk about filling needs. A lot of people think of us in terms of filling needs—skip it. Not so.

---

* This speech is reprinted by special permission from Arthur H. "Red" Motley.

We haven't been a needy people for 50 years in this country. We are a prosperous people. We are not a needy people. We are not engaged in filling needs—we're engaged in something far more important than that—we're engaged in making people want things. We're want creators not need fillers. Think of yourselves in terms of the most important people in America, because this want creating process which we, as sales people, understand is the fundamental motivating power behind all progress in all fields.

My grandmother died at 85 in the city of Minneapolis. She never owned a vacuum cleaner in her life, but her floor was so clean you could eat off it. My mother owned a vacuum cleaner—not because she was smarter than her mother or because the Motleys had any money, because we didn't. She owned that vacuum cleaner because a lot of sales people rang that door bell out on Pleasant Avenue so many times, pushed their way through that screen door so often, demonstrated that rig so effectively that Mama got to wanting that thing so badly that she put the arm on the old man to get the down payment up and she kept it there until he made every damn payment so they didn't take that rig away from her.

That's how we've got more vacuum cleaners than all the rest of the world combined. Not because a man in Ohio invented the vacuum cleaner—he did. Funny thing, though, he went broke, flat broke. Here was a better way for keeping floors clean, Lord knows the housewives in America needed it, but they didn't want it. He went broke, and he took his invention to a fellow by the name of Hoover, and Hoover nearly went broke. Why? Because he couldn't get any department stores or retail stores to handle it, because they said quite properly, "Nobody wants it, there's no demand for it, so why should we give it any floor space?" And so he had to go out and devise his own method of distribution, and he developed a door-to-door selling technique. And today every department store and specialty shop handles vacuum cleaners—why? Because a lot of people want them. That's why. And once they wanted it, nothing could stop them from getting it.

What makes America great We've got more automobiles than all the rest of the world combined. Not because we need them, but because the great automobile industry made our people want to go some place sitting down. That's right. And they made them want it so badly, that during the last great depression, they would almost face eviction from their homes rather than miss a payment on the old jalopy and run the risk of repossession. And what happened? Hundreds of thousands of good jobs in Detroit and other cities manufacturing automobiles and parts, and in the oil business and the gasoline business and the garage business and in the service business. That's the reason we've got more good jobs than all the rest of the world combined.

Let's understand that. Let's have done with all this nonsense about America having some particular patent on inventive genius or some particular access of natural resources—the only thing in the world we've got is the greatest thing in the world—we've developed a power to make people want things they don't need.

I've been married to the first and only Mrs. Motley for 22 years. Up to two years ago, I thought those first 20 years had been wonderful—every one of 'em. But two years ago, I began to wonder how we ever got through those first 20 years, because we didn't have a mink coat. I really began to worry about that. I really did. Little dearie got to wanting a mink coat two years ago so badly that it was no longer a luxury—it was an absolute necessity. And I was lucky to get off buying her just the top half—a jacket. What's wrong with that? What's wrong with Harper's and Vogue—those beautiful style magazines that dress up those gals in beautiful furs—so that they look at them and they want them? What's wrong with the great department store like Miller and Rhoades right here in Richmond putting those mannequins in the window dressed in furs and then running an ad in the Richmond paper saying, "Come on, girls, make a down payment in August and by January you'll have enough down on it that you can take it out and wear it while you pay for it the next ten years"? What's wrong with that? How else could we build 60 million good jobs? Some of them in trapping, and processing and lining manufacturers and sewing and distribution and servicing and storage . . . how else?

You are engaged in the most fundamental process in the world. Let's understand that process. It operates not alone in creature comforts—in the field of commerce; it operates in every field. You and I know that kids need an education, and what have we done? Why, we've built great educational factories like this one we are in here tonight, all over the land, even out in the rural areas. We've consolidated schools, we run buses into the far remote rural areas to bring the kids into the consolidated schools because we *know* the kids need an education. But we are also smart enough to know that no kid ever got an education unless he wanted it . . . unless some enlightened parent or teacher sold him the idea of getting in and digging for an education.

There isn't a man or woman in this room tonight that wouldn't agree with me that the principles of Jesus Christ are needed in the world as never before in the whole Christian era, and because we know they are needed we have built great educational factories in every town and hamlet in America —cathedrals, synagogues and churches. And we staff them with fine production people, ministers, rabbis and priests, and we've given them the greatest products in history—three great creeds, Catholic, Protestant and Jew—refined over the centuries, and what are we worrying about? We are worrying because the pews are half empty on Sunday. And the juvenile delinquency in some of the parishes. The need is there, what's wrong? Why, the church is forgotten in too many instances—but a sanctimonious demeanor, a deep bass voice or a turned around collar is not enough. In the days when church was vigorous and growing and militant, their great preachers were great salesmen—they didn't sit on their fanny in a store or in the factory, waiting for the customer to come in and take it off 'em—they went on foot and horseback—even back to Galilee and *sold and made converts* because needs were never enough—wants are the only thing that matter. And what's the difference between making a woman want a better way of keeping house, or making a child want a better education or making a citizen want a better moral character? What's the difference? You are engaged in a great work. Lift your sights. Understand what you are doing.

Let me close that point by telling you a story about my experience. I went to work for a publishing company selling space. *Colliers' Weekly.* They taught me how to sell. They taught me very well. I got a raise. I got transferred to the Detroit office. And then one day, because Detroit is a middle western and a friendly town, one evening the neighbors next door came in to call. And I heard Mrs. Motley describe to them how I made the Motley living. Oh, boy. She made the James boys sound like a couple of pikers. She brought out a magazine, turned to a four color refrigerator ad and said, "My husband sells those." The woman said, "That's very interesting." My wife said, "Do you know what they get for them?" The woman said, "No, I haven't any idea." My wife said, "$10,000." The woman said, "For how many?" My wife said, "Just one" and the woman fainted. I looked at the thing myself, and for the first time realized that I didn't know what I was doing. I didn't know *why.* That was important to anybody except the Motleys.

I'd heard all this criticism about advertising, consumer's research and all that stuff and I'd turn up my coat collar like this, hoping nobody would notice me because I had a nice job, it paid very well, thank you, and I didn't want there to be any change.

I don't turn up my collar and sneak down the back alleys any more, and in the three years following the discovery I made in 1931 I tripled my income as a salesman because for the first time I understood. I had to find it out myself. I went back and discovered that a man by the name of Kelvin in 1900, the turn of the century, discovered the principle behind mechanical refrigeration—and 25 years later, 1925, in the greatest of all markets, the United States of America, there were 3 or 4 little manufacturers, Copeland and Kelvinator, etc. making 75,000 of those mechanical ice boxes—selling them for $500 a piece, and none of them making any money.

Then something happened. A couple of big guys, General Electric and Frigidaire got into business. They did not sell a better box. But they did something far more important—they came into Richmond and every other community in America, and they got a distributor and he set up retailers and they hired retail salesmen and they hired showrooms and they had them put up a neon sign outside that said, "Refrigeration" and they used billboards around the town and they bought space in the local papers to tell the American housewife about this new and better method of preserving food—the protection, the waste, the elimination of spoilage—and in 1931, when this incident took place in Detroit, they are selling two million of those boxes. They are now $175 and even the Motleys have been able to afford one.

What happened to the ice man

For the first time, I knew that even Motley, this little pimple on the advertising sales fraternity in Detroit, was important. I was a part of something that was big, that was fundamental, that was making jobs and a better way of living for a lot of people. I was doing something that I didn't have to apologize for, and I didn't want my family or kids to apologize either, so I set the little woman down and I told her that story, and when I got all through, she looked me square in the eye and said, "Yup, but what happened to the ice man?"

I didn't know the whole story. What did happen to the ice man? I doubt there is hardly a man in this room that knows, and you should, because it's a great American story. They didn't go down to Washington and get somebody to pass a law to keep them in business. They didn't get down and scream and yell to their senator or congressman or the President about the fact that there was going to be unemployment in the ice business if they let these electrical boys take the kitchen market away from them. They did not. They did a typically American thing. They taxed themselves (and none of them were big guys because they were all local operators) for money, and they put a kitty together and they gave it to the Betel Institute at Ohio State for research to find out new uses for iceman's ice. And today their volume is twice as big as it was when the electrical boys threw them out of the kitchens of America. They created a new want, and in the creation of a new want, they doubled their business and maintained employment and protected the investment that made a good living for a lot of icemen and their families.

You have to believe

That's what I'm talking about that's what you are doing. I ask you to understand it. The second thing you've got to do is to believe in what you are doing. *Believe.* I'll treat this very briefly by telling you my own story. I kept the world safe for democracy in World War I in St. Paul. A very nice place in which to fight a war. We had no trouble up there and when I got out of the Boy Scouts in December, 1918, the only job I could get was in the iron mines of Northern Michigan. I find myself working for the Townsight Mine and Iron Works. The mines up there are closed shaft mines—it was dirty, backbreaking pick and shovel work, and besides that, I was scared to death every time that bucket went down into the ground. At the end of about 3 months, one night at the boarding house where I stayed, I met a fat, pink cheeked, sassy looking guy with a white shirt on and none of that red stuff under his nails, so I knew he was no miner—and I sat down next to him to see what made him tick. And I found out that he was a zither salesman. The old Chick Sales lap harp. He bought them for $5 wholesale out in Chicago and he never got less than $10 down, so he could not lose if he never collected another dime. It seemed like a wonderful idea to me.

I threw away the pick and shovel and became a zither salesman forthwith. This was a wonderful machine—you didn't play it with a pick. It had a couple of octaves of keys. You played it like you play a piano one handed. The keys tripped the hammers, the hammers would go down and hit the wires—the wires made beautiful music. The mines are going full blast in the summer of 1919—and there's no other music up there for those hunkies and their kids except this guy and his zither. I went like a house afire for 30 days. We gave away 30 sheets of music with every zither. At the end of 30 days, one of my customers came back and wanted more sheet music and then the cat was out of the bag. The thing only played in the key of C. When you got all through with "Smiles" and "God Save the King," you couldn't do a thing with Dardanella, Hindustan or any of the hot tunes of the day. You couldn't do a thing with them . . . no sharps, no flats, just the key of C. I was working to get a stake to go back to the University of Minnesota and I sold those things right up to September 15th, 1919. A funny thing, though. I never sold as many of them per day or week after I found out it would only play in the key of C.

If you think you are selling a service or a product that only plays in the key of C, unless you believe implicitly in that product, and the promises of that company behind the product, get another job, because you'll never go to town without belief in what you are doing. Spend a little time on it. Make sure, because in the process of making sure, you will resell yourself, rededicate yourself, and if your strength is parallel to mine, and any other top salesman I know of, you will begin to double your income.

The "pro" never stops learning And the third thing a good professional salesman has got to think of, and remember at all times, is the fact that because this is a profession, you are never through. You *must* have training. But that's not enough. You must have *more* training.

Professional—you heard me use that word. Three things if you are going to be a pro. Understand what you are doing in terms of benefits for others and yourself and your immediate superiors. Belief in the product and the company that you represent, and that takes some thought and some figuring—and the acceptance of the fact, like any good professional man accepts the fact that he is never through. That's what I mean by being a professional.

And how do you find out whether you are a professional? I'll give you a simple test. How do you act when you are not selling? Let me illustrate what I mean and watch for this. If you are a professional salesman, you are a salesman 24 hours a day for seven days a week. You don't just put it on when you get the body in front of the prospect and take it off when you leave his office. You don't put it on at nine and take it off at five. You are a salesman all the time. You eat, live, sleep, think and thrill to the prospect of being a want creator—which is the fundamental motivating force behind all human progress.

PART V

Miller, Monkmeyer

PART V
THE BOOK IN PERSPECTIVE

Communication in organizations is a complex and challenging process, and a number of aspects of communication such as writing and reading have not been covered directly in this book. This is attributable, in part anyway, to our wanting to keep the book to a reasonable length and to the fact that there are some excellent books already available on the subject. Nevertheless, experience has taught us that the skills most important to the organizational communicator are those that he uses in his personal interactions with others on the job. There are, of course, many different circumstances in which these interactions occur, and we chose to focus on the three formal channels that are most common: the interview, the conference, and the presonal presentation to an audience. There are some vital dimensions that distinguish these three channels from one another, but these are not always as well defined in practice as they are when we talk about them. For example, one may find oneself giving a personal presentation in a group conference, or a group interview may turn into a group meeting.

The underlying thrust of the book was aimed toward giving the organizational communicator more control over his own communicative behavior and over his interactions with others. In order to attain this, we felt that he must understand the organization as a context as well as understanding communication as a process. Chapter 1 began the analysis of the organization by identifying the basic components of organizations in terms of people, structure, technologies, and tasks. It was deemed particularly important that the organizational communicator understand the influence of structure on communication, and a review was provided of the principal structural characteristics common to nearly all organizations: hierarchy, span of control, division of labor, line and staff differences, chain of command, and role differentiation.

Chapter 2 examined the role of communication in organizations, and communication flow was pictured as a subsystem within the total organizational system. The most important point was that communication has four alternative functions in the organization: (1) information, (2) command and regulation, (3) persuasion, and (4) integration. These, too, are not always clearly distinct, but they do characterize the primary end products that communication can achieve. As we have written about interviewing, group conferences, and personal presentations, we have tried to keep the reader aware of the particular functions that could be achieved under the different circumstances. Finally, we stressed that most of the organizational communicator's personal contacts offered the potential for communication to flow upward as well as downward.

Chapter 3 established our frame of reference for the process of communication. It was defined as a joint process, with each person performing several different functions and having particular purposes behind his communicative behavior. Because each communicator has his own filtering patterns, the message sent is not always the message received; therefore it is highly desirable to provide timely opportunities for feedback whenever possible. Since the choice of a channel affects the interpretation of the message, we have tried throughout the book to evaluate the appropriate use of the interivew, the conference, and the personal presentation as different communication channels.

The interview, covered in Chapters 4–8, was defined primarily as a specialized dyadic pattern of communication in which the interviewer played the role of strategist as well as tactician, responding spontaneously to circumstances and situations. His role as strategist called for him to clarify the purpose, identify the content objectives, frame preliminary questions based on these objectives, structure the interview into some planned sequence or schedule, and arrange the interview setting. His role as tactician called for him to be sensitive to the nuances of the respondent, especially in terms of beginning the interview, motivating the interviewer to overcome any inhibitors to the interaction, probing incomplete or unsatisfactory answers, and concluding the interview. Both roles—as strategist and as tactician—are based on the idea that the interviewer should maintain control over the interaction.

The conference, examined in Chapters 9–12, is a channel involving group interaction. Its use has multiplied as organizations have become increasingly complex and the need to coordinate activities has been increased by the tendency to divide labor into narrower and narrower specialties. Nevertheless, the organizational communicator must be realistic about what groups can and cannot accomplish. Under certain circumstances groups yield better decisions, breed stronger commitments, and increase understanding. At the same time, however, they take a lot of time, diffuse responsibility, and breed conformity so that creativity may be stifled.

Despite the fact that most of us feel that we are unique and not completely predictable, when we interact in groups a kind of group anatomy develops that is ordinarily quite predictable. In the first place, a structure evolves and becomes a communication network. People adopt certain roles on the basis of their culture, formal agreements, and organizational precedents; they establish group norms of acceptable and unacceptable behavior; power is bestowed so that some form of management or leadership is set up; and some degree of cohesiveness among members will develop if the group is to be maintained. The organizational communicator can facilitate successful communication if he understands the limitations imposed upon him and upon the group by these factors. Specifically, he can take them into account as he plans the conference, regulates the size of the group, clarifies the group's purpose, prepares an agenda, and makes physical arrangements conducive to the kind of interaction he wants.

The third channel for the organizational communicator is the personal presentation, covered in Chapters 12–16. Like the other channels, personal presentations are related to the organization's communicative functions. They perform informative and instructive functions, demonstrative or integrative functions, and persuasive functions. Like the other channels, personal presentations call for an analysis of the receiver. The task, however, is more complicated in presentational settings in that having a larger number of receivers makes it difficult to know what the adaptation should be when they have different expectations, distractions, and points of view. Nevertheless, we have tried to suggest some alternatives for adapting to the audience in beginning the presentation, divulging and developing the subject, and ending the presentation. The truly professional organizational communicator will be meticulous in finding the best materials, preparing visual reinforcements for his ideas, polishing the basic outline he intends to follow, and delivering a dynamic presentation that is clear, ordered, and gives the listener a sense of progress, that is, that he is going somewhere with the idea.

Finally, we reiterate that these three channels offer the organizational communicator three different alternatives for his personal communication. He should learn to do each well. But in so doing he will need to recognize the relative merits and limitations of each. Unfortunately, there are no magic formulas that he can use, but we have tried to make the reader sensitive to some vital information about each. The reader who is already employed as an organizational communicator will have many real opportunities to test the validity of the information. However, for the reader who is a student or is preparing for the day when he will be working as an organizational communicator, we end the book with two case studies that can be analyzed with merit. In both cases the reader has to make some choices about what is communicated and through what channel it should be communicated. We have tried to write a practical book, and it is fitting that we end it by offering opportunities to practice your skills.

CASE 1
MAINTAINING STANDARDS OF PERFORMANCE*

Bill Jones is foreman of an assembly department and has 25 employees under his supervision. The operation is on a 3-shift basis. Of the 25 direct labor employees, 9 are male and 16 female.

Wage rates are high compared with rates paid by competitors and about the same as two other "best-paying" concerns in the community. The competitive situation is severe: Two of the largest competitors are adding capacity in order to obtain a larger share of the market. It is essential that costs be kept to a minimum.

About four months ago the product being produced in Bill Jones' department was redesigned, and intensive efforts have been necessary to overcome the problems of getting the new design into production and to meet the production schedule. That has now been accomplished.

During this period, however, manufacturing *losses* have risen sharply, and foreman Jones sees that his next big task is to get these losses back in line. The trend has been as follows:

Month	Minimum	Actual
January	4.0%	3.9%
February	4.0	4.1
March	6.0	7.8 (product redesigned)
April	5.0	8.0
May	4.0	7.1
June	4.0	7.3 (current rate)
July–December	4.0	

These standards were set up on the basis of past good practice in this department, with a fair allowance for the problems anticipated in getting the new design into production.

Foreman Jones studies his problem and makes up a list of the things he must do to get his employees to want to make a good record in meeting the production standard and reducing waste and spoilage.

1) **Make sure employees know what the standards are in terms of end results expected.**
2) **Explain why the standards are necessary and why it is important to them to meet these standards.**

* Used with the permission of Continental Can Company.

3) Explain how the standards are set and why they are reasonable.
4) Ask for suggestions on the best way of meeting these standards.
5) Show that it is possible to meet these standards and what must be done in order to meet them.
6) Express confidence in their ability to meet the standards.
7) Give frequent reports on progress being made.
8) Ask what problems they face in meeting the standards, and help them overcome these problems.
9) Give encouragement, and compliment them on good performance.
10) Point out poor performance and help them improve it. Show what happens to the group record when one person fails to do his or her part.

As the next step Jones plans the various ways in which he will communicate with his employees regarding each of the matters listed and draws up the following diagram:

Subject	Individual Interviews	Personal Presentations	Conferences	Articles in Mass Media
1.				
2.				
3.				
4.				
5.				
6.				
7.				
8.				
9.				
10.				

PROBLEM: If you faced this problem in your unit, what channels would you use to communicate each of these matters? Mark the diagram accordingly.

CASE 2
RESULTS OF A COMMUNICATIONS SURVEY

Pat Washington has been the manager of Plant 32, a very successful packaging plant, for four years. The plant, whose primary products are wrapping paper and paperboard boxes, employs 178 people. It is a relatively small plant in Acme Corporation, which has a total of 31,000 employees. Generally, Pat has had good rapport with his immediate employees and has made a favorable impression on the corporate staff. In fact, they occasionally make comments that lead him to believe he is expected to move higher in the organization.

Periodically the corporate industrial relations staff runs attitude surveys of the employees. Three months ago they wanted to check on communications throughout the company and asked if they could run a communication survey at Plant 32. Pat gave his approval and it was run. At the time the survey was made, the administrators made some rather vague promises to the employees that they would be told the outcome of the survey.

Yesterday Pat received the results and was told that it was up to him to communicate any or all of the results to his employees if he thought it would be useful. After examining the report closely, he feels that this must be handled very carefully so as not to create problems. Moreover, he hopes the survey can be used to help improve communications in the plant. Consequently he has arranged a meeting with Francis Redfield, the industrial relations supervisor, and they plan to develop the best strategy for communicating the results to the employees.

Essentially, they want answers to three questions: (1) What information should be communicated to the employees and in what form? (2) How can each kind of information best be presented? The choices seem to be interviews, conferences, a formal briefing or report, or a published report. (3) What kinds of responses or employee discussion should take place after the results are communicated?

The report Pat Washington received is reproduced here. It is presented in three parts: (1) Identification of Problems, (2) Levels of Satisfaction, and (3) Employee Suggestions for Improving Communications. What strategies do you think he should use?

REPORT

I. Identification of problems

All employees were asked, "What is the single greatest communication problem encountered on your job"? Their answers may be summarized as follows:

1) The most frequent response involved some dissatisfaction with supervisor-subordinate communication, and there were many complaints about communication with one's own immediate supervisor. Criticisms included such things as lack of availability, not knowing what the supervisor wants, failure to keep promises, failure to transmit information, lack of receptivity to the subordinate, and personality clashes.

2) A number of problems cluster around the lack of information needed to do one's job. Specifically, comments described poor timing, lack of coordination among departments, not knowing company policies and procedures, and the slow filtering of information down the hierarchy.

3) Coordination among departments is often a problem. Even though the respondents recognize how difficult this coordination can be, they think more can be done to smooth things over. Specifically, they feel that a system should

be set up so that some departments automatically receive information they think they need. There were complaints, particularly among the production people, that they often had to wait needlessly for supplies because inventories were not maintained.

4) There were many references to the problem of ambiguity in language that resulted in unclear communication and misunderstandings.

II. Levels of satisfaction

Employees were asked to rate their satisfaction with communication on each of the following items. A scale of 1–7 was used, with 1 being the highest level of satisfaction and 7 the lowest level. The responses were analyzed in terms of the following groups, and the results are given in Table 3.

III. Specific employee suggestions for improving communications

On the questionnaire employees were asked, "If the communication associated with your job could be changed in any way to make you more satisfied, please indicate how." The responses may be seen in the following list. It was felt that the best way of presenting these to management was just as the employees stated them, so that they might be properly evaluated.

1) I would appreciate a good kick if I deserve one or some good words if they are in order. My boss does not realize a good worker from a poor one. A loyal, steady employee is treated with less respect than your poor, late, often-absent employee. It seems that management has the feeling that the bad employee must have problems. They allow for this but screw the dependable fellow.
2) More information at the department level.
3) Better shift planning so employees can plan ahead.
4) Make sure operators and maintenance know what type of packaging, tagging, or marking should be used on their lines and make sure it is available to use when needed.
5) Constant policing by my supervisor is not necessary.
6) If the foreman wants me to put out every day, there is also a time when I expect an honest favor also.
7) A drink break or smoke break in between reliefs should help in this hot weather.
8) Have a more personal part in what is going on in the company.
9) Let us do our work without being harped at.
10) Fewer chiefs and more Indians.
11) Reports on short-term and long-term business forecasts, including the companies that we will be serving.
12) Try having the management listen.
13) I would like to be better informed about what is going on now and in the future about my department.
14) Questionnaires of this form are a fair means of communication. Let's have the results.
15) I would like to know when we are going to work extra days a little sooner.
16) A little more understanding; when you try to discuss something it's like talking to a brick wall.

P$_1$—Production (first shift) (number = 60)
P$_2$—Production (second shift) (number = 42)
P$_3$—Production (third shift) (number = 35)
M—Managers (number = 22)
OS—Office staff (number = 17)

TABLE 3   LEVELS OF SATISFACTION

Item	Very Satisfied	Satisfied	Slightly Satisfied	Neutral	Slightly Dissatisfied	Dissatisfied	Very Dissatisfied
Communication with supervisor	M P$_1$	OS	P$_2$		P$_3$		
Communication climate (people have good attitudes about communicating)	OS	M	P$_1$ P$_2$	P$_3$			
Personal feedback about how you are doing in your job			M OS	P$_1$ P$_2$	P$_3$		
Communication about the "big picture," i.e., what is going on in the company		M OS	P$_1$	P$_2$ P$_3$			
Horizontal communication with other workers and/or other departments	OS	P$_3$	M P$_1$ P$_2$				
Timing of communication		OS	P$_1$ P$_2$	M		P$_3$	
Information needed to do your job	OS	M P$_1$ P$_2$	P$_3$				
Company publications	OS	P$_1$ P$_2$	M	P$_3$			
Meetings				OS M P$_1$ P$_2$ P$_3$			
Opportunities to make suggestions in the company (the company listens)	M		OS	P$_1$ P$_2$			P$_3$

17) Nobody has really said if I'm doing something right or really wrong. I'd like to know.
18) Truth in communication would be most helpful.
19) There are no communication problems.
20) Better supervision.

21) Make the relationship between people more friendly.

22 Department-level suggestion boxes.

23) I only wish the foremen were a little more open-minded.

24) Daily notes telling you when things are done right and not just when they are wrong. This helps put a little pride into your work.

25) Inform us of all customer complaints when they are received.

26) Everyone should be expected to put in a full day's work.

27) Record all adjustments, repairs, and replacements on machines so you would know what has been done to the machine. It takes a little time to record, but it could save a lot of downtime.

28) Everyone should do the job the same way.

29) I'd like to know how the department is doing three or four times a year.

30) When a person gets a new job to perform, see that he is trained by some-one who has ability to teach.

31) There could be more communication, flowing down.

32) Supervisor should voice his grievances about me to me instead of my co-workers.

33) Have Quality Control report back sooner on our checks so we don't run for four hours with a defect.

34) Monthly meetings to help understand and solve problems and differences.

35) Choose supervisors for ability, not as a "payoff."

36) Better wages and a better boss in Shipping—one that can relate and get along with workers.

37) As long as the job is done and nothing is said, all is well.

38) There is absolutely no communication except local gossip and what happens at the club.

INDEX